Mark Powell

in company 3.0

INTERMEDIATE STUDENT'S BOOK

B1+

MACMILLAN

in company 3.0 at a glance

Third edition Student's Book:

15 Business communication units focusing on current business issues and everyday skills for the workplace

> **Learning objectives to track your progress**

> **Fluency and communication activities on every page**

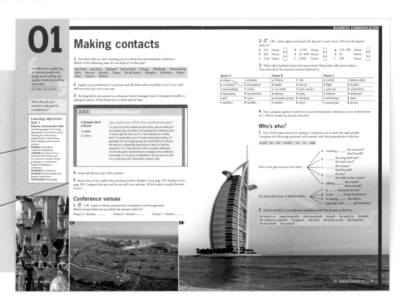

5 People skills units focusing on functional Business English language and interpersonal skills

> **Roleplay activities consolidate the skills learnt**

5 Management scenarios offering challenging case studies that simulate business situations and allow interaction with the language in a dynamic way

> **Engaging videos illustrate true-to-life scenarios**

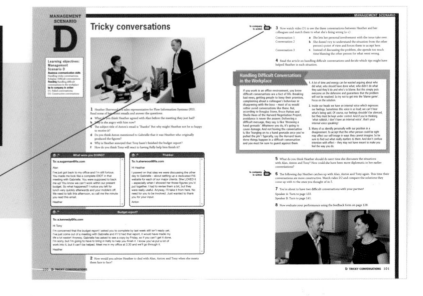

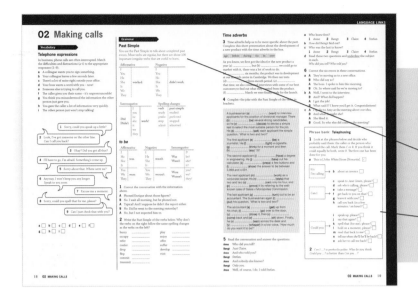

15 Language links
consolidating grammar and extending vocabulary from the Business communication units

Grammar reference with detailed explanations of key points

Phrase bank of key take-away phrases for quick revision

Extra material

- Additional material for communicative activities
- Self-evaluation forms for Management scenario activities
- Listening scripts

New Online Workbook and Student's Resource Centre

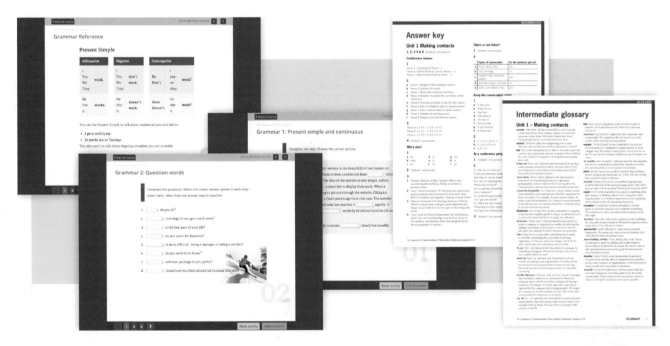

Online Workbook

Everything you need to build and expand on the Student's Book material outside the classroom, and all accessible online:

- Interactive activities to practise:
  - Vocabulary
  - Grammar
  - Reading
  - Writing
  - Listening
- Automatic markbook
- Grammar reference

Student's Resource Centre

An extensive collection of resources, all available to download:

- Student's Book audio
- 'In company in action' – Student's Book scenario videos
- 'In company interviews' – additional video material
- Glossary
- Answer key
- Phrase banks

Contents

Making contacts

How often do you attend or take part in a conference?

Learning objectives: Unit 1

Business communication skills
Describing people; Discussing appropriate conversation topics; Keeping the conversation going; Fluency: Networking with colleagues and business contacts

Reading A blog about conference attendance

Listening An extract from a business travel programme on conference venues; People gossiping at a conference; People socializing at a conference

Vocabulary Conferences

Grammar Present Simple and Present Continuous

Phrase bank Networking

1 Your boss tells you she's sending you to a three-day international conference. Which of the following cities do you hope it's in this year?

Abu Dhabi	Barcelona	Budapest	Buenos Aires	Chicago	Edinburgh	Johannesburg
Milan	Moscow	Mumbai	Prague	Rio de Janeiro	Shanghai	Stockholm	Sydney
Tokyo	Toronto	Warsaw				

2 Explain your preference to a partner and tell them what you'd like to do if you could add one extra day onto your trip.

3 The blog below was posted on a business travel message board. A business traveller is asking for advice. Write down two or three tips for him.

ASK ExecTravelBuddy.com

2 October 2014 3.56 pm

3 replies

52 views

Any advice for a first time conference-goer?

I'm going to my first conference next month, and am looking for some general tips and advice from experienced conference-goers on how to get the most out of it. The conference is in Rome, which I've never been to, so I'm quite excited about going. I'm generally a bit shy in large groups, but would like to try and use the event as a networking opportunity as well as a learning experience. It's a three-day event with a reception afterwards. I'm the only person representing my company at the conference. Fortunately, I'm not giving a presentation! But my boss has told me to come back with some useful contacts. Help!

4 Swap and discuss tips with a partner.

5 Read some of the replies this posting received. Speaker A see page 126. Speaker B see page 139. Compare the tips one by one with your partner. Which advice sounds the best to you?

Conference venues

1 🔘 **1.01** Listen to three extracts from a business travel programme. Which venues below do you think the extracts refer to?

Venue A = Extract _____   Venue B = Extract _____   Venue C = Extract _____

2 🖸 **1.01** Listen again and match the figures to each venue. What do the figures refer to?

a	321	Venue	☐	**d**	2,300	Venue	☐	**g**	170–780	Venue	☐
b	426	Venue	☐	**e**	10–30%	Venue	☐	**h**	95	Venue	☐
c	27th	Venue	☐	**f**	3,000	Venue	☐	**i**	200	Venue	☐

3 What other facilities does each venue have? Match the collocations below. They were all in the extracts you just listened to.

Venue A		Venue B		Venue C	
a unique	**1** activities	**a** 24-hour	**1** club	**a** central	**1** deluxe suites
b convention	**2** atmosphere	**b** health	**2** service	**b** flight	**2** location
c team-building	**3** centre	**c** car rental	**3** room service	**c** spacious	**3** connections
d banqueting	**4** tournaments	**d** express	**4** pools	**d** Internet	**4** restaurant
e golf	**5** space	**e** exclusive private	**5** checkout	**e** world-class	**5** views
f exhibition	**6** facilities	**f** outdoor	**6** beach	**f** spectacular	**6** access

4 Your company agrees to send you to an international conference at one of the venues in 1. Which would you choose and why?

Who's who?

1 One of the main reasons for going to conferences is to meet the right people. Complete the following questions and answers with the prepositions in the box.

at (x2)   by   for   in (x2)   on   to   with

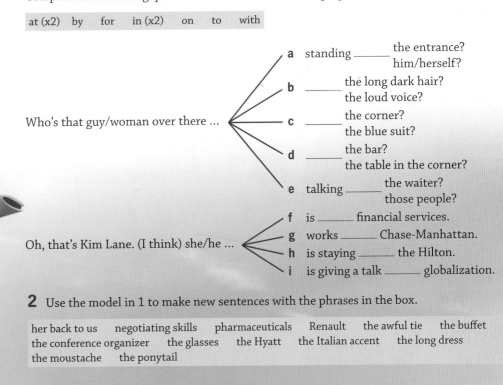

Who's that guy/woman over there …

a standing ——— the entrance? him/herself?

b ——— the long dark hair? the loud voice?

c ——— the corner? the blue suit?

d ——— the bar? the table in the corner?

e talking ——— the waiter? those people?

Oh, that's Kim Lane. (I think) she/he …

f is ——— financial services.

g works ——— Chase-Manhattan.

h is staying ——— the Hilton.

i is giving a talk ——— globalization.

2 Use the model in 1 to make new sentences with the phrases in the box.

her back to us   negotiating skills   pharmaceuticals   Renault   the awful tie   the buffet
the conference organizer   the glasses   the Hyatt   the Italian accent   the long dress
the moustache   the ponytail

3 🔘 **1.02–1.05** Listen to some delegates chatting at a conference reception. Decide which four people in the photo they are talking about and complete the information below.

1

Name: Karl Schelling

Company: _____

Position: _____

Based in: _____

Hotel: _____

Subject of talk: _____

Gossip: _____

2

Name: William Hall

Company: _____

Position: _____

Based in: _____

Hotel: _____

Subject of talk: _____

Gossip: _____

3

Name: Irena Stefanowitz

Company: _____

Position: _____

Based in: _____

Hotel: _____

Subject of talk: _____

Gossip: _____

4

Name: Margo Timmerman

Company: _____

Position: _____

Based in: _____

Hotel: _____

Subject of talk: _____

Gossip: _____

Taboo or not taboo?

1 Work with a partner. You meet some business people at a conference for the first time. Which of the following topics are:

- interesting?
- safe?
- conversation killers?
- a bit risky?
- taboo?

books   clothes   family   food and drink
gadgets   how work's going   jewellery
movies   music   people you both know
politics   religion   sport
the city you're in   the hotel you're staying at
the news   the weather   your country
your health   your holiday plans

2 🔘 **1.06–1.10** Listen to some people socializing at a conference. What are they talking about? Do they get on with each other?

	Topics of conversation	Do the speakers get on?
a		
b		
c		
d		
e		

Keeping the conversation going

1 🔘 **1.06–1.10** The expressions below were in the conversations you just listened to. Write in the first three words of each expression. Contractions (*it's, you'll, I'm*, etc) count as one word. If necessary, listen again and check.

a _____ first visit to Russia?
b _____ do, by the way?
c _____ you a drink?
d _____ business are you in?
e _____ these – they're delicious.
f _____ somewhere before?
g _____ me, I have to make a phone call.
h _____ talking to you.
i _____ your talk this morning.
j _____ enjoying the conference?
k _____ awful? Half a metre of snow this morning, I heard.
l _____ me a moment? I'll be right back.
m _____ go and say hello to someone.
n _____ many people here?
o _____ you anything from the buffet?

2 Look at the expressions in 1.

a Which would be good ways of opening a conversation?
b Which would help you to keep a conversation going?
c Which could you use to politely end a conversation?

At a conference party

Work as a class to keep the conversation going at a conference party at Disneyland®, Paris. It's a warm summer evening and the place is full of delegates. The conference theme is *Web 2.0: Business in the connected economy.*

1 Invent a fantasy business card for yourself! Include the following information:

- name (You could change nationality!)
- company (You could choose a company you've always wanted to work for!)
- brief contact details (mobile phone, email)

2 Write the questions below. Think of possible answers for each and make notes in the space provided.

Q So, who / work for?
A

Q How / business?
A

Q first time / Paris?
A

Q know many people here?
A

Q And what / do there?
A

Q Can / get / drink?
A

Q How / enjoying / conference?
A

Q So, where / staying?
A

Q Where / based?
A

Q Where / from originally?
A

Q giving / presentation?
A

Q Can / get / anything / buffet?
A

3 When everyone is ready:

- mingle with the other people in the class.
- introduce yourself to as many people as possible and show interest in what they tell you.
- use the questions in 2 to try to keep the conversation going. (Remember that you can talk about other people in the room as well as yourself.)
- exchange business cards and fix appointments with anyone you could do business with – see how many cards you can collect!

01 Making contacts

Conferences

When business people get together, they often just talk about work. This is called 'talking shop'. Complete the sentences with the pairs of words in the box.

down + factory	for + contract	in + distributor	of + job	off + workers	
out + product	to + office	under + takeover	up + plant	with + supplier	

a **A** I hear GEC are setting _____ a new _____ in Warsaw.

    B Warsaw? I thought it was Prague.

b **A** I understand you're _____ talks with a local _____ in Naples.

    B Yeah, that's right. In fact, we've already reached an agreement.

c **A** They say GM are laying _____ 5,000 _____ in the UK.

    B Is that right? Well, I knew they were downsizing.

d **A** Someone told me Sony® are bringing _____ a new _____ in December.

    B Yes, I heard that too. Some kind of multimedia entertainment system.

e **A** I hear you're thinking _____ leaving your _____ at Hewlett-Packard.

    B Well, yes. Just between us, I'm moving to Sony.

f **A** I understand you're being transferred _____ head _____ in Stockholm.

    B Well, it's not official yet, but I'm going after Christmas.

g **A** They say they're _____ threat from a hostile _____ bid.

    B Really? It's the first I've heard of it.

h **A** Someone told me they're doing a deal _____ a _____ in Tel Aviv.

    B Well, that makes sense. They do most of their business there.

i **A** I hear you're bidding _____ a new _____ in Singapore.

    B Yeah, we are. The negotiations are going quite well.

j **A** Someone told me they're closing _____ the Liverpool _____.

    B It doesn't surprise me. From what I heard, they're trying to centralize production.

Present Simple

About half of all spoken English is in the Present Simple. You use it to talk about actions and states which are always or generally true.

Affirmative		Negative		Interrogative			Spelling changes	
I		I			I		verb	he/she/it
You		You	don't	Do	you		go	goes
We	work.	We	work.	Don't	we	work?	watch	watches
They		They			they		push	pushes
He		He			he		miss	misses
She	works.	She	doesn't	Does	she	work?	fax	faxes
It		It	work.	Doesn't	it		try	tries

1 Correct the conversations using the information above.

a **A** Works he for the BBC?

    B No, he don't work for them anymore. He work for CNN.

b **A** Where work you?

    B I works for a design company in Frankfurt.

c At our firm, we doesn't work on Friday afternoons.

d On Mondays our CEO usually flys to Oslo.

2 Match the sentences (a–h) to their functions (1–4).

a I live just outside Munich. ☐

b He runs five kilometres every day. ☐

c Your presentation is this afternoon. ☐

d The United States has the world's strongest economy. ☐

e That's a good idea! ☐

f She works on Saturdays. ☐

g I love Vienna at Christmas. ☐

h My train leaves at 7.30. ☐

1 describes habits and routines

2 refers to schedules and timetables

3 expresses thoughts, feelings and opinions

4 refers to long-term situations or facts

Present Continuous

You use the Present Continuous to talk about current situations in progress and future arrangements:

- *They're **staying** at the Hilton.*
- *He's **giving** a talk on globalization at three o'clock.*

Affirmative		Negative		Interrogative			Spelling changes	
I'm		I'm not		**Am** **Aren't**	I		**verb**	***-ing* form**
							make	making
You're We're They're	working.	You **aren't** We **aren't** They **aren't**	working.	**Are** **Aren't**	you we they	working?	come	coming
							run	running
							drop	dropping
He's She's It's		He **isn't** She **isn't** It **isn't**		**Is** **Isn't**	he she it		forget lie	forgetting lying

3 Read the conversation.

A Alison?

B Yes. Who's calling? (a)

A It's Paco … About our appointment, we're meeting (b) on Thursday, right?

B That's right. Are you flying (c) to Heathrow?

A No. I'm working (d) in Zaragoza this month. So Gatwick's easier for me.

B Fine. Oh! The batteries are going (e) on my mobile. Can I call you back?

In the conversation, find examples of the following.

1 something happening right at this moment ☐ ☐

2 something happening around the present time ☐

3 a future arrangement ☐ ☐

Present Simple or Continuous?

Some verbs are not 'action' verbs and are not usually used in the continuous form.

be	believe	hear	know	like	mean	need
see	seem	think	understand	want		

4 Choose the best alternatives in the following conversation.

A What (a) *do you do / are you doing*?

B (b) *I'm / I'm being* an electrical engineer for Siemens.

A Really? Here in Munich?

B That's right. (c) *Do you know / Are you knowing* Munich?

A Oh, yes, great city. So, how (d) *do you enjoy / are you enjoying* the conference so far?

B Well, it's all right, (e) *I guess / I'm guessing*. (f) *Do you give / Are you giving* a talk?

A No, no. (g) *I only come / I'm only coming* to these things to get out of the office for a few days. Where (h) *do you stay / are you staying*, by the way?

B At the Avalon. (i) *I usually stay / I'm usually staying* at the Bauer Hotel in Münchenerstrasse, but it was full.

A Well, if (j) *you don't do / you aren't doing* anything later, do you want to go for something to eat?

Phrase bank: Networking

Match the sentence beginnings (a–k) to the pairs of endings (1–11).

a What do you   **1** introduce you to someone.
give you my card.

b Who do you   **2** enjoying the conference?
getting back to your hotel?

c Where are you   **3** nice talking to you.
a pleasure meeting you.

d How are you   **4** based?
staying?

e Isn't this   **5** with the beard?
in the dark suit?

f Who's the guy   **6** work for?
know here?

g I think he's   **7** a drink?
anything from the buffet?

h Can I get you   **8** a moment, I'll be right back.
I have to make a phone call.

i Let me   **9** do, by the way?
think of the venue?

j If you'll excuse me   **10** an amazing place?
weather awful?

k It's been   **11** in logistics.
giving a talk on PR.

a ☐   b ☐   c ☐   d ☐   e ☐   f ☐
g ☐   h ☐   i ☐   j ☐   k ☐

02 Making calls

How often do you use the telephone at work?

Learning objectives: Unit 2

Business communication skills Receiving calls; Leaving voicemails; Roleplay: Exchanging information on the telephone
Listening Planning a telephone call; Voicemail messages; Telephone conversations
Vocabulary Telephone expressions
Grammar Past Simple; time adverbs *ago, before, during, for, in, over*
Phrase bank Telephoning

1 How comfortable are you speaking English on the phone? Work with a partner. Complete the questionnaire with the verbs in the box in the correct form. Then discuss.

| have | keep | lose | misunderstand | shout | sound | try | want | wish |

BE HONEST!

Can you remember a time when you ...

A totally _____ what someone said on the phone?
Oh, yes ☐   No ☐

B really _____ rude and unhelpful because you were busy?
Oh, yes ☐   No ☐

C constantly _____ to ask the other person to repeat what they said?
Oh, yes ☐   No ☐

D just _____ putting off a call because you didn't want to speak English?
Oh, yes ☐   No ☐

E actually _____ at someone on the phone?
Oh, yes ☐   No ☐

F completely _____ track of the conversation?
Oh, yes ☐   No ☐

G just _____ you could talk to the other person face to face?
Oh, yes ☐   No ☐

H even _____ pretending you were out to avoid taking a call?
Oh, yes ☐   No ☐

I really _____ to kill the person on the other end of the phone?
Oh, yes ☐   No ☐

Making phone calls in a foreign language requires planning. It's especially important to know what to say right at the beginning of the call.

2 🔘 **1.11** Listen to the phone call. Why does the caller get angry?

3 🔘 **1.12** Listen to a better version of the same phone call and complete the following opening phrases:

_____, accounts _____. Marius Pot _____.

4 🔘 **1.13** Now listen to another phone call. Why does the caller sound so unprofessional?

5 🔘 **1.14** Again, listen to a better version of the same phone call and complete the following phrases:

_____ Ramon Berenguer _____ Genex Ace Pharmaceuticals.
_____ _____ _____ _____ Catherine Mellor, _____?
_____ _____ an invoice.

6 A lot of the English you need on the phone is just a small number of keywords used in different combinations. Work with a partner. How many telephone expressions can you make in two minutes using one word or phrase from two or more sections below (e.g. *Can I have your name, please?*)? Write them down.

Can	I you	ask check speak to take see if help have give speak up hold on get tell leave say spell read get back to	who's me you he/she him/her your name a message someone something a moment it that	please about it again with me with you back to me I called within the hour to call me back a few details on that is there for me later today calling when he'll/she'll be back a message

7 You overhear a colleague say the following things on the phone. What questions do you think she was asked? Use some of the telephone expressions you made in 6.

a Yes, I'd like to speak to Ifakat Karsli, please.

b Yes, it's Ivana Medvedeva.

c M-E-D-V-E-D-E-V-A, Medvedeva.

d Yes. Can you just tell her Ivana called?

e Yes, I'll tell him as soon as he gets in.

f Of course. Your reference number is 45-81099-KM. Okay?

g Sorry, is that better?

h Around three, I should think.

i Can we make that two hours?

j Certainly. Can you give me your number?

k Sure. When can I expect to hear from you?

l Sure. Just a minute. Where's my pen? Okay, go ahead.

8 1.15 Listen and check your answers.

Voicemail

1 1.16 Listen to six voicemail messages. Take notes. Which message is about:

a an order? ☐

b some figures? ☐

c a meeting? ☐

d a deadline? ☐

e a report? ☐

f a reminder? ☐

2 🔘 **1.16** Listen again and answer the questions.

Message 1	How many times did Cheryl phone yesterday?
Message 2	What's the good news about phase one?
Message 3	What did Zoltán include in his report?
Message 4	When was the delivery?
Message 5	When was the estimate due?
Message 6	What do you think is happening at three tomorrow?

3 🔘 **1.16** The messages in 2 contain the following verbs.

a phoned, corrected, faxed   **d** talked, despatched, delivered

b wanted, finished, explained   **e** called, discussed, expected

c started, emailed, included   **f** tried, waited, booked

The -ed endings of regular verbs in the Past Simple can be pronounced in three different ways: /d/, /t/ or /ɪd/. Listen to the messages again. Which verbs take the /ɪd/ ending? Why? Put them in the third column of the chart.

/d/	/t/	/ɪd/

Now put the other verbs in the correct column.

4 The following messages were taken by your secretary. Work with a partner. Can you recreate the original voicemails? The first one has been done for you as an example.

Svetlana (Paris)

Flight delay – late for meeting.

Start with item 2 on agenda.

Will join asap.

> *Hi, it's Svetlana. Listen, my flight's been delayed and it looks like I'm going to be late for the meeting. Can you start with item two on the agenda and I'll join you as soon as I can? Thanks! See you later.*

A

Seiji (Nagoya)

Negotiations going well – deadlocked on price. Authorize 14% discount on 50,000 units?

B

URGENT!

Jim (Expo in Dublin) Lost memory stick for presentation! Pls email PowerPoint slides asap!

C

Tony

Stuck in meeting at HQ. Conference arrangements progress? Pls contact speakers to confirm.

D

Kate (Seattle)

InfoTag querying our invoice for Q3. Ask accounts to check figures + reinvoice if necessary.

E

URGENT!

Alicia
Needs Turin report – tomorrow pm latest! Call back if problems.

F

Mike

Has appointment here Fri. Meet? Coffee? Ian sends his rgds.

pls = please
asap = as soon as possible
rgds = regards
HQ = headquarters
Q3 = third quarter

5 🔘 **1.17** Listen to the original voicemails and compare them with your answers.

Returning a call

1 1.18–1.19 Listen to two telephone calls and answer the questions.

Call 1

a Whose answerphone are we listening to?

b What does the caller want?

c Put the lines of the recorded message in the correct order.

1	Hello. This is Patterson Meats,
	but if you'd like to leave
	for calling. I'm afraid
	please do so
	your call right now,
	after the tone and I'll get back
	Sylvia Wright's office. Thank you
	I'm not able to take
	a message,
10	to you as soon as I can.

Call 2

a Who didn't come to the meeting?

    1 Bill Andrews   **3** Jonathan Powell

    2 Stephanie Hughes   **4** Melanie Burns

b Who does Tim already know?

    1 Bill Andrews   **3** Jonathan Powell

    2 Stephanie Hughes   **4** Melanie Burns

c What didn't the visitors from the UK see?

    1 the processing plant   **4** the freezer units

    2 the factory   **5** a presentation

    3 the packing department

d Tim was interrupted during the phone call. Complete what he said to Sylvia.

Sorry ―――――――――――――――――――――.

I just ―――――――――――――――――――――.

Where ――――――――――――――――――?

e What were the British visitors worried about?

f Would the product they came to see be popular in your country? Would you try it?

2 Put these irregular verbs from Call 2 into the Past Simple. You have 45 seconds!

be	come	do	get	give
go	have	meet	say	send
speak	take	tell	think	

3 One of the following extracts is from the phone call. The other is incorrect. Which is incorrect and why?

a So who else did come? Came Stephanie Hughes?

b So who else came? Did Stephanie Hughes come?

Finding out

Work with a partner. Phone each other in order to find out some information to help you:

- do business in a foreign city
- give a presentation
- attend a job interview.

Talk to your partner before you begin and decide on the subject of your phone calls. Think of the language you will need to use.

Begin your phone call in this way:

Hi, _____ (your partner's name). It's _____ (your name) here. How are things? … And how's business?

Then use the notes below to help you ask your questions. Ask other questions if you like.

> Remember to show interest in what your partner tells you.
> *Really?   I see.   Right.*
> *Uh huh.   Good.   Great.*
> *Oh, that's interesting.*
> Finish your call like this:
> *Anyway, look, I must let you go.*
> *Thanks a lot for your help.*
> *Speak to you soon.*
> *Bye now.*

1 A business trip

Listen, I'm going to _____ (city?) on business in a couple of weeks. I know you did some business there a while ago and I just wanted to ask you how it went.

a	Which airline / fly with?	**g**	meetings go okay?
b	business class?	**h**	language problems?
c	Where / stay?	**i**	chance / see much / city?
d	What / food like?	**j**	What / do / evenings?
e	What / people like?	**k**	invite / their home?
f	easy to work with?	**l**	take a present?

2 A presentation

Listen, I'm giving a presentation at _____ (a meeting? a conference?) in a couple of weeks. I know you had to give a presentation a while ago and I just wanted to ask you how it went.

a	talk / your own?	**g**	How many / visuals?
b	How long / take / prepare?	**h**	tell jokes?
c	How big / audience?	**i**	give / handouts?
d	How long / speak for?	**j**	take questions / the end?
e	nervous?	**k**	any difficult ones?
f	use PowerPoint?	**l**	How / deal with them?

3 A job interview

Listen, I'm going for an interview at _____ (company?) in a couple of weeks. I know you had an interview with them a while ago and I just wanted to ask you how it went.

a	How long / interview / last?	**g**	trickiest question?
b	How many interviewers?	**h**	ask / personal questions?
c	How friendly?	**i**	have / do / a test?
d	say what / looking for?	**j**	ask them / questions?
e	refer / your CV?	**k**	What / salary / like?
f	How interested / qualifications?	**l**	offer you / job?

02 Making calls

Telephone expressions

In business, phone calls are often interrupted. Match the difficulties and distractions (a–i) to the appropriate responses (1–9).

a A colleague wants you to sign something.

b Your colleague leaves a few seconds later.

c There's a lot of noise right outside your office.

d Your boss wants a word with you – now!

e Someone else is trying to call you.

f The caller gives you their name – it's unpronounceable!

g You think you misunderstood the information the other person just gave you.

h You gave the caller a lot of information very quickly.

i The other person just won't stop talking!

1 Sorry, could you speak up a little?

2 Look, I've got someone on the other line. Can I call you back?

3 Okay? Did you get all that?

4 I'll have to go, I'm afraid. Something's come up.

5 Sorry about that. Where were we?

6 Anyway, I won't keep you any longer. Speak to you soon.

7 Excuse me a moment.

8 Sorry, could you spell that for me, please?

9 Can I just check that with you?

a ☐ **b** ☐ **c** ☐ **d** ☐ **e** ☐ **f** ☐
g ☐ **h** ☐ **i** ☐

Grammar

Past Simple

You use the Past Simple to talk about completed past events. Most verbs are regular, but there are about 100 important irregular verbs that are useful to learn.

Affirmative			Negative		
I			I		
You			You		
He			He		
She	**worked**.		She	**didn't work**.	
It			It		
We			We		
They			They		

Interrogative			Spelling changes	
	I		**verb**	**past simple**
	you		study	studied
	he		prefer	preferred
Did	she	**work**?	stop	stopped
Didn't	it		admit	admitted
	we			
	they			

to be

Affirmative		Negative		Interrogative	
I		I			I?
He		He		**Was**	he?
She	**was**.	She	**wasn't**.	**Wasn't**	she?
It		It			it?
You		You			you?
We	**were**.	We	**weren't**.	**Were**	we?
They		They		**Weren't**	they?

1 Correct the conversation with the information above.

A Phoned Enrique about those figures?

B No. I wait all morning, but he phoned not.

A Typical! And I suppose he didn't the report either.

B No. Did he went to the meeting yesterday?

A No, but I not expected him to.

2 Write the Past Simple of the verbs below. Why don't the verbs on the right follow the same spelling changes as the verbs on the left?

hurry _____   play _____

occupy _____   enjoy _____

refer _____   offer _____

confer _____   suffer _____

drop _____   develop _____

flop _____   visit _____

commit _____

transmit _____

Time adverbs

3 Time adverbs help us to be more specific about the past. Complete this short presentation about the development of a new product with the time adverbs in the box.

| ago | before | during | for | in | over |

As you know, we first got the idea for the new product a year (a) _____, but (b) _____ we could go to market with it, there was a lot of work to do.
(c) _____ six months, the product was in development at our research centre in Cambridge. We then ran tests (d) _____ a three-month period. (e) _____ that time, we also conducted interviews with some of our best customers to find out what they wanted from the product.
(f) _____ March we were finally ready for the launch.

4 Complete the joke with the Past Simple of the verbs in brackets.

A businessman (a) _____ (want) to interview applicants for the position of divisional manager. There (b) _____ (be) several strong candidates, so he (c) _____ (decide) to devise a simple test to select the most suitable person for the job. He (d) _____ (ask) each applicant the simple question, 'What is two and two?'

The first applicant (e) _____ (be) a journalist. He (f) _____ (light) a cigarette, (g) _____ (think) for a moment and then (h) _____ (say) '22'.

The second applicant (i) _____ (have) a degree in engineering. He (j) _____ (take) out his calculator, (k) _____ (press) a few buttons and (l) _____ (show) the answer to be between 3.999 and 4.001.

The next applicant (m) _____ (work) as a corporate lawyer. He (n) _____ (state) that two and two (o) _____ (can) only be four, and (p) _____ (prove) it by referring to the well-known case of Gates v Monopolies Commission.

The last applicant (q) _____ (turn) out to be an accountant. The businessman again (r) _____ (put) his question, 'What is two and two?'

The accountant (s) _____ (get) up from his chair, (t) _____ (go) over to the door, (u) _____ (close) it, then (v) _____ (come) back and (w) _____ (sit) down. Finally, he (x) _____ (lean) across the desk and (y) _____ (whisper) in a low voice, 'How much do you want it to be?'

5 Read the conversation and answer the questions.

Anne Who did you tell?
Bengt Just Claire.
Anne And who told you?
Bengt Stefan.
Anne And nobody else knows?
Bengt Only you.
Anne Well, of course, I do. I told Stefan.

a Who knew first?
   1 Anne   **2** Bengt   **3** Claire   **4** Stefan
b How did Bengt find out?
c Who was the last to know?
   1 Anne   **2** Bengt   **3** Claire   **4** Stefan
d Read these two questions and underline the subject in each.
   Who did you tell? Who told you?

6 Correct the six errors in these conversations.
a **A** They're moving us to a new office.
   B Who did say so?
   A The boss. I spoke to him this morning.
   B Oh. So where said he we're moving to?
b **A** Well, I went to the interview.
   B And? What did happen?
   A I got the job!
   B What said I? I knew you'd get it. Congratulations!
c **A** I spoke to Amy at the meeting about our idea.
   B And what thought she?
   A She liked it.
   B Good. So who else did come to the meeting?

Phrase bank: Telephoning

1 Look at the phrases below and decide who probably said them: the caller or the person who received the call. Mark them *C* or *R*. If you think it could equally be both, write *B*. The first one has been done for you.

a This is [John White] from [Novartis]. ☐*C*

It's
I'm calling → **b** about an invoice. ☐

   c speak to Jane Green, please? ☐
   d ask who's calling, please? ☐
   e take a message? ☐
Can I → **f** get back to you on that? ☐
   g leave it with you? ☐
   h call you back (in a few minutes / an hour)? ☐

   i speak up, please? ☐
   j say that again? ☐
   k spell that (for me), please? ☐
Could you → **l** hold on a moment, please? ☐
   m read that back to me? ☐
   n tell me when she'll/he'll be back? ☐
   o ask her to call me back? ☐

2 *Can I ...?* is perfectly polite. Why do you think *Could you ...?* is better than *Can you ...?*

Keeping track

How do you ensure that the meetings you attend are productive?

Learning objectives: Unit 3

Business communication skills Checking and clarifying facts and figures; Fluency: Querying information; Clearing up misunderstandings
Reading Articles: two sportswear companies
Listening Extracts from meetings; A briefing meeting
Vocabulary Business phrasal verbs
Grammar Comparatives and superlatives
Phrase bank Checking understanding
🎬 **In company interviews** Units 1–3

1 When you take part in meetings in English, it is easy to lose track of what people are saying. Who do you generally find the hardest to understand?

native speakers   other non-native speakers   people who speak too fast
people with strong accents

2 Here are six simple ways of checking what someone has just said. Complete them with the pairs of words in the box.

catch + slow   follow + run   'm + go   missed + say   see + be   understand + explain

Sorry, I
a _____ that. Could you _____ it again?
b didn't _____ that. Could you _____ down a bit?
c don't _____. Could you _____ what you mean?
d _____ not with you. Could you _____ over that again?
e don't _____ you. Could you _____ through that again?
f don't quite _____ what you mean. Could you _____ a bit more specific?

3 Which of the phrases in 2 do you use when you:
1 didn't hear? ☐ ☐
2 didn't understand? ☐ ☐ ☐ ☐

4 Match the phrasal verbs (a–c) to their meanings (1–3).

a slow down   1 mention quickly
b go over   2 speak more slowly
c run through   3 examine, discuss

5 Can you remember the phrases in 2 when you need them? Work with a partner. Take turns to throw dice and try to produce the exact phrases using the words below to help you.

missed – say – again?

didn't catch – slow – bit?

don't understand – explain – what you mean?

not with you – go over – again?

don't follow you – run through – again?

don't quite see – mean – bit more specific?

Sorry?

1 In meetings where you are discussing facts and figures, saying 'Sorry?' or 'I don't understand' is not always enough. Sometimes you need to be more precise. Look at the following short extracts from meetings. Complete the second speaker's responses with the question words from the box.

how long   how much   what   when   where   who

a **A** The problem is money.
    B Sorry, _____ did you say?
    A The problem is money.
    B Oh, as usual.

b **A** We have to reach a decision by next week.
    B Sorry, _____ did you say?
    A Next week.
    B Oh, I see.

c A An upgrade will cost $3,000.
  B Sorry, _____ did you say?
  A Three thousand dollars, at least.
  B Oh, as much as that?

d A Ildikó Dudás spoke to me about it yesterday.
  B Sorry, _____ did you say?
  A Ildikó Dudás – from the Budapest office.
  B Oh, yes, of course.

e A The company is based in Taipei.
  B Sorry, _____ did you say?
  A In Taipei.
  B Oh, really?

f A The whole project might take 18 months.
  B Sorry, _____ did you say?
  A Eighteen months.
  B Oh, as long as that?

2 1.20 Listen to the conversations in 1 and check your answers.

3 Work with a partner to practise clarifying specific points. You are going to read about two famous sportswear companies started by two brothers in the same town. Speaker A see page 127. Speaker B see page 139.

4 How many comparative and superlative expressions can you find in the article you just read?

5 With a partner, complete the following quiz about comparative and superlative expressions. The article you just read should help you with most of them.

QUIZ

A Question: What do you call a company which is bigger than all the others except one?
Answer: The _____ _____ company.

B Question: What do you call a company which is more profitable than all the others except two?
Answer: The _____ _____ _____ company.

C Question: What's the opposite of 'one of the most profitable'?
Answer: One of the _____ profitable.

D Question: What's another way of saying 'easily the most successful'?
Answer: _____ _____ the most successful.

E Question: What's the opposite of 'things got better and better'?
Answer: Things got _____ and _____.

F Question: What are two other ways of saying 'much more than this'?
Answer 1: A _____ more than this.
Answer 2: A _____ _____ more than this.

G Question: What do you call a company which is 100% bigger than another?
Answer: _____ _____ big.

H Question: What do you call a company which is 50% smaller than another?
Answer: _____ _____ big.

I Question: What do you call a company which is bigger than another by a factor of four?
Answer: _____ _____ bigger.

J Question: What's another way of saying 'there has never been a more successful company'?
Answer: It's the _____ successful company _____.

K Question: What are two other ways of saying 'the number one brand of sports shoe'?
Answer 1: The _____ brand of sports shoe.
Answer 2: The world's _____ brand of sports shoe.

Didn't I say that?

1 People sometimes disagree about facts in meetings. One way of politely querying something is simply to repeat the part you think is wrong and ask a question. Look at the examples on the left.

2 Work with a partner. Take turns to read out the following false information. Query each other using the correct information in the box. The first one has been done for you as an example.

| 1997 | Finland | Google | Korean | music | software |
| Tata Motors | the Burj Khalifa | the Netherlands |

a The biggest Benelux country is Belgium.
   Belgium? Don't you mean the Netherlands?
b Hyundai is a well-known Japanese car manufacturer.
c China regained control of Hong Kong in 1998.
d Microsoft® is the world's leading computer hardware manufacturer.
e Jaguar cars are owned by Ford™.
f America has more mobile phones per household than any other country.
g MTV™ is the biggest news channel in the world.
h Yahoo® is the most popular search engine in the world.
i The tallest skyscraper in the world is the Taipei 101.

3 Write down a few false business facts of your own. Read them out to the rest of the class. Can they correct you?

4 **1.21** Listen to an extract from a meeting and tick the sentences which are correct.
a The meeting is being held to discuss last month's sales figures. ☐
b Overall, sales are up by 2.6%. ☐
c The best results are in Denmark and Norway. ☐
d 30,000 units have been sold in Scandinavia. ☐
e Last month was June. ☐
f John Munroe is head of Northern Europe. ☐
g Munroe is in Scotland at the moment. ☐

5 **1.21** Listen again and correct the mistakes in 4.

6 The following expressions are used to query information you are less sure about. They were all in the conversation you just listened to. Complete them with the words in the box.

| mistake | right | sound | sure |

a Are you _____?
b There must be some _____.
c That can't be _____.
d That doesn't _____ right to me.

7 How good is your business general knowledge? <u>Underline</u> the correct information below.

WORLD BUSINESS RECORDS

a According to Forbes magazine, the world's biggest public company (inc. sales, profits, assets and market value) is **Exxon Mobil / Royal Dutch Shell / General Electric**

b The world's best-selling mobile phone to date is **the iPhone / the Nokia 1100 / the Samsung Galaxy**

c The world's best-selling model of car to date is **the VW Beetle / the Toyota Corolla / the Ford Focus™**

d The world's oldest airline is **KLM / British Airways / Singapore Airlines**

e The world's most popular website is **YouTube / Facebook / Google**

f According to BrandZ, the world's largest brand equity database, the world's most valuable luxury brand is **Louis Vuitton / Gucci® / Cartier**

g The world's oldest bank is **the Banca Monte dei Paschi di Siena/ Sumitomo Mitsui / the Bank of England**

h The single invention with the highest global turnover is **the personal computer / the electric light bulb / the automobile**

i The world's biggest exporter of computer software is **the USA / Ireland / India**

j The country with the highest trade union membership is **France / Sweden / Russia**

k The world's richest country in GDP per head is **Qatar / Liechtenstein / Switzerland**

l Before it finally went into liquidation in 2006, Japanese architectural firm Kongo Gumi was the world's oldest family firm, having been in business for **350 years / 700 years / 1,400 years**

Answers on page 126

Now work with a partner to practise querying information. Take turns to read out your answers to the quiz. Query anything you think is wrong.

8 Sometimes what people say in meetings conflicts with what they said earlier.

A Eight out of ten members of staff liked the proposal. So, 90% is a good result.

B **Wait a minute.** Ninety per cent? **I thought you said** eight out of ten …

A Oh, yeah. Sorry, 80%, of course.

Work with a partner to practise pointing out discrepancies. Speaker A see page 135. Speaker B see page 140.

The briefing meeting

In company interviews Units 1–3

1.22 A mergers and acquisitions specialist has been transferred to the Tokyo office of his bank to work as part of a project team during a takeover bid. He is attending his first briefing meeting, but things don't go quite as he expected. Listen and complete his notes. Then check with a partner.

Sappore Bank Acquisition – Project team

Team leader: (a) _____
Position in company.: (b) _____

Me

Sharon (c) _____
Position in company.: (d) _____

Janet (e) _____
Job: (f) _____

Robin (g) _____
Job: (h) _____

- I'll be based at (i) _____.

- My main responsibility will be (j) _____.

- First project meeting scheduled for (k) _____.

- First round of negotiations begin on (l) _____.

03 Keeping track

Business phrasal verbs

Complete each conversation with one of the five words in the box.
Then match the phrasal verbs in the conversation to the verbs similar in meaning.

| down | off | on | out | up |

a The project meeting

A	Okay, that's item two. Let's move		to item three: new projects.
B	Now, just hold		a minute, Sylvia.
A	Kim, I'm counting		you to get us the Zurich contract.
B	But this is not the time to be taking		more work.

continue = _____ accept = _____ rely = _____ wait = _____

b The troubleshooting meeting

A	Right. Have you managed to sort		the problem with our computers?
B	To be honest, we haven't really found		exactly what the problem is yet.
A	Well, can I just point		that it's now affecting everyone on the first floor?
B	Yes, I know. We're carrying		tests on the system now. Give us a couple of hours.

say = _____ discover = _____ do = _____ solve = _____

c The union negotiation

A	The question is, will you agree to call		the strike?
B	Not if you're still planning to lay		a quarter of the workforce, no.
A	I'm afraid that's a decision we can't put		any longer.
B	Then, I'm sorry, we shall have to break		these negotiations.

fire = _____ end = _____ cancel = _____ postpone = _____

d The marketing meeting

A	We really must fix		a meeting to discuss our pricing strategy.
B	Our prices are fine. We're trying to build		market share, Otto. Profits can wait.
A	Yes, but our overheads have gone		nearly 20% over the last 18 months.
B	I know, but that's no reason to put		prices. We'll just lose customers.

rise = _____ raise = _____ arrange = _____ develop = _____

e The budget meeting

A	I'm afraid they've turned		our application for a bigger budget.
B	That's because group turnover's gone		again. So where are we supposed to make cuts?
A	We could start by cutting		the amount of time we waste in these meetings!
B	Now, calm		everybody. We need to be practical.

reduce = _____ relax = _____ reject = _____ decrease = _____

Comparatives and superlatives

Type	Adjective	Comparative	Superlative
1	cheap	cheaper	the cheapest
2	safe	safer	the safest
3	big	bigger	the biggest
4	early	earlier	the earliest
5	important	more important	the most important
6	good	better	the best

1 Classify the adjectives below as type 1–6.

clever ☐	high ☐	sad ☐
hot ☐	global ☐	thin ☐
dirty ☐	bad ☐	fat ☐
helpful ☐	wealthy ☐	late ☐
hard ☐	easy ☐	effective ☐
heavy ☐	rich ☐	reliable ☐

What generalizations can you make about one-syllable, two-syllable and three-syllable adjectives?

2 Use your own personal experiences to complete the following sentences. If necessary, use a dictionary to help you choose the right adjectives.

a The job I've got now is a lot _____ than my previous one. On the other hand, it's not quite as _____.

b I found _____ to be a fairly _____ city, but I think _____ is even _____.

c To be honest, I don't really like _____ music. I prefer something a bit _____.

d I'll never forget the view from _____. It's even _____ than the one from _____.

e I find _____ food fairly _____, but it's not quite as _____ as people think.

f I think the _____ building I've ever seen must be _____. Either that or _____, which was just as _____, but in a different way.

g The people in _____ are some of the _____ I've ever met – apart from the _____, who are even _____.

h I drive a _____ these days. In terms of _____, it's the _____ car I've ever had, but it's not as _____ as the _____ I used to have.

3 Complete the following humorous article with the comparative and superlative expressions in the boxes.

a–g

a lot more　　by far the lowest　　compared with even worse　　little safer　　much better　　world's highest

h–l

10% longer　　as famous as　　a little more significantly happier　　twice as likely

---

Phrase bank: Checking understanding

Look at the phrases and expressions below. Which do you use when you:

- understood differently?
- didn't hear?
- didn't understand?

a _____

Sorry, I ⟶ missed that.
　　　　　　 didn't catch that.

Could you just ⟶ say it again?
　　　　　　　　 go over that again?

b _____

　　　　　　 'm not (quite) with you.
　　　　　　 don't (quite) follow you.
Sorry, I ⟶ don't (quite) see what you mean.
　　　　　　 explain what you mean?
Could you just ⟶ be (a bit) more specific?
　　　　　　　　 say (a bit) more about that?

c _____

Isn't it
Don't you mean
Shouldn't that be ⟶ 12%?
I thought you said

What's the effect of using the words in brackets ( )?

How to live forever: six golden rules

Rule 1
Don't live in Iceland. With long dark winters, sub-zero temperatures and active volcanos, it has the (a) _____ suicide rate. Move to Palm Beach, Florida, where you have a (b) _____ chance of living to be over 100 – like the rest of the residents.

Rule 2
Don't go to Johannesburg. It's the murder capital of the world. Statistically, it's (c) _____ dangerous than São Paulo or New York. Milan's a (d) _____ but try not to breathe. The pollution's (e) _____ than in Mexico City.

Rule 3
Don't get sick in Equatorial Guinea. There's only one doctor to every 70,000 patients and no anaesthetic. If you have to be ill, be ill in Kuwait. It has (f) _____ death rate in the world. Only 3.1 people per thousand die annually, (g) _____ 11.2 in Britain.

Rule 4
If you're a man, think of becoming a woman. On average, women live (h) _____ than men. If you're a woman, stay single. Crime figures show women are (i) _____ to be killed by their partner than anyone else.

Rule 5
Become a 'chocoholic'. Chocolate isn't good for you, but it releases chemicals in the brain that make you (j) _____. And it's a medical fact that happiness prolongs life.

Rule 6
Become famous – like Elvis, James Dean and John Lennon. People will believe you're alive even after you're dead. Even if you can't be (k) _____ Marilyn Monroe or Kurt Cobain, you can be (l) _____ careful than they were. Don't act crazy! You won't actually live longer. It will just seem like it!

04 Listening

1 Have you had bosses like the CEO in the cartoon? Who's the *best* listener you know?

2 Complete the following sentences and share views with a partner.

a When someone is talking, I think it's rude to …

b One thing I find really irritating when I'm speaking to someone is …

c If I'm bored in a meeting, I often find myself …

d When people just won't get to the point, then it's okay to …

3 Read the article and answer the questions.

a In what context are the following statistics mentioned?

b Do any of them surprise you?

| 80% | 4–5 | 700wpm | ¾ | ½ | 25% | $50,000 | $14,000 | 2:1 |

"He's a good listener, but only to the sound of his own voice."

LISTEN UP!

Psychologist Eric Berne used to say that everyone in the world just wants to be listened to, but they seldom get what they want because so does everyone else! And this is especially true in the office. Research carried out by UK leadership institute Roffey Park shows that 80% of managers do not listen well. Part of the problem is that we think four to five times faster than we speak – about 700 words per minute. So no wonder our minds wander the minute someone else opens their mouth!

In their classic book on the subject, *Are You Listening?*, Ralph Nichols and Leonard Stevens estimate that the average employee spends about three-quarters of each working day in conversations with colleagues and clients – roughly half of this time requires them to listen and yet this is a skill at which most are only 25% effective. That means that in the case of an employee earning $50,000 a year, their company is actually paying them around $14,000 not to listen! But really bad listeners cost their companies millions more by damaging relationships, missing opportunities and making careless mistakes.
As the ancient Greek philosopher Epictetus wisely reminded us: 'We have two ears and one mouth, so that we can listen twice as much as we speak.'

4 1.23 As a group, listen to extracts from three conversations (a–c) and discuss what's going wrong. Summarize the main problem in each conversation.

Extract a _____

Extract b _____

Extract c _____

5 One way of making sure you're a good listener is to employ the L.I.S.T.E.N. method. With a partner, match the guidelines (a–f) to what you need to do (1–6).

a **L**ook interested

b **I**nquire

c **S**ummarize

d **T**est understanding

e **E**ncourage

f **N**eutralize your own attitudes

1 seek further information, probe with questions

2 resist the temptation to judge or criticize too soon

3 clarify any points which are unclear to you

4 establish eye contact, adopt an open, alert posture

5 paraphrase regularly to show you're paying attention

6 make polite noises, show support, repeat keywords

6 1.24–1.27 Now listen to extracts from four more constructive conversations. What's the main topic of conversation and which of the six listening skills in 5 is the listener using?

Extract 1 Topic: _____

Skill: _____

Extract 2 Topic: _____

Skill: _____

Extract 3 Topic: _____

Skill: _____

Extract 4 Topic: _____

Skill: _____

7 1.24–1.27 Can you remember in which extracts in 6 you heard the following? Listen again if you need to.

a So what you're saying is …

It sounds like you think …

In other words …

Okay, so the way you see it is …

So, for you, it's a question of …

Extract: _____

c Uh huh, go on.

Really?

Oh, that's interesting.

Right, I'm with you. Good point.

Hmm, nice idea. I like it.

Extract: _____

b Are you saying …?

Do you mean …?

What do you mean by …?

Sorry, I'm not quite with you.

How do you mean exactly?

Extract: _____

d How is that going to affect …?

But wouldn't that mean …?

Why do you say that?

Do you have figures for that?

Okay, fine. Just one question …

Extract: _____

8 Work with a partner. Each read out one of the meeting extracts below slowly and clearly. The other should listen and follow the instructions in brackets. Spend a few minutes preparing your questions and answers before you start. Some of the expressions in 7 might be helpful.

a Okay, well, in my opinion, our sales team is badly underperforming *(clarify)*. I think we definitely need to introduce some kind of incentive scheme *(encourage)*. We must also do something about poor performers *(clarify)*. At the same time, we have to build team spirit *(encourage)*. I'm concerned that there's currently too little communication and collaboration between team members *(summarize and ask one or two further questions)*.

b Okay, this is just an idea, but why don't we do more to celebrate successes amongst our sales staff *(clarify)*? This would be a great way to reinforce the idea that we're a winning team *(encourage)*. Perhaps we could also develop a mentoring system *(clarify)*. If junior staff could turn to more experienced team members for advice, I think it would improve overall performance and boost morale *(encourage)*. In fact, maybe mentors could get a bonus based on the performance of the people they're mentoring *(summarize and ask one or two further questions)*.

9 Work with a partner to practise your active listening skills. Both speakers see page 127.

The networking event

**Learning objectives:
Management
Scenario A**
Business communication
Identifying networker types;
Rules for successful networking;
Fluency: A networking event
Reading Making the most of
business networking events
In company in action
A1: The networking event;
A2: A useful contact

1 Flow Information Systems (FIS) is a London-based company that designs and sets up computer networks and databases for small and medium-sized firms. Anton Vega is the sales manager at FIS and he's about to attend his first breakfast networking event in London. Read the event's web page and answer the questions.

a Where and when is the event being held?

b What do you think CIO and MIS stand for?

c What's the event schedule?

d What's the dedicated website for?

SMALL BUSINESS NETWORKING EVENT
Help your IT business grow

A free networking workshop to help small business owners grow

**Monday 27th June – OXO2 Events Space Level Two
OXO Tower Wharf – South Bank – London SE1 9PH**

On 27th June, the CIO for Radcliffe Hotels (UK), Adrian Moore, joins us for the Small Business Networking Event at London's iconic OXO Tower. Adrian's short keynote, 'Cloud-Based Management Information Systems', will be followed by a gourmet breakfast as you mix and mingle with small business owners, IT directors and MIS providers from all over Europe. A dedicated website will be set up after the event to help you keep in touch and develop your new business relationships… **[more]**

---

2 How useful do you think these events are? Have you ever attended a similar event? If so, did you make any useful contacts?

3 Match the networker types (a–d) to their descriptions (1–4). Have you met anyone like this?

a The autobiographer

b The time waster

c The escape artist

d The hard seller

1 This person is so busy telling you all about themselves and their company, they barely have time to ask about you and yours.

2 This person talks business from the moment you meet and gives you their business card before you've even introduced yourself.

3 This person seems vaguely interested in what you have to offer, but is clearly not seriously considering doing business with you.

4 This person introduces you to someone (probably a time waster), and then leaves you with them whilst they go and talk to someone else.

In company in action

4 Now watch video A1 to see Anton networking at the event and put the types of people he meets in the order he meets them. How well does he deal with them – well (☺), okay (😐) or badly (☹)?

The autobiographer	☐	☺ 😐 ☹
The time waster	☐	☺ 😐 ☹
The escape artist	☐	☺ 😐 ☹
The hard seller	☐	☺ 😐 ☹

5 Discuss these questions with a partner.

a What can you remember about each of the people Anton spoke to at the event?

b How might he improve his networking skills?

6 Read the article on business networking events and complete the comments on the right. Then compare with a partner.

From Small Talk to Big Talk

Making the most of business networking events

In these days of social media, you might think that making personal contact is much less important than it used to be. Harvard business professor, Al Roth, disagrees and has shown that even the shortest conversation before discussing a deal will make potential business partners six or seven times more likely to co-operate. Here, then, are the rules of the game …

Rule number one: Start with small talk. In some cultures, business people think small talk is not as important as a real business conversation. But as communication specialist Debra Fine reminds us, 'without small talk, you rarely get to the real conversation'. The secret is to avoid boring small talk – the venue, the weather – and try to find something personal and positive to say to the people you meet. It could just be to compliment them on an item of clothing. But, if you've done your homework, you might be able to say something more personal or business-related. Either way, you've started a conversation and are ready to talk.

Rule number two: Have strategies for ending unproductive conversations. From time to time, we all get stuck in conversations that are going nowhere. It's rude to suddenly stop, but don't fall into the politeness trap and miss the opportunity to talk to others. Prepare a couple of good excuses for why you have to move on. If you're attending the event with a colleague, agree a way to signal to each other when you need 'rescuing'.

Rule number three: Find out what you can do for others. Instead of focusing on what other people at the event can do for you – which may make you nervous and overly anxious to do business – take Internet entrepreneur Guy Kawasaki's advice and try focusing on what you can do for them. This will both relax you and encourage you to listen, as well as make you more popular!

Rule number four: Keep it short and arrange to meet again. Don't drag out the conversation too long; you both want to meet other people at the event. Establish the basis for talking business now and arrange to talk again soon.

I think the article makes a good point about
_____
_____.

In my culture, the attitude to small talk is
_____
_____.

For me personally, the most important pieces of advice here are
_____
_____.

But I'm not sure I agree with the point about
_____
_____.

Next time I network with potential business contacts, I'll definitely try _____
_____.

In company in action

7 Now watch video A2 to see Anton having more success making a useful business contact. Which of the advice in the article in 6 has he taken?

8 Work with a partner to practise networking. Turn to page 128.

9 Now evaluate your performance using the feedback form on page 127.

Business travel

Have you had any 'remarkable' airplane journeys?

Learning objectives: Unit 5

Business communication skills Expressing likes and dislikes about travelling on business; Making polite requests and enquiries; Fluency: Dealing with travel situations; Identifying signs as British or American English; Roleplay: Greeting visitors

Reading Article from *Newsweek* about people who live in two cities; Article: travel tips

Listening Business travel conversations; Short exchanges in British and American English; Conversations at the airport

Vocabulary Business trips

Grammar Polite question forms

Phrase bank Business travel

1 Do you ever travel on business? If not, would you like to?

2 Combine one word from each section to make at least ten sentences. Start by making collocations from columns 3 and 4. Add your own ideas, if you like.

| I | don't like
can't stand
hate
dread
like
look forward to
enjoy
love | late
getting
losing
the endless
flight
meeting
tight
missing
finding out
strange
language
jet
getting away from
traffic
having
being away from
visiting | interesting people
problems
jams
lag
my luggage
food
queues
schedules
nights
lost
my family
the office
about different cultures
foreign places
new experiences
delays |

3 Look at these ways of emphasizing your opinions.

What I really like is *finding out about different cultures.*
What I hate most is *being away from my family.*
The thing I love most is *visiting foreign places.*
The best thing for me is *getting out of the office for a few days.*
The worst thing for me is *flight delays.*

Work in groups. Tell other people in the group what you like and dislike most about travelling.

On the move

1 🔘 **1.28** Listen to 18 short conversations involving people travelling on business. Where are the speakers? Write the numbers of the conversations under the correct location below.

In the taxi	At check-in	In departures
☐ ☐ ☐	☐ ☐ ☐	☐ ☐ ☐

On the plane	At customs	At the hotel
☐ ☐ ☐	☐ ☐ ☐	☐ ☐ ☐

2 Now match the question beginnings (a–h) to the endings (1–8). They were all in the conversations you just listened to.

a Could I
b Could you
c Would you mind
d Can you tell me
e Would you please
f Could I ask you
g Do you think I could have
h Is there somewhere I could

1 what time you stop serving dinner?
2 have your room number, please?
3 switch off your laptop now, please, sir?
4 not smoking, please?
5 to open your luggage, please, madam?
6 return to your seats?
7 send a fax from?
8 an alarm call at half past six tomorrow morning?

3 Which question beginnings in 2 could go before the following endings?

- borrow your mobile?
- buy some stamps?
- hurry or I'll miss my plane?

- which terminal I need?
- lending me some money until I find a cashpoint?
- to wait outside for five minutes?

> **AmE** lines = **BrE** queues
> **AmE** check bags = **BrE** check bags in

Travel tips

1 Bruce Tulgan is the CEO of Rainmaker Thinking Inc., the author of *Winning the Talent Wars* and an experienced business traveller. Complete his travel tips with the pairs of words in the box.

> business + pleasure   children + passengers   connections + flights   evening + destination
> magazines + newspapers   movies + view   receipts + cards   thing + problem
> travellers + lines   water + bags   work + plane

Bruce Tulgan's Top Tips

- Mix (a) _____ and _____. If I am going someplace nice, I try to bring my wife.

- Use hotel time wisely. Work out. Watch (b) _____ that your partner will never want to watch. Ask for a nice _____.

- Stay away from amateur (c) _____ whenever possible, especially in _____ and on planes.

- The most important (d) _____ I've learned is to be Zen when travelling. Whenever there is a _____, it helps to be almost emotionless.

- Avoid (e) _____ whenever possible – take direct _____.

- I try not to do 'serious' (f) _____ that requires concentration on the _____, because I find I am about half as effective as normal.

- For USA to Europe, leave in the (g) _____ whenever possible, sleep on the plane, wake up in the morning at your _____.

- Bring earplugs in case of (h) _____. Give very cold vibes to talkative _____.

- Drink tons of (i) _____. Pack very light. Never check _____.

- Use plane time wisely. Sleep, read, sort (j) _____ and business _____.

- Use airport time wisely. Stretch, walk, read (k) _____ and _____ while you're waiting. Make phone calls.

2 Discuss Tulgan's travel tips with a partner. Do you share his attitudes?

The nightmare journey

How well do you cope on business trips? Work with a partner to sort out a series of problems. Speaker A see page 130. Speaker B see page 135.

Transatlantic crossing

1 If your company asked you to relocate to Britain or the United States, which would you choose?

2 Look at the article below. What do you think the title means? Read the first paragraph to find out.

3 Now read the article and think about the questions below. Then discuss them with a partner.

4 Try to guess the meanings of the words and expressions in **bold** from their context.

The NY-Lon life

Ron Kastner is a classic New Yorker: first off the plane, first out of the airport. Carrying a single small bag, he walks straight through immigration and customs. He doesn't look like he's spent six hours in the air (business class will do that to you). He owns an apartment in the East Village in Manhattan, but tonight London is home: a flat in Belgravia, London's **wealthiest neighbourhood**. Kastner is a resident of a place called NY-Lon, a single city inconveniently separated by an ocean. He flies between the two cities up to five times a month. David Eastman lives there too. A Londoner who is a VP at Agency.com in New York, he travels the JFK–Heathrow route so often he's **on a first-name basis** with the Virgin Atlantic business class cabin crew.

As different as New York and London are, a growing number of people are living, working and playing in the two cities as if they were one. The cities **are drawn together by** a shared language and culture, but mostly by money – more of which **flows** through Wall Street and the City each day than all the rest of the world's financial centres combined. The **boom** in financial services attracted advertising agencies, accounting firms and management consultancies to both cities. Then came hotel and restaurant businesses, architecture and design, **real estate** and construction, air travel, tourism and other service industries.

Trevor Beattie, the London-based creative director of ad agency TBWA Worldwide, says, 'New York and London are both so **trendy** and so modern now in terms of fashion, art, photography, music.' 'We dream about each other's cities,' says Joel Kissin, a New Zealander who after 25 years in London bought a **penthouse** on New York's Fifth Avenue. 'If you're in New York, your dream is London and if you're in London, your dream is New York.'

a Is business class really that much better than economy?
b Would you like Ron Kastner's life?
c Do you have a favourite airline?
d Do New York and London share a culture? Or even a language?
e What other financial centres could eventually overtake London and New York?
f What are the other boom industries these days?
g Which two cities would you like to have homes in?

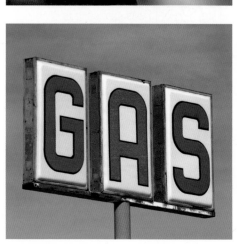

Where in the world?

1 Where would a business traveller see the following? Half of them are in New York and half in London. Write *NY* or *L* next to each.

a	Walk / Don't walk	____	**j**	Open Mon thru Fri ____
b	Freeway 2m	____	**k**	Parking lot ____
c	City center	____	**l**	Taxis: queue here ____
d	Rest rooms	____	**m**	Car park full ____
e	Underground	____	**n**	Chemists ____
f	Lift out of order	____	**o**	Truck stop ____
g	Gas station	____	**p**	Colour copies 10p ____
h	Motorway services 15m	____	**q**	Subway ____
i	Roundabout ahead	____	**r**	Trolleys ____

2 🔘 **1.29** Listen to the recording. Where do the conversations take place? Write the numbers in the boxes.

London ☐ ☐ ☐ ☐   New York ☐ ☐ ☐ ☐

In arrivals

1 🔘 **1.30–1.33** Listen to four conversations in which people meet at the airport and answer the questions.

	Conversation 1	Conversation 2	Conversation 3	Conversation 4
Have the speakers met before?				
What topics do they discuss?				
What plans do they make?				

2 Complete the following table with one word in each gap. All the expressions were in the conversations you just listened to.

You	(a) _____	be waiting for me.	… if that's	(f) _____	with you.
You		be tired after your long flight.	I hope that's		
You		be Alan Hayes.	He		his apologies.
(b) _____	me take those for you.		Susan	(g) _____	her love.
	me help you with your bags.		Martin		his regards.
We	(c) _____	you into the Savoy.	Luckily, I managed to		some sleep on the plane.
We		a table for 1.30.	I thought we could	(h) _____	some lunch.
So,	(d) _____	are things?	Now, let's see if we can		a taxi.
So,		is married life?	I was expecting to		Mr Hill.
So,		is business?	Thanks for coming to	(i) _____	me.
So,		was your flight?	I'd like you to		Graham Banks.
I	(e) _____	upgraded.	Pleased to		you.
I've		a taxi waiting outside.			

3 The red-eye is a long-haul night flight. Work with a partner to practise meeting a colleague off the red-eye in New York. Speaker A see page 136. Speaker B see page 138.

05 Business travel

Business trips

Think about the business trips you've been on in the past. The events below are listed in the order they usually happen. Complete them with the words in the boxes.

| check-in | destination | flight | lounge |
| movie | plane | shopping | sleep | the airport |

| a meal | arrivals | bags | control | customs |
| hotel | night | traffic | your things |

a confirm your _____

b take a taxi to _____

c queue at _____

d do some _____

e wait in the departure _____

f board the _____

g watch an in-flight _____

h try to get some _____

i arrive at your _____

j go through passport _____

k collect your _____

l go through _____

m be met in _____

n get stuck in _____

o check into your _____

p unpack _____

q go out for _____

r get an early _____

Polite question forms

When you make enquiries and requests, polite question forms and indirect questions are often more appropriate than imperatives and direct questions.

Imperative/direct question	Polite question form/indirect question
Where's the nearest taxi rank? (enquiry)	*Could you tell me where the nearest taxi rank is?*
Why is the flight delayed? (enquiry)	*Do you think you could tell me why the flight is delayed?*
	Do you happen to know why the flight is delayed?
Can I open the window? (request)	*Could I open the window?*
	Do you mind if I open the window?
	Would you mind if I opened the window?
Help me with my bags! (request)	*Could you help me with my bags?*
	Would you help me with my bags?
	Would you mind helping me with my bags?

1 You've just got a new boss. Your old boss was rude and a nightmare to work for. Fortunately, your new boss is much nicer. Look at some of the things your old boss used to say to you below and change them into what your new boss would probably say using a polite question form. Think carefully about word order and grammar.

a Coffee!

Could you _____?

b Remember to use the spell check in future!

Would you please _____?

c I want a word with you in private!

Could I _____?

d Where do I plug this mobile in?

Is there somewhere _____?

e Check these figures again!

Would you mind _____?

f How does this damn computer work?

Could you tell _____?

g What's the dialling code for Greece?

Do you happen _____?

h You'll have to work overtime this evening.

Do you think I could ask _____?

2 When you're rushing around on business, it's easy to sound more aggressive than you mean to. Use polite question forms or indirect questions to make these enquiries and requests sound more polite.

a I want a window seat.

_____

b Help me with my bags!

_____

c Where's a cashpoint?

_____

d Change this £20 note!

_____

e Don't drive so fast!

_____

f Lend me your mobile!

_____

g I need to recharge my laptop somewhere.

_____

h You'll have to give me three separate receipts.

_____

i What time is it?

_____

j How far is it to the airport?

_____

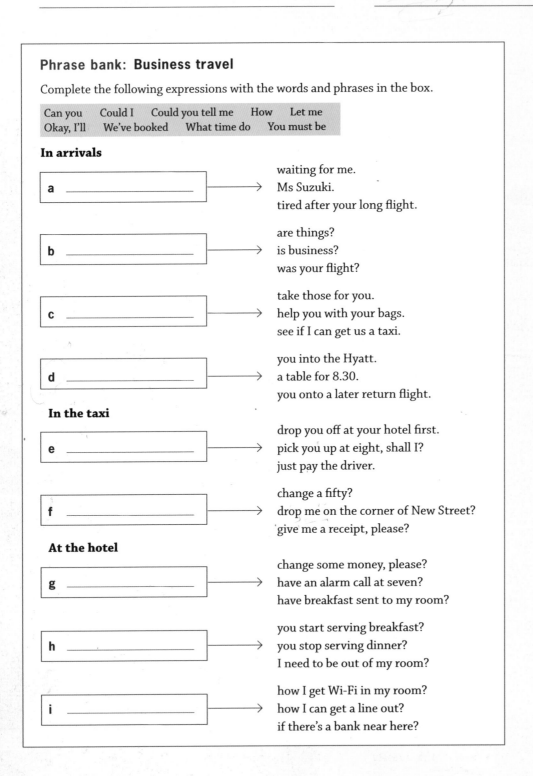

Phrase bank: Business travel

Complete the following expressions with the words and phrases in the box.

Can you	Could I	Could you tell me	How	Let me
Okay, I'll	We've booked	What time do	You must be

In arrivals

a _____ → waiting for me.
Ms Suzuki.
tired after your long flight.

b _____ → are things?
is business?
was your flight?

c _____ → take those for you.
help you with your bags.
see if I can get us a taxi.

d _____ → you into the Hyatt.
a table for 8.30.
you onto a later return flight.

In the taxi

e _____ → drop you off at your hotel first.
pick you up at eight, shall I?
just pay the driver.

f _____ → change a fifty?
drop me on the corner of New Street?
give me a receipt, please?

At the hotel

g _____ → change some money, please?
have an alarm call at seven?
have breakfast sent to my room?

h _____ → you start serving breakfast?
you stop serving dinner?
I need to be out of my room?

i _____ → how I get Wi-Fi in my room?
how I can get a line out?
if there's a bank near here?

06

> *The reason computers can do more work than people is that computers never have to answer the phone.*
>
> Anonymous

Do you prefer to make phone calls at work or send emails?

Handling calls

1 Work in groups and discuss the questions.

a What percentage of your time at work do you spend on the phone?

b How many of the calls you make and receive are essential?

c Can you not answer the phone? When you answer, is it:

- out of curiosity – it might be some good news for a change?
- with a sigh of relief – it must be less boring than whatever you're doing?
- because you're so indispensable, no one else is capable of dealing with it?
- force of habit – the phone rings, you pick it up?
- because if you don't, no one else will?
- for fear of what might happen to you if you don't?

2 Read the statistics below. What points are they making about phone calls at work?

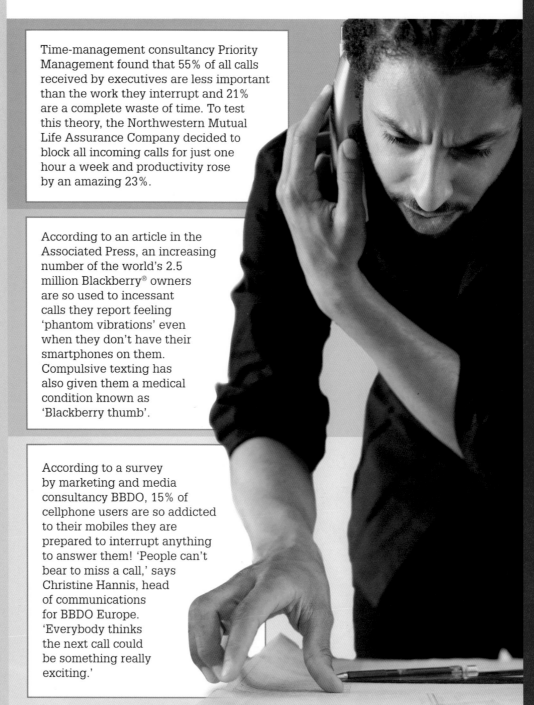

Time-management consultancy Priority Management found that 55% of all calls received by executives are less important than the work they interrupt and 21% are a complete waste of time. To test this theory, the Northwestern Mutual Life Assurance Company decided to block all incoming calls for just one hour a week and productivity rose by an amazing 23%.

According to an article in the Associated Press, an increasing number of the world's 2.5 million Blackberry® owners are so used to incessant calls they report feeling 'phantom vibrations' even when they don't have their smartphones on them. Compulsive texting has also given them a medical condition known as 'Blackberry thumb'.

According to a survey by marketing and media consultancy BBDO, 15% of cellphone users are so addicted to their mobiles they are prepared to interrupt anything to answer them! 'People can't bear to miss a call,' says Christine Hannis, head of communications for BBDO Europe. 'Everybody thinks the next call could be something really exciting.'

3 Complete the sentences with the pairs of words in the box.

| busy + ring | disturbed + hold | expecting + pick up | important + leave | out + divert |
| possible + answer | real + unplug |

a If I'm _____, I just let the phone _____.

b If I don't want to be _____, I tell my secretary to _____ all my calls.

c If _____, I try to _____ the phone before the fourth ring.

d If I'm _____ a call from the boss, I _____ the phone immediately.

e If I'm in the middle of something _____, I let them _____ a voicemail.

f If I'm having a _____ crisis, I _____ the damn thing!

g If I'm going to be _____ of the office, I _____ my calls.

4 How many of the statements in 3 are true for you? Compare with a partner.

Asking politely

1 Use the words and phrases in the box to make seven useful expressions which start with *if*.

| can | got a minute | got time | not too busy | not too much trouble | possible | would |

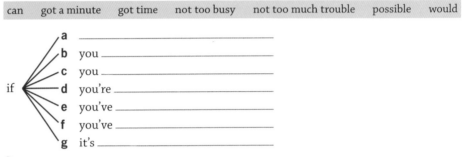

if
a _____
b you _____
c you _____
d you're _____
e you've _____
f you've _____
g it's _____

2 Divide the text into 12 things someone might phone to ask you to do.
All the requests start with *Could you …?*

Could you …?

emailmemyflightdetailsletmehaveacopyofthereportgetontooursupplierget
backtomewithinthehourtakeaquicklookattheproposalarrangeforsomebody
tomeetthematthestationsetupameetingwiththeheadsofdepartmentsend
theiraccountsdepartmentareminderfixmeanappointmentbooktheconference
roomforthreefaxthefiguresthroughtomeorganizeatouroftheplantforsomevisitors

3 Work with a partner. Make and answer polite telephone requests using the language
from 1 and 2 above. Speaker A see page 130. Speaker B see page 136.

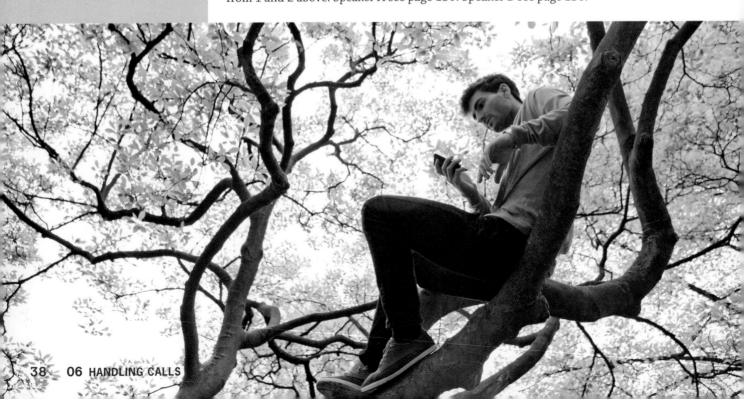

Unexpected phone calls

1 🔘 **1.34–1.37** Listen to four telephone calls and match them to their descriptions.

Call 1 **a** The caller is kept waiting.

Call 2 **b** A business contact calls to ask a favour.

Call 3 **c** A sales executive calls with a quote.

Call 4 **d** There is a communication breakdown.

2 🔘 **1.34–1.37** Listen again and answer the questions.

Call 1

a What's the misunderstanding?

b How does the man receiving the call deal with the problem?

c Do you ever have difficulties answering calls in English?

Call 2

a How does the person receiving the call avoid another call?

b Do you think he is really in a meeting?

c Do you ever pretend you're busy just to get someone off the phone?

Call 3

a How would you describe the telephone manner of the person receiving the call?

b What is the caller calling about?

c Have you ever been treated unprofessionally on the phone?

Call 4

a Where did the speakers meet?

b What does the caller want?

c Have you ever received a phone call from someone you have met but can't remember?

3 All the expressions below were in the telephone conversations you just listened to. Can you remember the first three words of each expression? *It's* and *I'm* count as one word.

Call 1

a _____ me through to Yves Dupont?

b _____ don't understand.

c _____ more slowly, please?

Call 2

a _____ those prices you wanted.

b _____ can't talk right now.

c _____ me back – say, in an hour?

Call 3

a _____ do for you?

b _____ when he'll be back?

c _____ speaking to?

Call 4

a _____ bother you.

b _____ who's calling?

c _____ me a contact number?

4 Use the phrases in the box to make nine responses to the statements below. All the responses were in the telephone conversations you just listened to.

> back later   back to you tomorrow   if I can reach him on his cellphone
> something out   someone who speaks better English   that right away
> to hear from you then   to you later   what I can do

a   I need to be on the next flight to Oslo.
b   I keep calling Mr Kirk at his office and getting no answer.
c   I'm afraid Angela's not here at the moment.
d   Could you fax me a map of the city centre?
e   I've got to go, I'm afraid. I've got a meeting.
f   I should be able to give you an answer by this afternoon.
g   I need somebody to come and have a look at my PC.
h   I'm sorry, I don't speak German.
i   I need those figures within the next 24 hours.

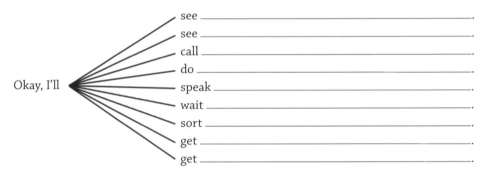

Okay, I'll
- see _____.
- see _____.
- call _____.
- do _____.
- speak _____.
- wait _____.
- sort _____.
- get _____.
- get _____.

5 Work with a partner to practise dealing with incoming phone calls. Speaker A see page 141. Speaker B see page 137.

6 a Complete the boxes below with the names of four people who typically phone you at work to ask you to do things. Write down what they usually ask you to do. Include private calls if you like.

   b Categorize each call: urgent (must be done now), important (but can wait), social (just keeping in touch), a nuisance (time wasting).

   c Swap boxes with a partner and practise phoning each other. What excuses can you give to avoid doing what they ask? Or what can you offer to do to get them off the phone?

Caller 1

Who's calling?

What do they want?

How important/urgent is it?

What excuses can you make to avoid doing it?

What can you do to help them out?

Caller 2

Who's calling?

What do they want?

How important/urgent is it?

What excuses can you make to avoid doing it?

What can you do to help them out?

Caller 3

Who's calling?

What do they want?

How important/urgent is it?

What excuses can you make to avoid doing it?

What can you do to help them out?

Caller 4

Who's calling?

What do they want?

How important/urgent is it?

What excuses can you make to avoid doing it?

What can you do to help them out?

06 Handling calls

Vocabulary

Office life

Complete the poem about a day at the office using the verbs on the right. Use the rhyme to help you.

To do today

First, there's a report to ¹ _____.
Then I'll ² _____ those figures through.
Flight details.
³ _____ emails.
Don't worry, I'll ⁴ _____ back to you.

check
get
do
fax

A memo now to ⁵ _____.
Nasty jobs to ⁶ _____.
Travel miles.
⁷ _____ files.
Can't stop now! I'm ⁸ _____ late.

update
circulate
running
delegate

⁹ _____ my calls till half past ten.
Should have ¹⁰ _____ my desk by then.
¹¹ _____ a copy.
¹² _____ a coffee.
¹³ _____ English class again!

cleared
grab
hold
cancel
print

Messages to ¹⁴ _____ to.
One moment, please, I'll ¹⁵ _____ you through.
¹⁶ _____ at three.
¹⁷ _____ PC!
¹⁸ _____ another interview.

meet
arrange
listen
put
crash

¹⁹ _____ up clients at the station.
²⁰ _____ a formal presentation.
²¹ _____ a list
Of deadlines ²² _____
²³ _____ off the negotiation!

give
make
break
missed
pick

²⁴ _____ supplier in Milan –
²⁵ _____ an appointment if you ²⁶ _____
²⁷ _____ that phone!
Must ²⁸ _____
The teleconference with Japan.

postpone
get
contact
fix
can

²⁹ _____ work at half past eight.
Must ³⁰ _____ home – I may be late.
³¹ _____ the car.
³² _____ the bar.
Damn it – why not ³³ _____?

phone
hit
celebrate
finish
leave

So, you ³⁴ _____ the presentation!
³⁵ _____ up the negotiation!
³⁶ _____ better?
³⁷ _____ a letter.
Now ³⁸ _____ in your resignation!

draft
hand
screwed
blew
feeling

Is your office anything like this?

Grammar

will

Will is a modal verb (like *can*, *must* and *should*).

Affirmative

I You He She It We They	will ('ll)	work.

Negative

I You He She It We They	will not (won't)	work.

Interrogative

Will Won't	I you he she it we they	work?

1 Correct the following sentences using the information above.

a Do you will help me?
b Stop making personal calls or I'll to charge you for them.
c I expect the company will to do well.
d I don't will accept anything less than 2%.
e Don't worry, he wills phone you back within the hour.
f I'll to take that call, if you like.
g I'll sending the figures right away.

2 Match the corrected sentences in 1 to their functions below.

1 a prediction about the future ☐
2 a spontaneous decision/reaction ☐
3 an offer ☐
4 a request ☐
5 a promise ☐
6 a refusal ☐
7 a threat ☐

3 Match the following to make five short conversations.

1 A I really need that report today.
2 A My plane gets in at seven.
3 A I'm just off to a meeting.
4 A Eva's off sick today.
5 A She wants to see you – now!

B I'll have to speak to her, I'm afraid.
B I'll be right there.
B I'll finish it this morning.
B I'll phone you later, then.
B I'll come and meet you at the airport.
A Good. I'll tell her you're on your way.
A Fine, I'll just give you my mobile number.
A Okay, I'll see if I can reach her at home.
A Great. I'll see you there, then.
A Okay, I'll look forward to seeing it.

You can often qualify sentences containing *will* with *if*.

- *I'll try to get you onto an earlier flight if I can.*
- *If you've got time, I'll show you round the factory.*
- *I'll send you a copy of our brochure if you like.*
- *If you prefer, I'll meet you at the station.*

4 Complete the conversation with the pairs of words in the box.

| busy + later | desk + look | give + right | leave + okay |
| make + know | nothing + away | try + time | wait + details |

József knocks on his boss's door and goes in. Tom is working hard at the computer and doesn't look up.

József Oh, sorry. If you're (a) _____, I'll come back _____.

Tom No, no, come in, József. If you (b) _____ me two minutes, I'll be _____ with you ... I'll just save what I'm doing ... Now, what can I do for you?

József Well, I just need you to check and sign these documents for me.

Tom Sure. If you leave them on my (c) _____, I'll have a _____ at them this afternoon.

József Fine. I'll just put them here, then.

Tom By the way, it's not urgent, but did you call Budapest about next week's meeting?

József Er, no. I'll (d) _____ to do it before lunch if I have _____.

Tom Okay.

József And I'll get someone to (e) _____ the travel arrangements if you let me _____ how many people are coming.

Tom Oh, right. I think it's four. If you (f) _____ a second, I'll give you the _____. ... Yeah, they're sending their manager and three sales executives.

József Okay, I'll see to it.

Tom Good. And I'll (g) _____ it to you to sort out the conference room, if that's _____. We'll need the usual AV equipment and refreshments.

József Of course. Well, if there's (h) _____ else, I'll get on with it right _____.

Tom Thanks, József.

Phrase bank: Polite requests

Look at the following requests. Which refer to people, which to events and which to documents or figures? Write *P*, *E* or *D*.

If	you can you're not too busy you've got a minute	could you	(a) get on to …	☐
			(b) take a quick look at …	☐
			(c) let me have a copy of …	☐
			(d) organize …	☐
			(e) set up a meeting with …	☐
			(f) fax through …	☐
			(g) check the arrangements for …	☐
			(h) get back to …	☐
			(i) send them …	☐

Offering assistance

Complete the following offers of assistance with the verbs in the box. You'll need some more than once.

| call | do | get | see | sort | speak |

Okay,	don't worry. no problem, leave it with me.	I'll	(a) _____ what I can do.	
			(b) _____ on to it straight away.	
			(c) _____ if I can reach her on her mobile.	
			(d) _____ something out.	
			(e) _____ back to you later.	
			(f) _____ you back with the figures.	
			(g) _____ to the people in marketing about it.	
			(h) _____ what I can, all right?	
			(i) _____ on to accounts.	
			(j) _____ someone to deal with it.	

Ending a call

Complete the expressions with the words in the box.

| catch | get | got | have | keep | speak |

a I'll _____ to go, I'm afraid.

b Well, I won't _____ you. I'm sure you're very busy.

c Okay, I'll let you _____ on. _____ to you later.

d Look, I've _____ a meeting. _____ you later, okay?

07 Making decisions

Nothing is more difficult, and therefore more precious, than to be able to decide.

Napoleon Bonaparte

Would you describe yourself as a decisive person?

Learning objectives: Unit 7

Business communication skills Doing a questionnaire on making decisions; Using fixed expressions in meetings; Fluency: Using the language of making decisions

Reading Article about James Bond films; Actor profiles: James Bond contenders

Listening Extracts from a documentary; An extract from a meeting; Interviews with James Bond contenders

Vocabulary Money and markets

Grammar Conditionals (future reference)

Phrase bank Decision-making

📼 **In company interviews** Units 5–7

1 Are you good at making quick decisions or are you a more methodical thinker? Answer *yes*, *no* or *it depends* to the following questions in under 90 seconds.

HOW DECISIVE ARE YOU?

a You're writing a report. The deadline's tomorrow, but it's your partner's birthday. Do you work late to finish it?

b You're with a major client who wants to stay out clubbing all night. You don't want to. Do you politely say good night?

c You're shopping for a suit, but the only one you like costs twice what you want to pay. Do you buy it anyway?

d A friend in banking gives you an investment tip. You could make or lose a lot of money. Do you take the risk?

e You're beating your boss at golf and he's a really bad loser. You could drop a shot or two. Do you?

f A good friend is starting her own business. She asks you if she can borrow $10,000. You can afford it. Do you lend it to her?

g You're offered twice your current salary to take a boring job in a beautiful city. Do you take it?

2 Who do you think is the most decisive person in your class? Make your decision, then look at the analysis on page 128 to check.

The art of decision-making

1 Discuss the following with a partner. How far do you agree with each point?

a Business is more about the ability to make decisions than about making the right decisions.

b The more decisions you make, the better decision-maker you'll become.

c Sometimes the best decision is no decision.

d If you discuss something for long enough, the right decision will eventually emerge.

e Most decisions are more a matter of emotion and gut instinct than logical reasoning.

f We are less in control of what we decide to do than we think we are.

2 🔘 1.38 Listen to a podcast on the art of decision-making in business. Take brief notes.

3 Compare your notes with a partner. To what extent are the views expressed in the podcast similar or different to the points you discussed in 1?

The decision-making process

1 Put the following stages in the decision-making process into the most likely order.

a consider the options ☐   d monitor the effects ☐

b define your objectives ☐   e implement your decision ☐

c collect information ☐   f choose the best course of action ☐

2 Look at the agenda for a decision-making meeting on the board below. Decide which two statements below were made at each stage in the meeting.

a **We're here to decide** whether to go ahead with the project.

b **One option would be** to do detailed market research.

c **The most important thing is**: can we make this profitable?

d **The advantage of** doing market research is we reduce risk.

e **Have a look at** these figures.

f **Above all, we must** be sure there's a market for our service.

g **What we've agreed, then, is to** start marketing this service now.

h **Another alternative is to** offer the service on a trial basis.

i **On the other hand**, market research takes time.

j **Our aim is to** find out if there's a good chance of success.

k **As you can see**, client feedback is very positive.

l **So, that's it – we're going ahead** with the project.

AGENDA

1 Objectives ☐ ☐

2 Priorities ☐ ☐

3 Data analysis ☐ ☐

4 Alternatives ☐ ☐

5 Pros + cons ☐ ☐

6 Final decision ☐ ☐

The language of meetings

1 The following expressions are useful in meetings, but some letters are missing from the final words. When you have completed them, the letters down the middle spell out a good piece of advice for the chairperson!

a Okay, let's get down to …

b Can I just stop you there for a …

c I totally …

d Perhaps I didn't make myself …

e What do you …

f With respect, you don't quite seem to …

g I agree with you up to a …

h If I could just finish what I was …

i Okay, let's move …

j I'm afraid that's completely out of the …

k Perhaps we can come back to this …

l Maybe we should take a short …

m Does anyone have any …

n Can I just come in …

o Sorry, I don't quite see what you …

p I think that's as far as we can go …

q We'll have to break off here, I'm …

2 **1.39** Listen to an extract from a meeting about a company relocating to the UK and tick the expressions in 1 as you hear them. Which one is not used?

3 Which expressions in 1 are used to:

1 open a meeting?

2 ask for an opinion?

3 interrupt?

4 prevent interruption?

5 get some fresh air?

6 speed things up?

7 ask for clarification?

8 disagree?

9 half-agree?

10 explain?

11 delay?

12 ask for ideas?

13 reject a proposal?

14 close a meeting?

4 Some managers are facing a cash flow crisis. Match the sentence beginnings (a–h) to their endings (1–8).

a I just don't see how we can go on

b No, I think we'll be okay,

c Maybe, but unless we do,

d In my opinion, we'd save a lot of money,

e Look, we're in a hi-tech industry. If we cut wages,

f No, wait. If we gave them a stake in the company,

g No, no, no. How is that going to work,

h Okay. Look, if we can't reach an agreement on this,

1 I suggest we break off here.

2 they might stay on. Or how about profit sharing?

3 our people will simply go and work for the competition.

4 if we keep overspending like this.

5 if we aren't making any profit?

6 we're going to be in serious financial trouble.

7 if we just reduced wages. Our wage bills are enormous!

8 providing we get this Russian contract.

The decision-making meeting

1 One of the toughest businesses is the film business, with millions of dollars made or lost on a single decision: who to cast as the star. First, work with a partner to match and check the meaning of the collocations below in a dictionary. Then read the article.

a current ⟶ brand
b profit ⟶ turnover
c best-selling margins

d combined earnings
e key awareness
f brand factor

g commercial news
h front-page series
i film success

NOBODY
DOES IT BETTER

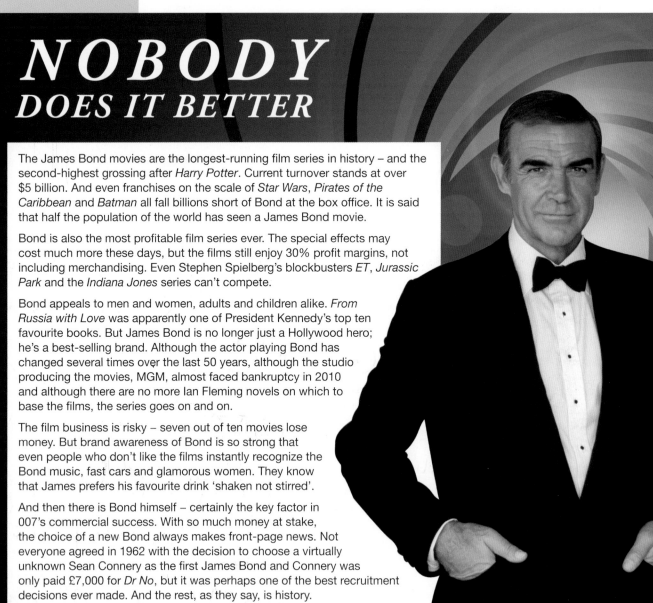

The James Bond movies are the longest-running film series in history – and the second-highest grossing after *Harry Potter*. Current turnover stands at over $5 billion. And even franchises on the scale of *Star Wars*, *Pirates of the Caribbean* and *Batman* all fall billions short of Bond at the box office. It is said that half the population of the world has seen a James Bond movie.

Bond is also the most profitable film series ever. The special effects may cost much more these days, but the films still enjoy 30% profit margins, not including merchandising. Even Stephen Spielberg's blockbusters *ET*, *Jurassic Park* and the *Indiana Jones* series can't compete.

Bond appeals to men and women, adults and children alike. *From Russia with Love* was apparently one of President Kennedy's top ten favourite books. But James Bond is no longer just a Hollywood hero; he's a best-selling brand. Although the actor playing Bond has changed several times over the last 50 years, although the studio producing the movies, MGM, almost faced bankruptcy in 2010 and although there are no more Ian Fleming novels on which to base the films, the series goes on and on.

The film business is risky – seven out of ten movies lose money. But brand awareness of Bond is so strong that even people who don't like the films instantly recognize the Bond music, fast cars and glamorous women. They know that James prefers his favourite drink 'shaken not stirred'.

And then there is Bond himself – certainly the key factor in 007's commercial success. With so much money at stake, the choice of a new Bond always makes front-page news. Not everyone agreed in 1962 with the decision to choose a virtually unknown Sean Connery as the first James Bond and Connery was only paid £7,000 for *Dr No*, but it was perhaps one of the best recruitment decisions ever made. And the rest, as they say, is history.

2 According to the article, what are the main reasons for the success of the Bond films? Tick the correct answers.

- the special effects ☐
- the 007 brand name ☐
- the actors playing Bond ☐
- the novels the films are based on ☐
- the Bond character ☐

In company interviews
Units 5–7

3 Now work in small groups to decide who's going to be the next Bond! First, make a list of the qualities you think an ideal Bond actor should have. Then look at the actor profiles on the next page and read the agenda of the casting meeting. You may find the expressions on pages 44 and 45 useful in your decision-making meeting.

CASTING MEETING

1 Appoint a chairperson
2 Review actor profiles
3 Discuss alternatives
4 **1.40** Listen to interview extracts
5 Make final decision

name and age
Peter Aston-Sharpe   40
nationality
English
marital status
divorced
height
1.83 m
physical pursuits
scuba-diving, aikido black belt, pilot's licence
experience
Leading actor for the last eight years with the Royal Shakespeare Company, Stratford. Has also done a lot of TV work, playing mostly romantic leads in costume dramas. Has starred in several fairly low-budget, but successful, British films.
achievements
Won a BAFTA award for his part in *Shadows*, a psychological thriller.
usual fee
Doesn't earn much in the theatre, but was paid $3 million for his last TV series about an international jewel thief.
comments
Superb dramatic actor who's also good at comedy. Hasn't done an action movie before.
Some say he can be moody and difficult to work with. Ex-wife says: 'He's just the sort of male chauvinist pig you need to play Bond.'

name and age
Jon McCabe   35
nationality
Scottish
marital status
single
height
1.83 m
physical pursuits
shooting, climbing, riding
experience
Mixed martial arts champion turned male model. Very little acting, but his recent supporting role in a London gangster movie won praise on both sides of the Atlantic. Has just completed filming a high budget science-fiction movie in which he plays a cyborg-assassin.
achievements
MMA champion three years running in light-heavyweight division.
usual fee
As a model, he earns $15,000 a day, but he accepts his inexperience and is prepared to do his first Bond film for what he calls 'minimum wage'.
comments
A charismatic and very funny man. Not well known outside Europe.

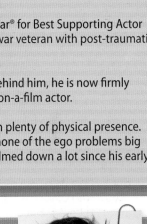

name and age
Sam Landon   37
nationality
American
marital status
single
height
1.90 m
physical pursuits
body-building, kick-boxing, jet-skiing
experience
Discovered by Hollywood while working as a cocktail waiter in LA. Has starred in several high-action blockbusters, although his last film, a comedy, was poorly received. Best known for his cop movie character, Detective Eddie Stone.
achievements
Surprise winner of an Oscar® for Best Supporting Actor for his role as a disabled war veteran with post-traumatic stress disorder.
usual fee
A run of box-office hits behind him, he is now firmly established as a $10 million-a-film actor.
comments
A big Hollywood star with plenty of physical presence. Seems easy-going, with none of the ego problems big stars usually have. Has calmed down a lot since his early 'hell-raising' days.

name and age
Charles Fox   44
nationality
English
marital status
married
height
1.88 m
physical pursuits
canoeing, passion for cars and motorbikes
experience
Big British star who has not yet quite lived up to his potential. Was considered for the leading role in *Robin Hood*, but lost out to Russell Crowe.
achievements
Won a Golden Globe for his portrayal of a classical musician who's also a serial killer. Voted 'World's Most Attractive Man' two years running by *Top Woman* magazine.
usual fee
Makes $3–5 million per film.
comments
A very versatile actor – action, romantic and dramatic roles, but not much comedy. Apparently very keen to get the Bond part. He wanted it last time it was on offer, but was unable to break his contract with another studio. According to his agent, 'Charles is obsessed with Bond.'

4 If you are unable to reach a decision, see page 139 for Plan B.

07 Making decisions

Money and markets

1 All the verbs and adjectives in the box can be used to talk about bigger or smaller increases and decreases in prices. Fit them into the diagram.

| cut | falling | freeze | hike | plunging |
| raise | rising | slash | soaring | stable |

Verbs   **Adjectives**

```
+   a _____      f _____
↑   b _____      g _____
0   c _____ prices  h _____ prices
↓   d   cut              i _____
–   e _____      j _____
```

2 Put the two sets of adjectives below in order of scale from the smallest to biggest.

| huge | modest | reasonable | record |

```
+                          a _____
↑                          b _____
  The company made a       c _____  profit.
–                          d _____
```

| crippling | heavy | moderate | slight |

```
+                          e _____
↑                          f _____
  The company suffered     g _____  losses.
–                          h _____
```

3 Make collocations containing the word *market* by writing the words in the box before or after it. Add an article if needed.

be forced out of	break into	challenger	competitive
declining	dominate	enter	flood	forces	growing
leadership	mass	niche	research	saturation	share
supply

```
┌─────────────────┐              ┌──────────────┐
│ break into (the)│              │   research   │
│                 │    market    │              │
│                 │              │              │
└─────────────────┘              └──────────────┘
```

4 Complete the following sentences using some of the collocations you made in 3.

a Market _____ occurs when the demand for a product is satisfied, but you continue to _____ that market.

b Even a very small or _____ market can be profitable if you totally _____ it.

c Pepsi has always been the number 2, the market _____ threatening Coke's® global market _____.

d The PC market has been so fiercely _____ that many European firms have _____ it altogether.

Conditionals (future reference)

You can connect two related ideas in one sentence using *if*. Look at the conversation below.

A **If we take on another project**, we'll need more staff.

B But we'll need a bigger office **if we employ more people**.

C No, not **if we hire teleworkers**, we won't.

The sentences in the conversation are examples of conditionals. The *if*-clause (underlined) introduces a possibility (e.g. *we take on another project*). The main clause shows what the speaker thinks the result of that possibility will be (e.g. *we'll need more staff*).

The *if*-clause can come at the beginning or end of a sentence. When it comes at the beginning, it is followed by a comma (,). When it comes at the end, there is no comma after the main clause.

1 Match the sentence beginnings to their endings in the following extracts from a meeting about a product that is still in development.

Extract 1

A Look, Jean, the product is still in development. If we rush the launch through,

B I realize that. But if I gave you another six weeks,

A Well, we might be able to

B Ian, you know if I give you more people,

A Well, if you can't give me any more staff,

B You realize we may lose our technological lead

A Yes, but I'd prefer to be second onto the market

B Hmm. You wouldn't say that

a could we have it ready for the Seoul Trade Fair?

b if it means we make a superior product.

c if we don't get this product out before our competitors?

d we won't have time to run the final tests.

e if we had more people working on the project.

f there's no way we're going to be ready. I'm sorry.

g if you had to deal with the marketing department!

h I'll have to take them off other projects. And I can't do that.

Extract 2

A Well, if we're going to meet our deadline without extra staff

B Okay, fair enough. And if I get you that bigger budget

A I promise. But if we spent more,

B We'll let Finance worry about that. If we can solve this problem with a bit of overtime,

A Excellent. Because we're missing the publicity event of the year

B You're telling me! If we didn't have a stand at the fair,

A Okay. That's decided then. I'll get us to the launch stage on time

B Great. Now, if you're not rushing off home,

a it would be a disaster.

b if we're not at Seoul.

c can you promise me we'll be ready on schedule?

d I'll buy you that drink I owe you!

e I'll do what I can to get you the budget for that.

f wouldn't that affect our profit margins?

g I'm going to need a bigger budget, Jean, so I can pay my people overtime.

h if you get head office to okay a budget increase.

2 Look again at the extracts in 1. Which of the grammatical structures below come in the *if*-clause, which in the main clause and which in both?

can + infinitive	could + infinitive	going to + infinitive
may + infinitive	might + infinitive	Past Simple
Present Continuous	Present Simple	will + infinitive
would + infinitive		

if-clause	Main clause

As well as *if*, we can use other words to connect two related ideas in a conditional sentence.

- ***Unless*** *we reach a decision by this afternoon, it may be too late.* (= If we don't reach a decision …)
- *The product will be ready in time* ***provided/providing (that)****, / **as/so long as** everyone does overtime.* (= … if, but only if, everyone does overtime.)
- ***Suppose/Supposing*** *the tourist industry is affected, what'll we do then?* (= What if the tourist industry …)

3 Rephrase the sentences below using the word(s) in brackets.

a If they offer you a promotion, what will you do? (supposing)

b We'll go ahead with the new design, but only if the market research is positive. (provided that)

c We'll lose the contract if we don't lower the price. (unless)

d You can go to the conference, but only if you give a talk. (as long as)

Phrase bank: Decision-making

Match each of the six stages of a decision-making meeting (a–f) to two things you might say (1–12).

a Define your objectives

b Set priorities

c Analyze data

d Present alternatives

e Weigh up pros and cons

f Make final decision

1 **The most important thing is**: will there be synergy?

2 **As you can see**, they do have exactly the expertise we need.

3 **So, that's it**: we've decided to go ahead with a full alliance.

4 **One option would be to** work with them on just this project.

5 **We're here to** decide whether to proceed with this alliance.

6 **The main advantage of** an alliance is reduced costs.

7 **Have a look at** this feasibility study.

8 **What we've agreed, then, is to** accept their proposal.

9 **Our aim is to** reach a final decision by the end of this meeting.

10 **Another alternative is to** form a more strategic alliance.

11 **On the other hand**, this would be a very serious step to take.

12 **Above all**, we must be sure our two cultures are compatible.

a ☐☐ b ☐☐ c ☐☐ d ☐☐ e ☐☐ f ☐☐

08

Influence

1 Have you ever been in a meeting like the one in the cartoon? What happened?

MIKE SHAPIRO

"I realize you were just saying what everyone was thinking ... and if you do it again, you're fired."

2 In your company, are all levels of management involved in decision-making or are decisions mostly handed down from the top? Where's your firm on the scale below?

TOP-DOWN ⟵————————————————⟶ INCLUSIVE

3 Is it possible to be influential even if you are not in a position of authority?

4 In your experience, how is getting what you want from peers and subordinates different from getting what you want from your superiors? Share your thoughts with a partner.

5 Work in groups of three. Each read the introductory paragraph and one other paragraph in the article on the next page. Discuss what you've read (in particular the parts in **bold**) and compare it with what you talked about in 1–4.

6 1.42 Now listen to short extracts from six conversations. Decide what the topic is and then tick the boxes in the chart below according to whether the speaker is managing up (↑), down (↓) or sideways (→).

	Topic of conversation	↑	↓	→
a				
b				
c				
d				
e				
f				

The ups and downs of management

It's a fact of business life that very few managers ever reach the boardroom. But nowadays we're all encouraged to be 'leaders' and leading from the middle is a lot more challenging than leading from the top! As a middle-manager, then, partway up the corporate ladder, you need to adopt three separate management styles, each requiring very different tactics.

1. MANAGING DOWN Some companies are obviously more hierarchical than others. But, whilst the command-and-control approach may occasionally be necessary when dealing with subordinates, those who report to you will generally prefer to be **motivated** rather than dictated to. So vary the tasks you delegate, emphasize how **mission-critical** those tasks are, allow a certain amount of autonomy and don't be slow to **praise** good work. Show you **understand the pressure** your team's working under. And don't forget your **non-verbal communication** – even a touch on the shoulder lasting just 1/40th of a second has been scientifically proven in most cultures to increase people's willingness to comply with a request.

2. MANAGING SIDEWAYS Before trying to persuade your peers, make sure you've built a **good working relationship** with them first. Of course, you don't want to abuse your friendship, but psychological research confirms that liking someone does make us much more responsive to their requests – as does the feeling that we are somehow in their debt and **owe them a favour**. So don't hesitate to remind the other person of the last time you helped *them* out – especially if it was recent. Research also suggests that people like to seem **consistent** in their behaviour. So don't hesitate to remind them of **the last time** *they* helped *you* out either! And never underestimate the power of **flattery**. Used with sincerity, it always works!

3. MANAGING UP The main thing when attempting to influence your boss is to **put yourself in their shoes** – if you were them, what would most interest you about the proposal you're about to make? So, do they like their managers to **do non-job-related work**, for example? If you know your boss is particularly **cost conscious**, point out the savings your idea will achieve. If, on the other hand, they're more **customer-centric**, focus on **improving client services or product benefits**. If they like to keep up with the latest management practices, refer to what your competitors are already doing – appeal to **consensus**. But if they prefer to **stand out from the competition**, talk instead about what no one else is doing yet – appeal to **uniqueness**. Remember, too, that those in authority will tend to respond well to the **views of other authorities** – so provide one or two convincing pieces of **data from reliable expert sources**.

7 🔊 1.42 The expressions below are in the order you heard them in the extracts you just listened to. Listen again and decide what influence tactics in the article are being used.

a I realize you already have a lot of work on this week, but … ↓

b It's absolutely essential that we get back to the client on this by Friday. ↓

c I think you may find it an interesting change from what you normally do. ↓

d I know how you like to encourage your trainers to gain some outside experience. ↑

e You said yourself we need to make savings and with business a little slow this quarter … ↑

f I know I already owe you one for standing in for me last time. →

g To be honest, you're much better at this sort of thing than me, anyway. →

h Just about everybody who's anybody is going to be there – all our competitors, for sure. ↑

i Now, I know you're worried about the cost, but have a look at this report I just received. ↑

j Listen, mate, I've got a bit of a problem and I was hoping you might be able to help me out. →

k You remember a couple of weeks ago I took the Morelli account off your hands …? →

l You said how much you enjoyed it last time. And it would be a real help to me if … →

m I was very pleased with the way you handled the Korean deal. ↓

n I think you're ready to take on a bit more responsibility. ↓

o What do you say? Do you think you're up to it? ↓

8 Work with a partner to practise your influencing skills in some of the same situations as the ones you just listened to. Speaker A see page 126. Speaker B see page 129.

Meetings on the go

1 Alan Sugarman is a sales representative for Flow Information Systems (FIS).
Read the email he sent to Heather Sherwood, another sales representative, and
answer the questions.

a What's Alan's problem? How urgent is it?

b What's the favour he's asking for?

c How does he sound?

- positive
- desperate
- angry

d How easy is it to say *No* to requests like Alan's?

Help!

To: h.sherwood@fis.com

Hi Heather

Hope it's all going well with the people from ABI. I'm really sorry to bother you
while you're in the middle of negotiations, but I have a big favour to ask you and,
unfortunately, I need an answer pretty quickly.

As you know, I'm due to speak at the Infotech conference in Paris next week, but I
just received some bad news from home. You remember how I told you about my
grandfather? Well, it seems his condition has got worse. I really need to fly out to the
States to help my family. So (I guess you know what's coming) do you think you'd be
able to stand in for me in Paris?

Please don't say 'No' straightaway. It's only a 20-minute presentation and I've got all
the slides together. Can we at least talk about it when you get back on Wed? You're
my last hope!

Speak to you in a couple of days. Good luck in Milan!

Alan

In company
in action

2 Alan doesn't get an immediate reply from Heather, but two days later he catches up
with her in the corridor at the FIS office in London. Watch the first part of video B1 to
see their conversation, and tick the different strategies Alan uses to try and get Heather
to stand in for him at the conference in Paris. Which strategy seems to be the most
successful?

- flattery ☐
- threat ☐
- incentive ☐
- emotional pressure ☐
- appeal to fairness ☐

In company
in action  **3** Shortly after her talk with Alan, Heather bumps into her assistant Tony in the kitchen. Watch the second part of video B1 to see their conversation and evaluate their behaviour on the scales below.

HEATHER			TONY		
ineffectual	authoritative	aggressive	submissive	accommodating	disrespectful

4 If you were Heather, would you have handled the two conversations differently? If so, how?

5 Read the article on handling meetings on the go. Which of the advice in the article did Alan, Heather and Tony take or fail to take?

How to Handle Meetings ON THE GO

How many of *your* meetings take place in office corridors, at the coffee machine or water cooler? In today's fast-paced business environment, chances are quite a few! Not that the corridor meeting is anything new. Way back in the 1970s, executives at Hewlett-Packard were encouraged to get out of their offices, and walk around the workplace solving problems and building relationships. They called it MBWA – management by wandering around. Forty years later, the management culture at companies like GE, Disney®, 3M®, PepsiCo, LucasFilm and Walmart is largely based on MBWA. But if you're going to hold meetings on the run, there are one or two things you should know:

1 Be careful not to have a corridor meeting when you're in a rush to get somewhere else or the person you're talking to is. Bosses won't thank you for making them late for an important meeting or even for their game of golf.

2 Feeling hurried also means you probably won't be paying full attention and will be more likely to make decisions you'll regret. So before you say *Yes* just to make your escape, make sure you really mean 'yes'. It would be better to say 'OK, let me think about it and I'll get back to you'.

3 Sometimes, if you're busy, you'll automatically say *No* to more work and may miss a fantastic opportunity to advance your career. But if you really do mean 'no', just say *No*. It helps to give a reason for saying *No*, but keep it brief and vague. If you go into lengthy explanations, you're inviting the other person to start negotiating with you. And you haven't got time for that!

In company
in action **6** Now watch video B2 to see Tony having a more constructive conversation with Anton, the sales manager. How do you rate Anton's leadership skills?

7 After speaking to Tony, Anton has a meeting with Alan about the Infotech conference in Paris. What do you think the meeting is going to be like? What would be the best approach for Anton to take?

In company
in action **8** Finally, watch video B3 to see Anton talking to Alan and check your predictions in 7.

9 Work with a partner to practise making the most of meetings on the go. Turn to page 126.

10 Now evaluate your performance using the feedback form on page 130.

09 Small talk

A friendship founded on business is better than a business founded on friendship.

John D Rockefeller, American industrialist

Do you think it's important to build friendships in business?

Learning objectives: Unit 9

Business communication skills Completing a questionnaire on cultural awareness; Talking about experiences; Roleplay: Engaging in small talk
Listening Pre-meeting conversations
Vocabulary Exaggeration and understatement
Grammar Past Simple or Present Perfect
Phrase bank Engaging in small talk

1 What exactly is small talk? How important do you think it is in business?

2 How culturally aware are you? Try a cultural sensitivity test. Speaker A see page 129. Speaker B see page 137.

Getting down to business

1 In *When Cultures Collide,* cross-cultural consultant Richard D Lewis talks about the role of small talk in international business. The diagram below shows how long it takes different nationalities to get down to business. Try to complete the diagram with the names of the countries in the box.

Finland France Germany Japan Spain and Italy UK USA

a ________ →

Formal introduction. Sit down. Begin.

b ________ →

Formal introduction. Cup of coffee. Sit down. Begin.

c ________ →

Informal introduction. Cup of coffee. Joke. Begin.

d ________ ————→

Formal introduction. Cup of tea and biscuits. 10 mins small talk (weather, sport). Casual beginning.

e ________ ————→

Formal introduction. 15 mins small talk (politics, scandal). Begin.

f ________ ————————→

Formal introduction. Formal seating. Green tea. 15–20 mins small talk (pleasantries). Signal from superior. Begin.

g ________ ————————————→

20–30 mins small talk (football, family) while others arrive. Begin when everyone's there.

Mins 0 5 10 15 20 25 30

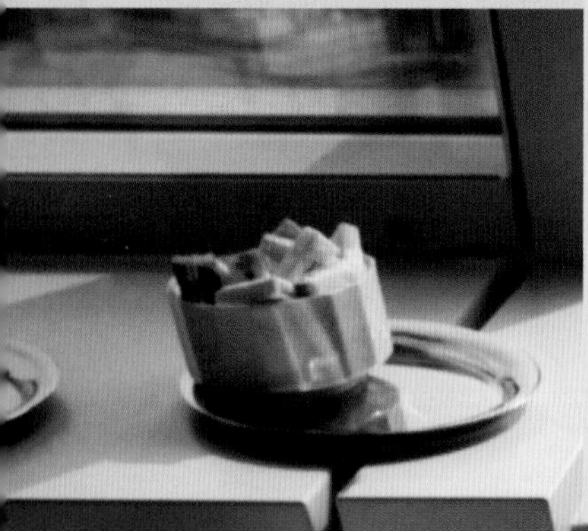

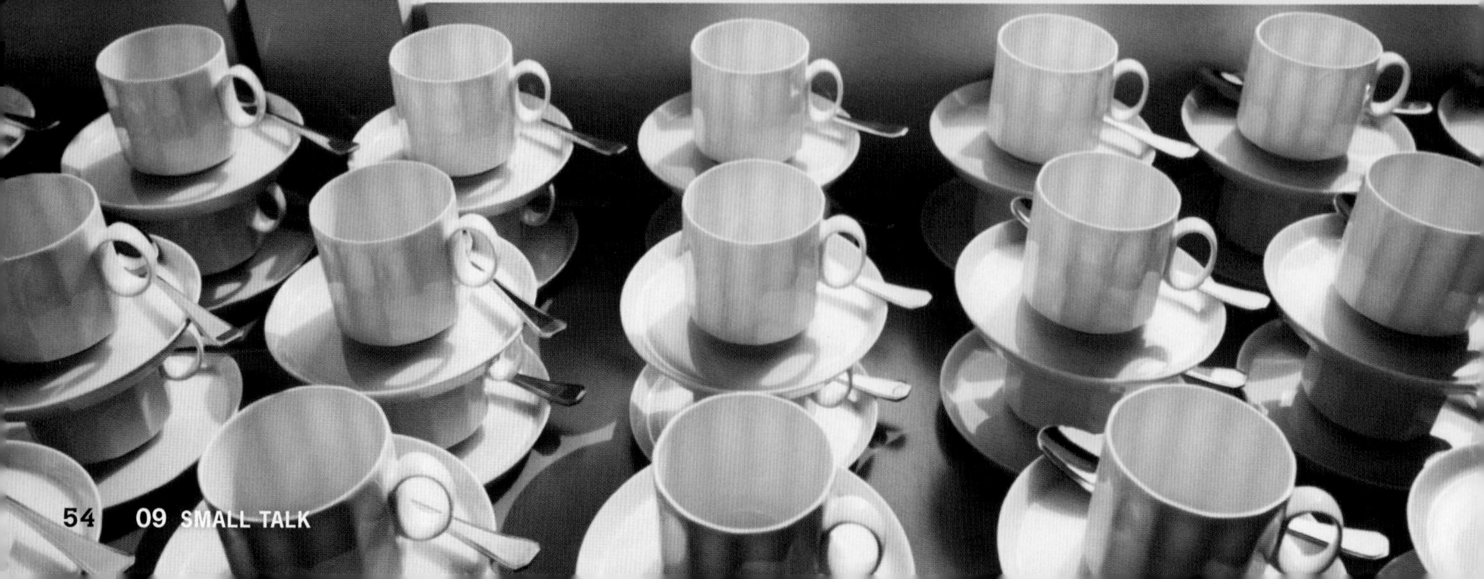

2 2.01–2.07 Listen to extracts from seven meetings. Check your answers in 1 by matching each extract to the correct country.

3 2.01–2.07 Listen again and answer the questions. There is one question for each extract.

a Where exactly is Tom Pearson asked to sit?

b How long is Dr Alan Winter going to spend in Berlin?

c What was Miss Sterling's father's job?

d What kind of snack is served at the meeting?

e Why was Catherine in Finland before?

f In the joke, what score do both the man and the woman get in the test?

g What commonly happens in their meetings these days?

4 Put your own nationality on the diagram, if it's not there already. If it is there, do you agree with where it's placed?

5 2.01–2.07 Look at these excerpts from the conversations you just listened to and <u>underline</u> the best grammatical choice. Then listen again and check.

a **A** *Did you try / Have you tried* green tea before, Mr Pearson?

   B Er, yes, I *did / have*. I *had / have had* it last time I *was / have been* here. I like it very much.

b **A** I'd like to introduce you all to Dr Alan Winter, who *came / has come* over from the Atlanta office to spend a few days at our research centre. Welcome to Berlin, Dr Winter.

   B Thank you very much, Wolfgang. It *was / has been* kind of you to invite me.

c **A** … And then Juventus *scored / has scored* the winner. It *was / has been* an incredible goal! *Did you see / Have you seen* the Lazio game last night, Miss Sterling?

   B Yes, I *did / have*. *Wasn't it / Hasn't it been* a great match? One of the best I *ever saw / have ever seen*.

d **A** Rain *stopped / has stopped* play again yesterday, I see.

   B Sorry?

   A The cricket. They *cancelled / have cancelled* the match.

   B Oh, they *didn't / haven't*! Well, we certainly *didn't see / haven't seen* much cricket this summer.

e **A** I think this is your first time in Finland, isn't it, Catherine? Or *were you / have you been* here before?

   B Actually, I *came / have come* here on holiday once, but that *was / has been* a long time ago.

f **A** That's a terrible joke, Marty.

   B No, you see, he *copied / has copied* her test, right?

   A Marty, we *heard / 've heard* the joke before. It's ancient. Okay, everybody, time to work.

   B I *thought / have thought* it *was / has been* funny.

g **A** What I do worry about is what's going on between our vice-president and our head of finance.

   B They're having an affair?

   A *Didn't you hear / Haven't you heard*? I *thought / have thought* everybody *knew / has known*.

   B No! No one ever tells me anything.

Talking about experiences

1 A good way to socialize in English is to talk a little about some of the experiences you've had. You're going to play *The Experiences Game*. Prepare by thinking about what you could put in the gaps on the board. Some of the verbs and adjectives in the boxes below may be useful, but you'll need to change their grammatical form.

| be | eat | go | happen | hate | have | hear | know |
| like | love | meet | read | see | spend | stay |

amazing	attractive	beautiful	boring	brilliant	delicious	disgusting	dull
entertaining	exciting	fabulous	fascinating	frightening	funny	great	hard
intelligent	interesting	lousy	luxurious	marvellous	nasty	nice	relaxing
strange	stressful	stupid	terrible	ugly	violent	wonderful

2 Play the game with a partner. Choose a box to start on and then move around the board talking about your experiences.

PEOPLE
I've _____ some
_____ people, but there
was this one guy/woman I
_____ in _____
who …

JOBS
I guess the _____ job I've
ever _____ was when I
was a _____. What I really
_____ about that job was …

HOLIDAYS
The _____ holiday I've
ever _____ was when I
_____ to _____.
I/We probably _____ most
of the time …

JOKES
One of the _____ jokes I've
ever _____ is the one about
_____. I'm not sure if I can
tell it, but I'll try!

HOTELS
I've _____ in some
_____ hotels, but the
one in _____ was really
_____. The _____
thing about it was …

RESTAURANTS
The _____ restaurant
I've ever _____ in is
called _____. Last time I
_____ there, I had …

CITIES
I suppose the _____ city
I've ever _____ to must
be _____. What I really
_____ about it was …

BOOKS
One of the most _____
books I've _____ recently
is _____. Basically, it's
about …

FILMS
One film I have _____ which I
really _____ is _____.
A lot of people think _____ is a
_____ actor/actress, but I …

WEIRD STUFF
One of the _____ things
which has ever _____ to
me is when I was in _____.
What _____ was …

3 In conversation, we often want to describe our experiences. What do the following adjectives describe? Choose nouns from the boxes.

| ~~city~~ | clothes | economy | movie | people |
| weather |

| book | car | holiday | hotel | job | news |

a sophisticated/cosmopolitan/industrial
city

b marvellous/changeable/miserable
_____

c strong/weak/depressed _____

d smart/designer/casual _____

e friendly/hard-working/enterprising
_____

f exciting/classic/unforgettable
_____

g great/shocking/latest _____

h secure/challenging/well-paid
_____

i economical/luxury/flashy
_____

j relaxing/beach/sightseeing
_____

k comfortable/poor/luxurious _____

l dull/brilliant/well-written _____

At a conference dinner

Work with a partner to practise small talk at a conference dinner.

You are sitting next to each other at a conference dinner in a city you both know well, and have just sat through an incredibly long and boring opening speech. You have not been introduced.

First decide:

- where the conference is being held
- what the conference theme is
- why you are there (e.g. to give a presentation, to network, to do deals).

Then look at the conversation notes below and prepare what you are going to say.

Speaker A
Start the conversation:
'I think that must be the longest opening speech I've ever heard! I'm _____ (name), by the way. I don't think we've met.'

Speaker B
'Pleased to meet you. I'm _____ (name).'
Continue the conversation by asking about one or more of the following:
- what your partner thought of the conference (fun? dull?)
- talks your partner's been to (any interesting ones?)
- the dinner you've just eaten (local dishes, drinks)

Speaker A
Continue the conversation by asking about one or more of the following:
- your partner's company (location, main activities)
- your partner's job (how long she's/he's had it)
- where your partner's staying (service, comfort, convenience)

Speaker B
Continue the conversation by talking about one or more of the following:
- the city (architecture, people, prices, local economy)
- the weather (typical for the time of year?)
- shopping (the best places you've found to buy presents)

Speaker A
Continue the conversation by talking about one or more of the following:
- sightseeing (a place of interest you've visited)
- the nightlife (a restaurant, bar or club you've been to)
- a recent item of news (politics, sport, scandal)

Speaker B
Break off the conversation:
'Oh, wait a minute, it looks like the next speaker is going to begin. Let's hope this one's better than the last.'

09 Small talk

Exaggeration and understatement

Are you the sort of person who tends to exaggerate or are you a master of understatement?

Exaggeration

A *I hear it was a fairly dirty hotel.*

B *Yeah, **it was absolutely filthy**!*

Understatement

A *I hear it was a fairly dirty hotel.*

B *Well, **it wasn't exactly the cleanest** I've ever stayed in.*

1 Respond to the following statements using the words in the box to exaggerate.

boiling enormous fascinating freezing gorgeous tiny

a A I suppose Helsinki was pretty cold.
  B _____

b A Thailand is an interesting country.
  B _____

c A So, he's got a big house in the country?
  B _____

d A It's actually a very small place.
  B _____

e A It's quite a beautiful sunset.
  B _____

f A Of course, Turkey's hot in summer.
  B _____

2 Now do the same to understate.

a A It's a dull book, isn't it?
  B (interesting / read)
  _____

b A So it was quite an ordinary meal?
  B (amazing / had)
  _____

c A Well, that was a boring party!
  B (exciting / been to)
  _____

d A It's been a stressful week.
  B (relaxing / had)
  _____

e A It was a pathetic joke.
  B (funny / heard)
  _____

f A Isn't Chicago dangerous?
  B (safe place / been to)
  _____

Past Simple or Present Perfect

The Present Perfect is a present tense. You use it to talk about:

- things that start in the past and continue up to the present.
  *We **haven't seen** much cricket this summer.*
- people's experiences, no matter when they happened.
  *I've **tried** green tea before.*
- things that have an obvious connection to the present.
  *Dr Winter **has come** over from the Atlanta office.*
  (= he's here now)

Affirmative/Negative

I You We They	have haven't	
		worked.
He She It	has hasn't	

Interrogative

Have Haven't	I you we they	
		worked?
Has Hasn't	he she it	

1 Read the three sentences below.

*The Thomke family **came** to America from Switzerland 40 years ago and **started** a business. (1)*
***Since** the 1980s they **have been** extremely successful. (2)*
*In fact, **for** the last five years, they **have been** the market leader in their field. (3)*

a Which of the sentences above refers to:
  a point in time? ☐   a period of time? ☐   both? ☐

b Which two pieces of information are basically **history**? Which tense is used?

c Which two pieces of information are most relevant to the family's **current success**? Which tense is used?

2 Look at the following time expressions, and decide which are used before *ago*, after *for* and after *since*. Fill in the table. Some expressions can be used more than once.

2001 a couple of days a long time a week Christmas half past four last month over an hour the 1990s the day before yesterday the oil crisis Thursday years

... ago	for ...	since ...

3 Using the rules you've worked out so far, try the following quiz about the people who said the sentences (a–f). Write *Yes*, *No* or *Maybe*.

a *I lived in Lisbon.*
Does he live there now? _____

b *I lived in Helsinki for six months.*
Does she live there now? _____

c *I've lived in Toronto.*
Does he live there now? _____

d *I've lived in Taipei for three years.*
Does she live there now? _____

e *I've been in all morning and she hasn't phoned.*
Is he in now? _____ Is it still morning? _____

f *I was in all morning and he didn't phone.*
Is she in now? _____ Is it still morning? _____

4 Complete the conversation with the verbs in brackets in either the Past Simple or Present Perfect.

Tibor, a sales manager, is planning to send his staff on a team-building survival course.

Tibor Right, now (a) _____ you all _____ (get) my email yesterday about the training course?

Fydor Er, yes … (b) _____ (be) it a joke?

Tibor I certainly (c) _____ (not mean) it to be a joke, Fydor. No, I (d) _____ (notice) recently that we need to work as a team more. Last year's interpersonal skills course obviously (e) _____ (not be) as successful as I (f) _____ (hope) and so I (g) _____ (now decide) to send you all on a management survival course.

Fydor At the Death or Glory Training Camp.

Tibor That's right. (h) _____ you _____ (hear) of it?

Fydor No.

Eva Erm, you (i) _____ (say) in your email, Tibor, that you won't be coming on the course with us yourself. Is that right?

Tibor Er, unfortunately, yes. Obviously, I (j) _____ (want) to join you, but I'm going to be much too busy, I'm afraid. For one thing, I still (k) _____ (not do) the quarterly sales figures.

Ivan Tibor, why (l) _____ you _____ (not tell) us about this at the departmental meeting last week?

Tibor Well, I (m) _____ (not make up) my mind until today. But I, er, (n) _____ (think) it would bring us all together.

Fydor It (o) _____ (already bring) us together. None of us wants to go!

Tibor Now, look, Fydor, don't be so negative. Wait until you (p) _____ (have) a chance to think about it. I (q) _____ even _____ (not show) you the course brochure yet. Anyway, what do the rest of you think?

Eva I think it's the most ridiculous thing you (r) _____ (ever ask) us to do. And, I mean, the interpersonal skills training (s) _____ (be) bad enough. I am not being dumped on a freezing hillside and told to find my way back to civilization with a fruit knife, a chocolate bar and a ball of string!

Phrase bank: Engaging in small talk

Listed below are some questions which might keep the conversation going at a business event. Complete them with the verbs in the box in the correct form. You'll need to use some of them more than once.

be	come	enjoy	find	go	give	have
hear	make	meet	read	see	stay	try

Are you →
a _____ the conference?
b _____ near here?
c _____ on after the conference?
d _____ a presentation?
e _____ to the keynote tomorrow?

Have you →
f _____ to Brasilia before?
g _____ to any interesting talks?
h _____ any useful contacts?
i _____ the (latest) news?
j _____ much of the city?
k _____ any nice restaurants?
l _____ the local cuisine/wine?
m _____ Dr Wendel?

Haven't we →
n _____ (somewhere) before?
o _____ wonderful weather (so far)?

Did you →
p _____ a good day?
q _____ any interesting people?
r _____ to the conference last year?

Didn't I →
s _____ your name on the programme?
t _____ an article by you in *Businessweek*?

10 Email

Do you take time to proofread your emails?

**Learning objectives:
Unit 10**

Business communication skills Discussing email likes and dislikes; Guidelines for writing email; Simplifying a lengthy email; Writing: Exchanging emails
Reading Emails
Listening Voicemail messages
Vocabulary Computers
Grammar Future forms
Phrase bank Email

1 When do you email rather than pick up the phone? Discuss with a partner.

2 You're going to listen to some business people being interviewed about what they love and hate about email. First divide the following phrases into love and hate. Label them *L* or *H*.

I'm a big fan of …   I'm not crazy about …   I'm not keen on …   It drives me nuts.
It's really cool.   That really bugs me.   The really neat thing is …   What I can't stand is …
What really annoys me is …

3 Working with a partner, see if you can predict what the interviewees will say. Make notes below according to how likely you think they are to mention it.

	What I love about email	What I hate about email
Sure to mention …		
Might mention …		

4 🔘 **2.08** Now listen and tick off the likes and dislikes. Make a note of any you missed.

5 What's your own special 'pet hate' with emails? Tell the rest of the class what really bugs you about it.

Writing emails

1 How important is the ability to write in business? Read this extract from the book *E-Writing*. Do you agree?

The importance of writing stands to reason. Your boss, co-workers or customers don't follow you around on the job. They don't see how you handle people or projects day to day. They simply see the results of your work – database notes, email, reports, proposals. Clear writing reflects clear thinking. Your writing becomes your face on the page or screen. Not only must your writing be clear, correct, complete and concise, but it also has to connect. Your entire relationship with co-workers or customers may rest solely on your email exchanges. In a world of emotional disconnection, people long to be treated as special, important individuals.

2 With a partner, think of short, simple ways in which you can 'connect' with the people you email.

3 There are no universally accepted rules for writing email, but here are some useful guidelines. Match the rules (a–h) to the reasons why they are useful (1–8).

a Create a subject line with impact.
b Write short sentences.
c Keep paragraphs short.
d Don't always trust your spell check.
e Put your signature on the message.
f Proofread the message before sending it.
g Use headings, bullets and numbering.
h Add one personal touch to your message.

1 It saves people scrolling down to see if there's more text.
2 These will guide the reader and make the message easier to grasp.
3 It can't tell the difference between *your* and *you're*, or *theirs* and *there's*!
4 It is more likely that someone will read your email.
5 On one level, *all* business is personal.
6 There's less chance the reader will miss anything.
7 It creates a more professional image if there are no silly errors.
8 You don't need complex grammar or punctuation.

4 People you know well may send you emails with certain grammar words missing. What three types of grammar word are missing in these examples?

It's a great idea.
I'm presenting it to the board today.
I'll speak to you later.

Now put the missing words back into the email below.

Hello

Hi Rosa – been in meetings all day, so just got your message plus attachment. Sounds great – particularly like your suggestion about discount rates. One or two points a bit unclear perhaps, but basically good stuff. Could add something about packaging. Nice job, anyway.

See you Friday. Leo

---

5 Emails generally contain fewer fixed expressions and are less formal than business letters. Rewrite the following extracts from business letters as emails with the expressions in the boxes in place of the words and phrases in **bold**.

Bad news:	Cheers.	Could you do me a favour and ...?	Good news:	from ...
Got your message on ...	Hi ...	Shall I ...?	Sorry about ...	Sorry, but I can't make ...

A

Dear Louisa,

Thank you for your letter of the 12th September. **Unfortunately, I shall be unable to attend** the meeting on the 21st. **I would appreciate it if you could** send me a copy of the minutes.

Best wishes,

Tom Hunt

B

I'm delighted to tell you that as of 2 Jan we are offering substantial discounts on all orders over €1,000. **If you wish, I would be happy to** send you further details and a copy of our new catalogue.

C

I regret to inform you that the board turned down your proposal. **I would like to apologize for** not getting back to you sooner on this, but I've been in Montreal all week.

About ...	Are we still okay for ...?	Following ...	If you have any questions, let me know.
I'm sending you ... as an attachment.	please ...	See you ...	Speak to you soon.	Thanks.

D

I am writing to confirm our appointment on 3rd May. My flight gets in about 11 am. **With regard to** my presentation on the 4th, could you make the necessary arrangements? **I enclose** a list of the equipment I'll need.

I look forward to meeting you next week.

Charlotte De Vere

E

Further to our telephone conversation this morning, **I'd be grateful if you could** send me a full description of the problem and I'll pass it on to our technical department.

Thank you for taking the time to do this. If I can be of any further assistance, please do contact me again.

I look forward to hearing from you

6 Rearrange the information in the email below and rewrite it to make it clearer. Give it paragraphs and a suitable subject line.

> Otto
>
> How are you doing? Got the joke you sent me – very funny. I've emailed you those statistics you wanted, by the way. Hope they come in useful for your presentation. Spoke to Cheryl in accounts the other day. She sends her regards. On the subject of accounts, did you send your quarterlies in? I don't seem to have them. Let me know how the presentation goes. And don't forget those figures.

7 Make the email below simpler and clearer by deleting as many unnecessary words as possible without changing the meaning.

> Dear Mr Nordqvist,
>
> On behalf of myself and my colleague, Karen Sharpe, may I take this opportunity to thank you and your team once again for your kind hospitality during our brief stay in Malmö. Karen and I both felt that the two-hour meeting we had with you at your headquarters last week was, without doubt, a great success, and we very much look forward to discussing our ideas with you in much more detail than we were able to in that extremely short but highly productive meeting.
>
> I am sure you will be pleased to know that I passed on your valuable comments to our Managing Director, Diane Lee, and she assures me that she will certainly be in contact with you over the next couple of weeks or so. In the meantime, let me just say that it was a very great pleasure meeting you, your managers and enthusiastic staff, and exploring the possibilities of some kind of a joint venture between us in the not-too-distant future.
>
> With my very best wishes,
>
> Sam White, Senior Product Manager, Thermoflex (UK)

8 Having edited the email in 7 down to a more manageable size, add one or two personal touches at appropriate points in the message. You know that Niels Nordqvist has just been promoted to vice-president (finance) and that his wife has just had their first child.

Changing arrangements

1 🔘 **2.09–2.11** Sarah is organizing a business trip to Japan for herself and her colleague, Peter. She has left three voicemail messages for Koichi, her contact in Nagoya. Listen and answer the questions.

Message 1

a When will Sarah and Peter arrive in Nagoya?

b Why are they going to be two days late?

Message 2

a Why can't Sarah and Peter stay at the Radisson?

b What does Sarah ask Koichi to do?

Message 3

a How long will the presentation be?

b What software and hardware do they need?

2 Complete the extracts from the messages in 1.

a Peter and I _____ arrive in Nagoya on Monday …

b That _____ possible now, I'm afraid …

c So, we _____ get there by Wednesday …

d Peter and I _____ stay at the Radisson …

e … I _____ email you about this yesterday.

f We _____ keep the presentation itself quite short …

g … we _____ use PowerPoint …

h … we _____ need a projector and screen …

3 Which of the extracts (a–h) in 2:

1 are predictions? _____

2 refer to current plans or intentions? _____

3 refer to past plans or intentions? _____

4 Write the email that Koichi might write in response to Sarah's messages.

You've got mail

Work in groups of three or four to exchange emails.

- Write a short email message (no more than 60 words) to each member of your group, starting with one of the introductory expressions on the left. Make sure the information in your email is connected to your own job or experience. Include your email address, that of the person you are emailing and a suitable subject line.
- After five minutes, place your message in the 'inbox' at the front of the class and take out any messages addressed to you.
- Write a reply to each message you receive directly below the original message. Invent any information you have to.
- After another five minutes, put your replies back in the 'inbox' and take out any addressed to you.
- Repeat the above procedure until you have dealt with at least five different topics.
- In your group, compare the sequences of emails you have produced.

Change of plan. I was going to …, but …

Have you heard …?

Don't want to be a pain, but …

I was thinking of …

I want to go on a training course to …

I've just heard …

I'm giving a presentation about …

A few of us are planning to …

10 Email

Computers

1 Combine the words in the box to make at least ten computer terms. Some are written as two words and some as one.

ad	banner	base	board	data	desk	disk
engine	hard	help	home	key	menu	'page
search	sheet	site	spread	top	web	

2 Match the verbs (a–n) to the phrases on the right that they collocate most strongly with.

a	surf	a program
b	enter	files off the Net
c	run	on an icon
d	download	data into a computer
e	click	a computer
f	transmit	the Internet
g	crash	a virus
h	install	the trash
i	burn	an attachment
j	send	the Web
k	empty	text
l	browse	to a better model
m	upgrade	CDs
n	cut and paste	software

3 Complete the song about computers with the verbs on the right. Use the rhyme and rhythm to help you. Have you experienced similar problems?

My PC is Giving Me Problems

(to the tune of *My Bonnie Lies Over the Ocean*, traditional)

My PC is giving me problems.
My PC is giving me hell.
It says it's got Intel inside it.
But its Intel inside is not well.

Chorus
***Bring back, bring back, oh bring back my
typewriter, please, oh please.***
***Bring back, bring back, oh bring back my
typewriter, please.***

It ¹ _____ on me three times this morning.
And wouldn't connect to the ² _____.
It ³ _____ my trash without warning.
It's some kind of ⁴ _____, I bet.

virus
Net
crashed
emptied

I ⁵ _____ head office a memo
Sent an ⁶ _____ in Microsoft® Word,
But HQ's computers are Apple®
And that's when an ⁷ _____
⁸ _____.

attachment
error
occurred
emailed

I ⁹ _____ on an icon to
¹⁰ _____
A ¹¹ _____ that iMacs® can read
But lost half the ¹² _____ on my hard disk
So somehow I must have miskeyed.

program
files
download
clicked

Now my spreadsheet has lost all its
¹³ _____.
And sadly no ¹⁴ _____ were made.
I phoned up the ¹⁵ _____ at Compaq.
They told me I need to ¹⁶ _____.

upgrade
helpline
data
backups

They finally sent a ¹⁷ _____,
Who debugged my ¹⁸ _____ with ease,
But something's gone wrong with my
¹⁹ _____,
'Cause when I ²⁰ _____ 'd's it prints
'c's.

type
printer
technician
desktop

I guess I'm ²¹ _____ illiterate –
I don't know my ²² _____ from my RAM.
My ²³ _____ skills are a disaster
And my email has filled up with
²⁴ _____.

keyboard
spam
computer
ROM

I think I should ²⁵ _____ down my PC.
Admit that I'm going ²⁶ _____.
Arrange to see Human ²⁷ _____
And tell them I want to ²⁸ _____!

Resources
retrain
shut
insane

Future forms

In English, there are many ways of talking about the future. The differences between them have less to do with time than with the speaker's attitude to the future event. Study the following examples, all of which refer to the same point in time: next Sunday.

- *I'm 40 on Sunday.* (1)
- *I fly home on Sunday.* (2)
- *I'll let you know on Sunday.* (3)
- *You won't have a problem getting a taxi on Sunday.* (4)
- *I'm going to a wedding on Sunday.* (5)
- *No! I'm not working on Sunday!* (6)
- *It's going to snow on Sunday.* (7)
- *I'm going to have a good rest on Sunday.* (8)

The form we choose can depend on such things as:

- whether we are talking about a fact or an opinion
- how sure we are
- whether we have already made plans or arrangements
- how determined we are
- whether we want the thing to happen.

1 Match the sentences (1–8) on page 65 to their main function (a–h).

a a fixed arrangement ☐
b a scheduled or timetabled event ☐
c an informed prediction ☐
d an offer or promise ☐
e a plan, intention or decision ☐
f an indisputable fact ☐
g a refusal ☐
h an opinion about the future ☐

In practice, the difference in meaning between certain future forms is often very small.

2 Match the sentences (1–8) on page 65 to the sentences (a–h) which are similar in structure and function.

a My plane leaves at five. ☐
b I'm going to go on a diet. ☐
c It's going to be a difficult meeting. ☐
d It's Christmas in three weeks. ☐
e I'll get back to you within the hour. ☐
f We're getting a new car on Friday. ☐
g There'll be a lot of traffic on the roads. ☐
h I'm not giving someone like him the job. ☐

3 Look at the following structures for expressing intention. Put them in order of certainty.

| aiming to | going to | hoping to | intending to | planning to |

more certain ↑ I am/was ⟵ a _____
                              b _____
                I am/was ⟵ c _____
                              d _____
less certain ↓ I am/was ⟵ e _____

asap = as soon as possible
BTW = by the way

4 <u>Underline</u> the most appropriate verb forms in the conversation below.

It's 8 pm. Cleo is just leaving work, when she sees the light on in Eric's office.

Cleo Hello, Eric. Are you still here?

Eric Hi, Cleo. Yeah, I'm just checking everything for my talk tomorrow.

Cleo Oh yes, (a) *you'll give / you're giving* your presentation to the board. Are you nervous?

Eric Not yet. But (b) *I will be / I am* if I don't get this PowerPoint thing to work properly.

Cleo Oh, I use PowerPoint a lot. (c) *I'll help / I'm going to help* you if you like.

Eric Thanks, but I think I've had enough for tonight. The presentation (d) *isn't being / isn't* till 11, so (e) *I'll still have / I'm still having* a couple of hours tomorrow morning to get things ready.

Cleo Well, some of us (f) *will go / are going* out for a Chinese meal and then maybe to that new club if you want to join us.

Eric Hmm, sounds like (g) *you're having / you're going to have* a pretty late night. I think (h) *I'll give / I'm giving* it a miss this time.

Cleo Well, (i) *we go / we're going* for a drink first. Why don't you come? (j) *It'll take / It's going to take* your mind off tomorrow.

Eric Well, maybe you're right. Look, (k) *I'm just checking / I'm just going to check* this thing one last time and (l) *I'm / I'll be* right with you.

Cleo Okay. See you there.

Phrase bank: Email

Match the following informal email expressions and acronyms (a–p) to their functions (1–16).

a Hi.
b Got your message, thanks.
c Sorry, but I can't make it.
d Could you do me a favour?
e Are we still okay for Fri?
f About the conference, …
g Good/Bad news.
h See attachment.

1 Cancelling a meeting
2 Introducing a topic
3 Requesting information/action
4 Giving positive/negative information
5 Greeting
6 Referring to an extra document
7 Confirming a meeting
8 Replying to an email

a ☐ b ☐ c ☐ d ☐ e ☐ f ☐ g ☐ h ☐

i asap
j Following our phone call, …
k I'll chase it up.
l BTW
m Fri's fine by me.
n Let me know how it goes.
o I'll be in touch.
p Cheers.

9 Adding an extra point
10 Offering to contact someone again
11 Saying goodbye
12 Confirming an appointment
13 Showing interest
14 Referring to an earlier conversation
15 Offering to look into something
16 Requesting/Offering urgent action

i ☐ j ☐ k ☐ l ☐ m ☐ n ☐ o ☐ p ☐

11 Presenting

How often do you give presentations at work? Do you enjoy them?

1 Think of successful talks you've been to in the past. What made them so successful? Complete the list of elements that make a good presentation with the words in the boxes.

To be a good presenter, you need:

appearance	contact	humour	knowledge	talk

a a well-structured _____
b thorough subject _____
c a smart and professional _____
d a good sense of _____
e good eye _____

attitude	language	preparation	visuals	voice

f an enthusiastic _____
g a strong _____
h a creative use of _____
i expressive body _____
j careful _____

2 With a partner, discuss the elements in 1 and rank them in order of importance. Use the phrases in the box in your discussion.

Another important thing is …	… can make a real difference.
I think … is pretty important too.	It helps if …, but it's not essential.
What you need most of all is …	You don't need …, as long as …

3 Add your own ideas to the list in 1.

Delivery

1 Read the text below. Is it good advice?

> **Did you know …** that almost 30 million business presentations are given every day? And yet, in surveys, most managers say they are more afraid of public speaking than anything else – even death! To overcome nerves, a lot of presentation trainers advise you to 'just be yourself'.

2 **2.12** Listen to three people speaking. Concentrate on the way they sound. Do you think they are having a conversation or giving a presentation? Write *C* or *P* next to each extract.

Extract a ☐   Extract c ☐   Extract e ☐
Extract b ☐   Extract d ☐   Extract f ☐

3 Discuss with a partner. How is speaking to an audience – even a small one – different from speaking to a group of friends? Think about the following:

- how clearly you speak
- how quickly you speak
- how often you pause
- how emphatic you are

4 **2.13** Guy Kawasaki is the co-founder of Alltop.com, Garage Technology Ventures and the former 'chief evangelist' at Apple®. Read the following extract from a talk he gave at Stanford University on entrepreneurship. The extract is unpunctuated. Mark (|) where you think Kawasaki paused. Then listen and check.

The first thing I figured out and learned sometimes the hard way about entrepreneurship is that the core the essence of entrepreneurship is about making meaning many many people start companies to make money the quick flip the dotcom phenomenon and I have noticed in both the companies that I have started and funded and been associated with that those companies that are fundamentally founded to change the world to make the world a better place to make meaning are the companies that make a difference they are the companies to succeed my naïve and romantic belief is that if you make meaning you'll probably make money but if you set out to make money you will probably not make meaning and you won't make money.

5 **2.13** Listen again and <u>underline</u> the STRONGLY stressed words.

- Is there a connection between what we stress and where we pause?
- What's the effect of pausing:
  - less often?
  - more often?

A team presentation

1 Look at the following information from First Direct. You are going to use this information to practise delivering a presentation. Mark the pauses and stressed words. With a partner, first 'present' the information clearly and professionally. Then 'present' the information enthusiastically and dramatically. Which sounds better?

Presenter 1
When you join First Direct, you experience something unbelievable. A bank designed around you, which doesn't expect you to fit round it.

Presenter 2
A bank which recruits people who like to talk. A bank which gives its people all the information they need to enable them to help you. A bank which believes in sorting your money out for you without you having to ask.

Presenter 1
Funny kind of bank? Unbelievable? Even a little magical? Yes, but also efficient, safe and secure.

Presenter 2
You can, naturally, choose when, where and how to deal with your money. We're open 24 hours a day. Our people are ready to talk to you, whenever you call.

Presenter 1
And wherever you might be in the world, you can bank online. Receive information online. Buy online. We can even send banking messages to your mobile phone.

Presenter 2
Join First Direct and feel good about your bank; it's your money, after all.

2 In the extract above, find examples of:

a repetition
b rhetorical questions
c grouping points in threes
d pairs of contrasting points.

3 Match the items (a–d) in 2 to why they are effective (1–4).

1 You invite your audience to try to anticipate your answer. ☐
2 You create a satisfying sense of completeness. ☐
3 You make sure your audience doesn't miss your main points. ☐
4 You emphasize what you're saying by using the power of opposites. ☐

Structuring a presentation

1 The following expressions help you to give a clear structure to a presentation. Complete them with the prepositions in the box.

about	back	for	of	off	on	to	up

a To start _____, then, …
b To move _____ to my next point, …
c To go _____ to what I was saying, …
d To turn now _____ a different matter, …
e To say a bit more _____ that, …
f To give you an example _____ what I mean, …
g To digress _____ a moment, …
h To sum _____, then, …

2 Which of the expressions in 1 are used to:

1 return to an important point? ☐
2 repeat the main points? ☐
3 talk about something unconnected? ☐
4 begin the presentation? ☐
5 expand a point? ☐ ☐
6 change the subject? ☐ ☐

Using visuals

1 You can draw attention to your visuals by using the phrases below. Complete them with the words in the box.

> give   have   mean   point   see   show

a _____ a look at this.
b As you can _____, ...
c I'd like to _____ out ...
d The figures clearly _____ ...
e To _____ you the background to this ...
f So, what does this _____ in terms of ...

2 Which parts (a–g) of the graph on the left do the following verbs refer to?

rise ☐   level off ☐   fluctuate ☐   peak ☐
recover ☐   bottom out ☐   fall ☐

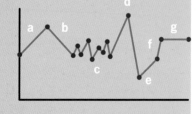

A technical problem

1 🔘 **2.14–2.16** Listen to a stock trading company manager describe how his team solved a problem with the company's website.

Part A

a <u>Underline</u> the two things the manager does to open his presentation.
   1 asks a question
   2 tells a joke
   3 tells a story
   4 quotes some figures
b What's the significance of the following facts and figures?
   1 nine
   2 250,000
   3 three
   4 60,000

Part B

c What three problems was the company having with its website?
d Having improved the website, what are E-Stock's two current objectives?

Part C

e Which graph (a–d) on the left does the speaker refer to?
f What three things does the manager do to close his presentation?
   1 sums up his talk
   2 quotes a well-known person
   3 refers people to his report
   4 invites questions

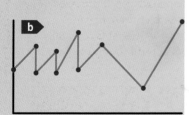

2 Read the following sentences from the presentation in 1.

a When we first **went** online, we **were getting** over 250,000 hits a day.
b The problem **was** not the service we **were offering**, but the website itself.
c A fault we **hadn't noticed** in the programming **caused** 1,500 people to invest in a company that didn't even exist.
d The next thing **was** Internet advertising, winning back the customer confidence we'**d lost**.

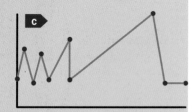

In which of the sentences above do the verbs in **bold** refer to things:
- happening at the same time? ☐ ☐
- happening one after the other? ☐ ☐

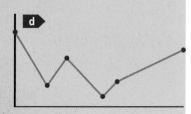

Giving a short presentation

Choose one of the situations below and prepare a short presentation.

Situation 1

You have been given the job of introducing a celebrity guest speaker who has come to give a motivational speech to your company. You can choose anyone you like from the worlds of business, sport, entertainment, media, science or politics.

Use some of the frameworks below to help you prepare, but change whatever you need to. Try to use contrasts, repetition, rhetorical questions and groups of three in your speech. You should aim to speak for about two minutes. Your guest speaker is making a surprise appearance, so don't announce who it is until the end of your introduction. See if people can guess who it is!

It was ... who said ... Our guest this evening is a perfect example of that.

How do you describe someone who ..., who ... and who ...?

She/He showed the first signs of ... at the age of ...

And at the age of ..., she/he had already ... and was beginning to ...

Highlights of his/her career include ..., ... and ... When asked ..., she/he said ...

Not only is our guest ..., she/he is also ... A good example of that is when ...

Truly, in the world of ... no one has done more to ..., to ... and to ...

Ladies and gentlemen, please give a warm welcome to ...

Situation 2

You have been chosen to present the Business World award for most innovative product of the last quarter-century. You can choose any product you like from household to electrical goods, cars to clothes and machines to medicines.

Use some of the frameworks below to help you prepare, but change whatever you need to. Try to use contrasts, repetition, rhetorical questions and groups of three in your speech. You should aim to speak for about two minutes. Nobody at the awards ceremony knows what the winner is, so don't announce the winning product until the end of your introduction. See if people can guess what it is!

Once every ... years or so a product comes along which totally changes the way we ...

... is/was such a product. Not only is/was it ..., it is/was also ... and ...

How do you begin to describe something which literally revolutionized the ... industry?

When I tell you that it sold over ... million units, you will not be surprised.

... once said that this product was the most ...

I could also tell you that it is/was ... and that ... But that would fail to do it justice.

The ... is quite simply the best ... ever invented.

Ladies and gentlemen, the winner of the award for most innovative product is ...

In company interviews
Units 9–11

11 Presenting

Vocabulary

Presentations

Communication skills

1 Complete the collocations by writing the nouns in the right-hand boxes. They are all things you might do in a presentation.

a graph	a point	an issue	figures	jokes	questions

make stress	(a)	describe refer to	(d)
quote compare	(b)	tell crack	(e)
address raise	(c)	field deal with	(f)

Trends and change

2 Read the following news headlines and mark each of the verbs and nouns of change according to what it describes: ↘, ↗, ↑, ↓, →, ↘↗, ∿, ∧, ∨. The first three have been done for you as examples.

a	Housing slump [↓] as interest rates climb [↗] to 7%.
b	Oil prices reach new peak [∧] as fear of terrorism increases [ ].
c	Asian stocks recover [ ] after sudden fall [ ] to monthly low [ ].
d	As China rises [ ], pollution soars [ ] to all-time high [ ].
e	Spanish market stabilizes [ ] after two-month slide [ ].
f	Wild fluctuations [ ] in the price of paper destabilize [ ] the publishing industry.
g	Stocks rebound [ ] after substantial losses [ ] in early trading.
h	Steady decline [ ] in white-collar jobs in the West caused by outsourcing boom [ ].

Grammar

Past Continuous

Affirmative/Negative			Interrogative		
I He She It	was wasn't	working.	Was Wasn't	I he she it	working?
You We They	were weren't		Were Weren't	you we they	

1 Match the examples of the Past Continuous (a–d) to what they describe (1–4).

a I met my wife while I **was working** as a teacher in Barcelona.

b He **was studying** to be a doctor when he dropped out of university and decided to go into business instead.

c We **were going** to Vienna for a training weekend, but it was cancelled.

d You **were** always **working** late when you had that job in the City.

1 a past action which was interrupted or not completed ☐

2 the background to a more important event ☐

3 repeated actions in the past ☐

4 previous plans ☐

2 Correct the following conversation. Three of the verbs in the Past Continuous should be in the Past Simple and vice versa.

Inge Ah, Peter. I was wondering if I could speak to you?

Peter Hello, Inge. Er, sure. I just went out for lunch, but, er, what was it about?

Inge Well, I was seeing Dieter the other day and he told me you're leaving.

Peter Oh, well, yeah. Actually, I was deciding a month ago, but I didn't think anybody was knowing about it yet.

Inge Oh, yes. The whole department talked about it when I came in today. They still talked about it when I left.

The Past Continuous can suggest a continuing feeling or attitude, so you can use it when you want to put gentle pressure on someone to do something.

- *I **was wondering** if you could help me.*
  (And I still am. So will you help me?)
- *I **was looking** for something cheaper.*
  (And I still am. So have you got anything cheaper?)
- *We **were hoping** for a bigger discount.*
  (And we still are. So how about a bigger discount?)

Past Perfect

Affirmative/Negative			Interrogative		
I You He She It We They	had hadn't	worked.	Had Hadn't	I you he she it we they	worked?

- *By the time I arrived at the party, everyone **had left**. (1)*
- *I was halfway to the airport before I realized I'd **forgotten** my passport. (2)*

3 Look at the examples on page 72.

a What happened first: my arrival at the party or everyone else's departure?

b Put the events in chronological order: getting halfway to the airport, forgetting your passport, realizing your mistake.

The Past Perfect is often used to look back from a time in the past to an earlier time.

Past Simple, Past Continuous or Past Perfect

4 Complete the following anecdote by underlining the most appropriate verb forms. Read the whole sentence before you make your choice.

'Apparently, there was this guy working for a financial services company in the City. Anyway, it (a) *was being / had been* a really tough year, so he (b) *decided / was deciding* to take a nice long holiday. He (c) *just cleared / was just clearing* his desk when he (d) *suddenly remembered / had suddenly remembered* what (e) *was happening / had happened* the last time he (f) *was / was being* off work. He (g) *was coming / had come* back to an inbox containing hundreds of emails. So this time he (h) *came up / had come up* with a bright idea to prevent it happening again.

What he (i) *did / was doing* was this: he (j) *set / had set* his computer to automatically send a message to anyone emailing him, telling them that he (k) *was / had been* in the Caribbean for two weeks and not to email him again till he (l) *got back / was getting back*. Then, just as he (m) *was leaving / had left* the office, he (n) *thought / was thinking* he would email his best friend and tell him all about his holiday plans.

Unfortunately, his best friend, who (o) *was going / had gone* on holiday the day before, (p) *was setting up / had set up* his computer in exactly the same way. So the two PCs (q) *proceeded / were proceeding* to email each other every few seconds for the whole fortnight, while these two guys (r) *were enjoying / had enjoyed* themselves on holiday, totally unaware. I (s) *heard / had heard* that so many messages (t) *were finally building up / had finally built up* on the company's server that it (u) *crashed / was crashing*, costing the firm millions! True story. Austin in accounts told me.'

Phrase bank: The language of presentations

The following expressions are all useful in presentations, but some letters are missing from the final words. When you have completed them, the letters down the middle should make a good piece of advice for a presenter.

a Can everybody hear me …

b Right, let's get …

c Let me introduce …

d I've divided my presentation into three main …

e Just to give you a brief …

f I'll be saying more about this in a …

g I'm sure the implications of this are clear to

h There's an important point to be made …

i Okay, let's move …

j I'd like you to look at this …

k As you can see, the figures speak for …

l To go back to what I was saying …

m Are there any questions you'd like to ask at this …

n I'd like to look at this in more …

o Let's just put this into some kind of …

p Perhaps I should expand on that a …

q To digress for a …

r So, to sum …

s That brings me to the end of my …

t Thank you. I'm sure you have many …

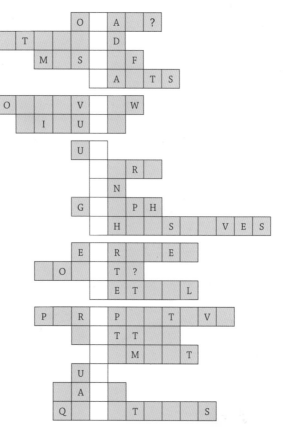

12 Impact

1 How many business presentations have you sat through like the one in the cartoon?
Share some of your experiences with the rest of your group.

© MARK ANDERSON, WWW.ANDERTOONS.COM

"Okay, I'm now going to read out loud every single slide to you, word for word,
until you all wish you'd just die."

2 Why do so many presenters fill their visuals with data and then simply read them out?
What are they trying to achieve?

3 What creates impact in a presentation? And what kills it? With a partner, make two
lists. Then compare lists with the rest of your group.

BRAVO!	BORING!

4 You are going to read a text about 'the four Cs of presenting with impact'.
Cover the text and work with a partner.

- Predict the four Cs. Then look at the text and check your predictions.
- Student A read paragraphs 1 and 3. Student B read paragraphs 2 and 4.
  <u>Underline</u> any points you included in 3.
- Share and discuss what you read with
  your partner.

The FOUR Cs of
Presenting with Impact

1. CONFIDENCE Many presenters suffer from pre-talk nerves. If you're one of them, don't despair! The art of appearing confident can be learned. Step one: slow down. Nothing says 'I'm nervous' more than hurried speech. Step two: ignore the usual advice about making sure to smile. Yes, a genuine smile reflects confidence, but a forced one only makes you look more anxious. So smile when there's something to smile about. Otherwise, don't. Step three: try adopting a confident pose just before you're due to speak. Research at Columbia University has shown that this raises testosterone levels in both men and women by nearly 20%, making them feel markedly more confident. It also cuts the stress hormone cortisol by a quarter, helping to calm those nerves. So stand tall, head up, hands on hips and let your body chemistry do the rest!

2. CREDIBILITY Whilst you may not be a household name, you can significantly boost your professional credibility just by doing four things. First, make sure you give your audience at least one really valuable piece of information they didn't know. They will delight in passing this on to others and they'll love you for it! Second, create the opportunity to mention high-profile projects you've been involved with. This tells them you know your stuff. Third, pause before your most important points. This gives your audience time to appreciate the significance of what you're about to say. And, fourth, never compete with your visuals. A good visual should only tell half the story – leaving you to tell the other half. So keep those slides simple and store the details in your head – where they're supposed to be!

3. CLARITY When giving a presentation, less is more. So, keep it short and simple. And if you can't, then break it into short and simple sections! Avoid unnecessary jargon. Decide if a single visual could take the place of a ton of data. And try to anticipate potential objections before they're raised – nothing makes you look better prepared! If the purpose of your presentation is to sell something, then it'll need a clear and logical structure. The Stanford Method, known as N.A.B.C., provides that structure. N – what's the **need** for what you're offering? A – what's your **approach** to meeting that need? B – what are the **benefits** to your customer or company? And C – what, if anything, are your **competitors** doing to meet that same need?

4. CHARISMA To really fire up an audience, let your hands do some of the talking. Neuroimaging technology has shown that the same areas of the brain light up when we gesture as when we speak. So gestures help us speak more fluently! Increase your impact further by using 'power-language'. Former Apple® CEO Steve Jobs was a master of this. For him, no success was ever just 'big'; it was 'huge'. No product was ever just 'attractive'; it was 'gorgeous'. And, finally, tell stories. In an experiment at Stanford University, only 5% of an audience were able to remember the statistics they'd been presented. But 63% could remember the stories! While giving a serious talk on the global threat of malaria, philanthropist Bill Gates released some mosquitoes into the auditorium, saying: 'There's no reason why only poor people should have the experience!' Of course, the mosquitoes weren't infected, but his audience were tweeting about it for months afterwards! This is what presentation coach and author Nancy Duarte calls a S.T.A.R. moment – something they'll always remember!

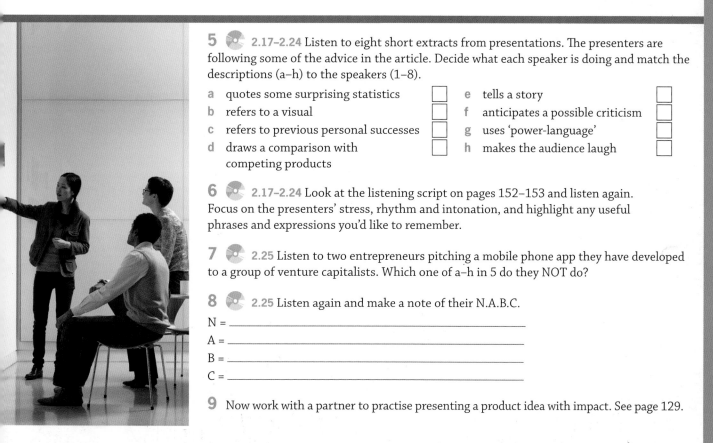

5 🔘 2.17–2.24 Listen to eight short extracts from presentations. The presenters are following some of the advice in the article. Decide what each speaker is doing and match the descriptions (a–h) to the speakers (1–8).

a quotes some surprising statistics ☐
b refers to a visual ☐
c refers to previous personal successes ☐
d draws a comparison with competing products ☐

e tells a story ☐
f anticipates a possible criticism ☐
g uses 'power-language' ☐
h makes the audience laugh ☐

6 🔘 2.17–2.24 Look at the listening script on pages 152–153 and listen again. Focus on the presenters' stress, rhythm and intonation, and highlight any useful phrases and expressions you'd like to remember.

7 🔘 2.25 Listen to two entrepreneurs pitching a mobile phone app they have developed to a group of venture capitalists. Which one of a–h in 5 do they NOT do?

8 🔘 2.25 Listen again and make a note of their N.A.B.C.

N = _____

A = _____

B = _____

C = _____

9 Now work with a partner to practise presenting a product idea with impact. See page 129.

Morale problems

1 Gabrielle Tate is marketing director for Flow Information Systems (FIS). Read the email she sent to Anton Vega, the sales manager, and answer the questions.

a For how many months has Anton's unit failed to meet its sales quotas?

b Is there any excuse for its poor performance?

c Could the low sales figures be the result of something else?

d What two meetings does Anton now need to arrange?

e How would you describe Gabrielle's tone in the email?

Sales quotas for Q2-3

To: a.vega@fis.com

Anton

I'm rather concerned that your unit has failed to meet its sales quotas for the second quarter running. Of course, I understand that in the present financial climate we're all struggling to grow our client base, but your team is now significantly underperforming in comparison with our other sales units. I suggest we meet sometime tomorrow morning to discuss this.

Incidentally, I've heard rumours that your team are having morale problems again – some of your reps not doing their fair share of the work, others overloaded and people generally unhappy with the quality of the leads they're getting from our telemarketing team. If this is true, it's no wonder the sales figures are down. You might want to hold a motivation session quite soon, because I'm sure I don't need to remind you that low morale in a sales unit is fatal.

Let me know when you'll be free to meet in the morning.

Gabrielle

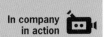

In company
in action

2 After a tense discussion with Gabrielle the following day, Anton decides to set up a meeting with his team. Watch video C1 to see the meeting and tick the things he does wrong.

a He blames people. ☐
b He refuses to listen. ☐
c He makes threats. ☐
d He loses his temper. ☐
e He divides the team. ☐
f He becomes abusive. ☐

3 How should Anton have done things differently in the meeting?

4 Before you read the article on motivating a team, check with a partner that you are familiar with the words and phrases in the box. Then see if you can work out the meaning of the ones you don't know from the context as you read. They are in the order you meet them in the article.

> incentives   bonuses   fringe benefits   deadlines
> dismissal   routine   initiative   contribution
> pat on the back   working relationship   P4P

Motivating Your Team

A question many managers ask themselves is: what's the best way to motivate my team? Should I use the carrot or the stick?

The carrot approach offers employees incentives such as a higher salary, bonuses or fringe benefits like free health care – great if you can afford it! And the stick approach imposes schedules, deadlines and perhaps the threat of dismissal if targets are not met on time – a sure way to become unpopular! But the real problem is that both the carrot and stick are extrinsic motivators – external punishments and rewards designed to make us work harder. And in most office environments, these are simply no longer effective.

In his best-selling book *Drive*, Dan Pink explains that whilst people in dull routine jobs may improve their performance for more pay, people in jobs that demand creativity and initiative actually find such incentives stressful and end up performing worse! What 'knowledge workers' like these need is intrinsic motivation – the freedom to make their own decisions, a feeling of mastery in the skills they use and a sense of belonging to something bigger than themselves to which they can make a positive contribution. So what can managers do to provide their people with the intrinsic motivation to improve their performance?

Psychologist Dan Ariely says they need to stop having a 'market relationship' with their staff (I pay you to work hard for me) and begin to develop a 'social relationship' with them as well (I value the contribution you make). You might think a thousand-dollar bonus would be more motivating than a small thank-you present and a pat on the back from the boss, but you'd be wrong. In fact, Ariely claims that if a working relationship is strong, paying for performance (P4P) can actually destroy it, not strengthen it. Imagine, he says, offering to pay your mother-in-law for a beautiful meal she just cooked for you. She'd never speak to you again! In the workplace too, good social relationships need to be sustained and you can't put a price on them.

5 Make a note of two points you most agree with and one you disagree with from the article. Then compare notes with a partner.

Agree: _____

Agree: _____

Disagree: _____

In company in action

6 Now watch video C2 to see Anton try to repair some of the damage he did in his first team meeting. Rate his closing presentation.

Rapport   ☺ ☺ ☹
Impact   ☺ ☺ ☹
Delivery ☺ ☺ ☹

Compare your ratings with your partner.

7 What did he do right this time?

8 Practise delivering a motivation session. Turn to page 134.

9 Now evaluate your partner's performance using the feedback form on page 136.

13 Being heard

What do you think makes an effective meeting?

**Learning objectives:
Unit 13**
**Business communication
skills** Discussing attitudes
to meetings; Completing a
questionnaire on assertiveness
in meetings; Roleplay:
Interrupting a speaker;
Discussing meeting styles in
different countries
Listening People talking about
their attitudes to meetings;
Meetings in different countries
Reading Meeting styles in
three countries
Vocabulary Meetings
Grammar Modal verbs
Phrase bank Interrupting and
preventing interruption

1 Work with a partner. Complete and discuss the statements below.

| chat | criticize | discuss | exchange | find | make | waste |

Meetings are:

a an ideal opportunity to _____ points of view.

b the best place to _____ key decisions.

c a safe environment in which to _____ important issues.

d a rare chance to _____ with people from other departments.

e the only way to _____ out what's really going on.

f an open invitation to _____ each other.

g the perfect excuse to _____ an entire morning!

Which is closest to the kinds of meetings you have?

2 2.26 Listen to eight business people from different countries complaining about meetings. Match the extracts (1–8) to the correct topics (a–h).

a there's no fixed agenda ☐

b preparation is lacking ☐

c only the boss's opinions count ☐

d it's all about status ☐

e the follow-up is never clear ☐

f meetings go on too long ☐

g no decisions are made ☐

h interruption is a problem ☐

3 Read the statements in 2 again. Which of them apply to the kinds of meetings you have?

4 How assertive are you in meetings? What if the meeting is held in English?

5 Complete the questionnaire with the words in the box. Then discuss each point.

conflict   conversation   people   room   rubbish   silences   things   time

Questionnaire

a You shouldn't interrupt too much – it just creates _____.   **agree** ☐   **disagree** ☐

b If someone's talking _____, I'm afraid you just have to stop them.   **agree** ☐   **disagree** ☐

c You should always try to avoid embarrassing _____ in meetings.   **agree** ☐   **disagree** ☐

d You must always think before you speak – take your _____.   **agree** ☐   **disagree** ☐

e You can't expect everybody to see _____ your way all the time.   **agree** ☐   **disagree** ☐

f You mustn't let other _____ push you around.   **agree** ☐   **disagree** ☐

g You don't have to wait until the _____ stops before you speak.   **agree** ☐   **disagree** ☐

h If people refuse to listen, you can just walk out of the _____.   **agree** ☐   **disagree** ☐

For comments on your answers see page 131.

6 Each sentence in 5 contains a modal verb. Match the modal verbs (a–h) to their meanings (1–6).

1 it's a good idea ☐
2 it's a bad idea ☐
3 it's necessary ☐ ☐
4 it's not necessary ☐
5 it's acceptable ☐
6 it's not acceptable ☐ ☐

Cultural differences

1 In *Riding the Waves of Culture*, communications expert Fons Trompenaars shows how different cultures have different discussion styles. The diagram below illustrates his results. The lines represent the two speakers and the spaces represent the silences. When lines and spaces overlap, this shows that people are speaking at the same time.

Culture 1 — Long silences / No interruption

Culture 2 — Short silences / Some interruption

Culture 3 — No silences / Constant interruption

2 Work with a partner. On the diagram in 1, where would you typically place:

a Asians?
b Northern Europeans?
c Southern Europeans?
d Middle Easterners?
e North Americans?
f Latin Americans?
g Africans?
h Australasians?
i your own nationality?

3 🔘 **2.27–2.29** Listen to extracts from three business meetings. Which of the cultural types are they?

Extract 1 _____

Extract 2 _____

Extract 3 _____

Interruption strategies

1 What do you think is the most effective way to do the following? Tick your answers.

Interrupt in meetings

I raise my hand. ☐

I cough. ☐

I say *Errrrrm* ... ☐

I say the speaker's name. ☐

I just start speaking! ☐

Prevent interruption

I gesture that I haven't finished. ☐

I raise my VOICE! ☐

I avoid eye contact with the other person. ☐

I just keep talking! ☐

I glare at the person interrupting. ☐

2 Put the expressions (a–i) in the correct order. They were all in the conversations you just listened to.

a a / just / minute _____

b me / let / finish _____

c no / me / out / hear _____

d on / hang / second / a _____

e again / to / sorry / interrupt _____

f could / if / finish / I / just _____

g here / can / just / I / in / come / ? _____

h just / I / something / say / can / ? _____

i what / I / finish / could / just / saying / was / I / ? _____

3 Label the expressions in 2 'interrupting' or 'preventing interruption'. Which two can be both?

Hang on a minute!

1 Work with a partner. You are going to practise interrupting and preventing interruption. Speaker A see page 140. Speaker B see page 137.

2 Try the activity again, this time without the time limit. The reader should try to deal with each question before moving on.

Meeting across culture

1 Work in four groups. Choose one of the scenarios on pages 81–82 describing a British salesman's experience in four different countries. Read the text and do the vocabulary exercises in your group. Then look at 2.

SAUDI ARABIA

Brilliant white walls, luxurious carpets and the soft hum of air conditioning. A British salesman sits a little uncomfortably in the office of a Saudi manager. An hour passes in little more than small talk – recent news, horse racing, the Royal Family. The salesman casually compliments his host on his taste in art and, after several futile attempts to refuse, ends up accepting a valuable-looking vase as a gift.

When the meeting finally gets underway, there are almost constant interruptions and it is difficult to stick to any kind of agenda. People drift into the office unannounced, talk loudly and excitedly, and leave. Several subjects seem to be under discussion at once. It is sometimes difficult to be heard above the noise. The salesman smiles uncertainly as he accepts a third cup of hot sweet tea.

Five days later, a second meeting is in progress. This time the questions are more direct. A senior Arab manager is present on this occasion, but says very little. The arrival of yet another visitor holds up the conversation by a further 40 minutes. The salesman tries hard to hide his frustration.

Meeting three. Terms are negotiated in a lively haggling session. The salesman finds the Saudis more easily persuaded by rhetoric than hard facts. They clearly want to do business. The question is whether they want to do business with him. Their initial demands seem unrealistic, but slowly they begin to make concessions. As the Arabs say, 'When God made time, he made plenty of it!'

a Match the following to make collocations from the text.

stick to	the conversation
hold up	concessions
negotiate	an agenda
make	terms

b Find the words or phrases which mean:
start (paragraph 2)   argument about a price (paragraph 4)
be happening (paragraph 3)   impressive speech (paragraph 4)

GERMANY

Rain beats against the mirror-glass windows of a Frankfurt office block. The British salesman's appointment was fixed for 9.30. At 9.29, he's shaking the hand of his prospective client and stepping into the spotlit orderliness of the German's office. Technical diagrams and flow charts cover the magnetic whiteboard. A secretary brings machine coffee in Styrofoam cups and it's straight to business.

The salesman starts to set up his PowerPoint presentation, but there's a problem with the disc and he ends up borrowing the German's top-of-the-range Fujitsu. He tries to make a joke of the problem – rather unsuccessfully. When he finally gets going, objections seem to be raised to nearly everything in his proposal. 'Are you sure this is a more efficient system?' 'Do you have figures to back that up?' 'Ah, we tried that before and it didn't work.'

Sixty minutes have been allocated to the meeting. An electronic alarm on the German's watch marks the hour. Shortly afterwards, there's a call from reception to say the salesman's taxi has just arrived. He is accompanied to the lift, staggering under the weight of six technical manuals, a 200-page printout of production quotas and a promotional video.

Over the next 18 months, the Germans have an endless supply of questions. Dozens of emails are exchanged and diagrams faxed before any agreement is reached. After the deal goes through, the salesman is surprised to be invited to dinner at the German manager's family home. But he never gets to meet 'the big boss'.

c Match the following to make collocations from the text.

raise	agreement
allocate	objections
exchange	time
reach	emails

d Find the words or phrases which mean:
get something ready (paragraph 2)   support a fact (paragraph 2)
start (paragraph 2)   be completed (paragraph 4)

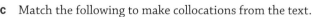

BRAZIL

São Paulo. 2 am. A jet-lagged British salesman and his better-dressed Brazilian client wait outside the elegant restaurant in which they've hardly talked business all night. Their car is driven right up to the door. This is a good part of town, but you don't want to be walking to the parking lot in a smart suit and expensive watch. The Brazilian suggests a nightclub, but tomorrow's meeting is scheduled for 9 am.

By 9.35 the following morning, the meeting's about to begin. The salesman is introduced to everyone round the table in turn. A number of them seem to be related. The conversation ranges from football to families to traffic problems and back to football. The atmosphere's relaxed, but the salesman's barely started his technical presentation before someone cuts in. Soon everybody's joining in the discussion with wildly creative ideas of their own. If this is a negotiation, it's hard to see how the Brazilians are working as a team.

The salesman is surprised to find his hosts so enthusiastic about his product. Did he really win them over that easily – or will there be problems later on? The meeting has overrun. He decides to press them for a decision. All eyes turn to the boss. 'We needn't worry about the contractual details at this stage,' says the senior Brazilian manager, smiling, his hand on the Briton's shoulder. 'I'm sure we can work something out. Let's think about the future.'

e Match the following to make collocations from the text.

talk	a decision
schedule	a team
work as	business
press for	a meeting

f Find the words or phrases which mean:

interrupt (paragraph 2)   continue for too long (paragraph 3)

persuade (paragraph 3)   find a solution (paragraph 3)

CHINA

A formally laid-out boardroom overlooking the Hai He River in downtown Tienjin. After months of preparation and endless requests from the Chinese for further background information about his company, a British salesman and his team have at last been granted a meeting with a potential client. For a first meeting, the salesman is surprised to see such a large group of executives in attendance. Following protocol, the Chinese had entered the room in strict order of seniority, led by an elderly gentleman the salesman immediately identified as the boss. But he is mystified when this gentleman takes almost no part in the meeting.

After a few minutes of chit-chat and an official welcome speech, business begins. The meeting is highly structured. There's lots of nodding, but the salesman is not sure if this shows agreement, understanding or is simply a matter of courtesy. An interpreter provides an ongoing summary, which breaks the flow of conversation. And when one of the Britons interrupts to clear up a misunderstanding, there seems to be disapproval amongst the Chinese, but this is quickly covered up.

Unfortunately, the impressive figures the salesman quotes during his presentation do not overly impress his clients today and talk of contracts is politely dismissed as premature as the Chinese become more resistant. The size and importance of the Chinese market are repeatedly emphasized as is the need to involve the state government in any final decision. Substantial discounts and product customization seem to be expected. When the meeting breaks up, small groups form and the discussion continues. Has any decision been made or not?

g Match the following to make collocations from the text.

be granted	a misunderstanding
follow	a meeting
clear up	figures
quote	protocol

h Find the words or phrases which mean:

surprised and confused (paragraph 1)   politeness (paragraph 2)

small talk (paragraph 2)   happening too soon (paragraph 3)

2 Form new groups with people who read different scenarios. Discuss the different attitudes to the topics in the box:

communication style   decision-making   delegation   follow-up   formality   hierarchy
interruption   power and status   relationship-building   technical matters   time

In which of the four countries would you feel most at home?

13 Being heard

Meetings

1 Complete the collocations by writing the nouns and noun phrases in the right-hand boxes. They are all things you might do before, during or after a meeting.

a decision   a point   agreement   an action plan
an opinion   comments   details   ideas   the agenda

set stick to	(a)	reach be in	(e)
brainstorm exchange	(b)	make invite	(f)
hold express	(c)	draw up implement	(g)
raise clarify	(d)	go into sort out	(h)
		come to reconsider	(i)

Comments and opinions

2 In meetings, certain expressions help you to introduce your comments and indicate your opinions more clearly. Look at the following five extracts from meetings. Replace the phrases in **bold** with ones in the box which have a similar meaning.

As a matter of fact   Clearly   Essentially   Frankly
If you ask me   In short   In theory   Incidentally
Luckily   On the other hand   Overall   Strangely enough

1 A **Personally**, / (a) _____, I think this whole project has been a waste of time.
   B **To be honest**, / (b) _____, I tend to agree with you.
   A **However**, / (c) _____, we've put too much money into it to cancel it now.
2 A **By the way**, / (d) _____, did you get in touch with our agent in Warsaw?
   B **Actually**, / (e) _____, she phoned me. I'll talk to you about it later.
3 A **Obviously**, / (f) _____, we don't want to have a strike on our hands.
   B **Fortunately**, / (g) _____, we may not have to. I spoke to the union rep this morning.
4 A **In general**, / (h) _____, did people like the idea of open-plan offices?
   B **Funnily enough**, / (i) _____, they didn't. We may have to rethink our proposal.
5 A **To sum up**, / (j) _____, by year-end we should be nearing the break-even point.
   B **Basically**, / (k) _____, then, we're going to make a net loss?
   A **Technically**, / (l) _____, yes. But that's because we're channelling so much money back into the business.

Modal verbs

can   could   may   might   must   shall   should   will   would

You don't add an -s in the third person singular.

Modal verbs are followed by the infinitive without *to*. (NB After *ought*, use *to* + infinitive: *She ought to go*.)

Couldn't he attend the meeting?

You don't use *do* or *does* to make questions.

You don't use *do* or *does* to make negatives.

You use modal verbs to express many different functions. (See page 84.)

be able to   be allowed to   have to

Be able to, *have to* and *be allowed to* are often used in place of modal verbs.
You use these verbs to express concepts that are not possible with modal verbs.
 • *Will you be able to finish the report tomorrow?* (*will you can* is not possible)
 • *I had to attend a meeting last night.* (*must* has no past form)

1 Modal verbs say as much about the speaker's attitude as about the factual content of the sentence. Match the modal verbs in **bold** to their main functions.

A They **should** be here by now. (a) *5*
B I**'ll** phone and check. (b) *6*
A No, wait a minute, that **must** be them. (c) *2*

A **Could** I leave early tomorrow, do you think? (d) *3*
B Well, I **might** need you to check the monthly figures. (e) *4*
A But I **have to** pick up the kids from school. (f) *1*

1	expressing obligation
2	expressing certainty
3	asking for permission
4	expressing possibility
5	expressing probability
6	taking the initiative

Now do the same with these:

A You **mustn't** load that software onto your company PC! (g) *11*
B But I **can't** do this job without it. (h) *9*
A Well, you **ought to** speak to IT, then. (i) *7*

A I'm getting a drink from the machine. **Can** I get you anything? (j) *12*
B Oh, thanks. **Could** you get me a Coke® or something? (k) *10*
A Sure. What's this? You **don't have** to give me the money! (l) *8*

7	giving advice
8	saying something isn't necessary
9	expressing inability
10	making a request
11	prohibiting something
12	making an offer

2 Try to complete the following modal verbs quiz in less than five minutes.

a 'You mustn't do that.'

Will there be trouble if you do it?

b 'You don't have to do that.'

Will there be trouble if you do it?

c Put these sentences into the past:

1 'I can't talk to you now.'

2 'I hope we'll meet again.'

3 'I must fly to Geneva.'

d What's the opposite of 'That can't be right'?

e What does 'She should be here at nine' mean?

1 She's supposed to be here at nine.

2 I expect she'll be here at nine.

3 Either.

f 'I could do it' refers to:

1 the past.

2 the present.

3 the future.

4 It depends.

g 'They needn't have done it.' Did they do it?

h 'They didn't need to do it.' Did they do it?

i Are these two sentences possible?

1 'I could swim by the age of two.'

2 'I was able to swim by the age of two

j Are these two sentences possible?

1 'I took the exam three times and finally I could pass.'

2 'I took the exam three times and finally I was able to pass.'

Phrase bank: Interrupting and preventing interruption

1 Add the expressions below to the diagram according to whether they are ways of interrupting, preventing interruption or both.

Can I just come in here? (a)   Can I just say something? (b)
Could I just finish what I was saying? (c)   Erm, ... (d)
Hang on a minute. (e)   Hold on a second. (f)
If I could just finish ... (g)   ~~Just a moment. (h)~~
Let me finish. (i)   No, hear me out. (j)
Sorry to interrupt (again). (k)   Wait a minute. (l)

Interrupting   Preventing interruption

2 Which of these statements means (1) you want Juan to stop speaking, and (2) you want someone else to stop speaking, so Juan can say something?

a Thanks, Juan.   **b** Thanks. Juan?

How does your voice go up and down when saying the two expressions above? Which sounds like this: ↘↗? And which sounds like this: ↗↘?

3 Put the lines of the conversation in the correct order. The first one has been done for you.

a Yes, what is it? ☐
b You were saying ... ☐
c Can I come back to those later? ☐
d Can you give us the figures for that? ☐
e Where was I? ☐
f Can I stop you there? ☐ *1*
g Okay, sorry. Go on. ☐

14

Snail mail

Writing without thinking is like shooting without aiming.

Arnold Glasow

Do you still consider writing letters a good method of communication?

1 According to management guru Henry Mintzberg, even in the age of the electronic office most of us still spend a third of our time doing routine paperwork. What kind of documents cross your desk in a typical day?

2 Different managers are talking about the paperwork they have to do. Complete what they say below with the documents in the box they are referring to.

> contracts　copies　diagrams　figures　forms　invoices　letters　mail
> memos　Post-it®　questionnaires　receipts　record　report　trade journals

a The first thing I do when I get into the office is get myself a coffee and check the morning _____.

b Whenever I have important _____ to write, I usually draft them several times before finally sending them.

c One thing I can't stand is filling in _____ – they never give you enough space to write your answers!

d I try to read as many _____ as possible – just to keep up with what's going on.

e I work in the legal department, so that means a lot of drafting and drawing up of _____.

f I work for a design firm, so I often find myself faxing _____ of plans and _____.

g I have to keep a _____ of all my expenses, so I always ask for _____ – I have a pile by the end of the month!

h I try to settle _____ as quickly as possible, but I query them immediately if the _____ don't add up.

i I used to circulate _____ to other people in the department, but these days I just email them on the intranet or stick a _____ on their desk.

j In my job, I have to design market research _____, which usually means putting together some kind of _____ afterwards.

Communication channels

1 Underline the correct preposition in each situation below.

You want to:

a introduce your company *to* / *for* a prospective client.

b complain *about* / *of* the service at a hotel you stayed in.

c give instructions *of* / *on* how to get to your office.

d confirm an appointment *for* / *on* tomorrow morning.

e sum *off* / *up* what was agreed at a recent meeting.

f deal *with* / *about* a complaint from an important customer.

g follow up *with* / *on* a sales presentation you made.

h raise the subject *with* / *of* a salary increase with your boss.

i thank someone you stayed with *for* / *on* their hospitality.

j ask *with* / *for* a signature on a contract.

k send *off* / *out* a job application and CV.

l share a joke you found on the Internet *with* / *about* a friend!

2 What would you do first in each situation in 1? Discuss with a partner.

- write a letter
- speak to the person face to face
- send an email
- send an SMS
- make a phone call
- send a fax
- arrange a meeting

In a rush

1 Read the business letter below. The person who wrote it was in a rush to finish it and made a lot of mistakes. With a partner, try to find as many mistakes as you can. These could relate to spelling, grammar, punctuation or wrong/unnecessary words. There are 16 mistakes – how many can you find? An important element of a business letter is also missing – do you know what it is?

> Xenod Communications
> In touch with technology
> 22st February
>
> Re Enquiry about the DigiCom System
>
> My dear Ms Ramalho,
>
> thank you for your letter from 9th Feb and for your interest in the new Xenod digital comunication system.
>
> I am such sorry you were disabled to attend our presentation in São Paulo last month, but I am delighted to tell you we are planning another one in Brasilia on 30th April.
>
> In the mean time, I enclose a copy of our last catalogue and currant prize list.
>
> If you have any questions or would like further informations concerning our company and its products, please don't hesitate but contact me again.
>
> I look forwards to hearing from you.
>
> Yours fatefully,
>
> Rudolf Kinski
>
> pp Brian Green
>
> XENOD Communications   Unit 45   Pinewood Industrial Park   Oxford OX7 T42
>
> Tel. (44) (0)1865 356 777   email xenod-communications@email.net   website www.xenod.co.uk

2 🔘 **2.30** The person who wrote the email asked a colleague to check it for him. Listen to eight extracts from their conversation. Do they make the same corrections you did?

Could I see you a moment?

Work with a partner to practise checking each other's business letters. Both speakers see page 131.

What's missing?

1 Work with a partner. Replace the missing words in the following sentences from business letters. In sentences a–j, one word is missing. In k–t, two words are missing. The first one has been done for you as an example.

a How are things *with* you?

b I apologize not replying sooner.

c Further our telephone conversation yesterday, …

d See you the weekend. Best wishes, Jim.

e I thought I'd send you a copy this article.

f Sorry I wasn't there meet you when you called.

g Sincerely, Brian Green

h It was great pleasure meeting you last week.

i Take care yourself.

j How's going?

k Thank you your letter 6 May.

l Get back to me soon you can.

m I look forward hearing you.

n With reference your fax 3 June, …

o I am writing regard your recent advertisement.

p I'll be touch the next couple of weeks or so.

q I can be any further assistance, do please contact me again.

r Let know when you're next Zagreb.

s It was nice talking you other day.

t Please pass my regards your sales manager, Ms Fontaine.

2 Now write the letters of the sentences in the box below according to whether they usually come at the beginning or end of a business letter, and whether they are formal or informal.

	Formal	Informal
Beginning		
End		

Crossed in the post

Work in groups to practise sending and receiving letters. Every ten minutes, you will have to 'mail' the letter you have written to another group and reply to the one you receive. Use the phrases and expressions below as the basis for your letters, but add extra points if you like. If necessary, phone the other group to confirm your arrangements with them.

Group A

1 Preparation

In your group, invent a sales meeting you had with a potential client. Decide what you were trying to sell, what the main features and benefits of the product are, and how it compares with the competition.

2 Following up a sales meeting

Dear • Thank you • taking the time • see us • your offices in • During our meeting • I hope • able • show you the benefits of • As you saw • really is a superior product in terms of • I think • meets your requirements very well • Need further information • feel free • contact • again

3 Putting off a potential contact

Dear • Enjoyed meeting you in • Everyone agreed • very interesting discussion • Unfortunately • not in a position • carry things further • the moment • Busy time of the year for us • When • had time • consider • more detail • will contact • again

4 Reviving a cold contact

Dear • How are things? • Hope • got over your busy period • As • haven't been in touch • a while • wondering • had more time • consider our conversation • conference • January • In fact • have some news • might be • great interest to you • When • convenient time • talk?

5 Responding to a sales pitch

Dear • Thank • your letter • copy new product brochure • Very impressed • specifications • like • place • initial order for …

OR

Dear • Thank • letter • Afraid • decided • purchase • another supplier this time • Have kept • product details • file …

Group B

1 Preparation

In your group, invent a company you met at a conference who might be interested in using your service. Decide what the service is and how you compare with your competitors.

2 Following up a business contact

Dear • A pleasure meeting you in • Hope you got back safely • I was wondering • you'd like • discuss further what we talked about • conference reception • I've spoken • my boss • very interested • exploring the idea further • If you're interested • happy • set up a meeting

3 Putting off a prospective supplier

Dear • Thank you • coming • talk to us about • Very much enjoyed • presentation • extremely interested in • At the moment, however • considering several alternative products • haven't yet • final decision • Be in touch in due course • Thank you once again

4 Reviving a cold sales lead

Dear • As someone who • previously shown interest in • wanted you to know • now a new, improved version of the • at an even more competitive price • added features include • This means you can • Enclosed • copy • new product brochure • Look forward

5 Responding to a business opportunity

Dear • Thank • letter • Jun 15 • Now had time • discuss your proposal • head office • like • arrange • meeting • explore • more detail …

OR

Dear • Thank • letter • Having considered • proposal more fully • sorry • inform you • not able • proceed at this time …

Jan

Feb

Jun

July

14 Snail mail

Prepositions

Prepositions (*in*, *at*, *of*, *for*, *through*, etc) are a restricted group of short words, each having many different purposes. They usually take their precise meaning from the words around them.

Apart from their standard uses to refer to time, place and movement, prepositions also combine with verbs, nouns and adjectives to form a lot of useful phrases and expressions. Such phrases are best learned 'whole' as items of vocabulary.

Prepositional phrases

1 Twenty-three prepositions are missing from the following letter. How many can you find? Write them in.

> Dear Mr Savage
>
> Thank you your letter 12th April. I'm very sorry the difficulties you've had getting one our engineers come and repair the alarm system we installed January. Please accept my apologies. I am as concerned the delay as you are.
>
> The manager who is responsible our after-sales service is new the department and not yet familiar all our procedures, but this is no excuse such a long delay. Rest assured, he is now aware the problem and will arrange an engineer call whatever time is most convenient you. Obviously, this will be free charge. I have also authorized a 10% refund the purchase price.
>
> If you are still not fully satisfied the system, please contact me personally and I shall be happy supply you a replacement.
>
> My apologies once again the inconvenience this has caused you.

Preposition + noun + preposition

2 Complete the following extracts from business letters, faxes and emails with the nouns in the box. Pay particular attention to the prepositions on either side of each noun.

> accordance   account   addition   agreement   behalf
> case   effect   favour   pressure   regard   terms
> touch   view

a I am writing with _____ to your advertisement in *Marketing Week*.

b We are basically in _____ with the main points in your proposal.

c I've been in _____ with our distributors in Poland concerning your enquiry.

d There are one or two points in _____ to those we discussed which we now need to address.

e No one at the meeting was in _____ of the idea.

f The goods have been insured in _____ of damage in transit.

g There will be a 3% price increase with _____ from 1st January.

h Plan A has been rejected on _____ of the considerable costs involved.

i We decided, in _____ of the political difficulties, not to export to Iraq.

j We are again under _____ from head office to reduce overheads.

k Certainly, in _____ of experience, she's the best candidate we've seen so far.

l We are investigating the complaints in _____ with our normal procedures.

m May I, on _____ of myself and the whole team, thank you for making our visit so enjoyable.

Multi-verb expressions

When we combine two verbs in a sentence, the second verb can follow several patterns:

1 Modal verbs are followed by the infinitive without *to*:
   • We **must make** *a decision on this today*.
2 Non-modal verbs are followed either by the infinitive with *to*:
   • We **agreed to review** *the situation in a month*.
   or by the *-ing* form:
   • They **regretted borrowing** *the money*.
3 Some verbs, normally followed by the *-ing* form, change when there's an indirect object:
   • *I advise* **repackaging** *the product*.
   • *I advise* **you to repackage** *the product*.
   • *I suggest* **breaking** *off the meeting here*.
   • *I suggest* **we break** *off the meeting here*.

4 Some non-modal verbs can be followed by both the infinitive with *to* and the *-ing* form. But be careful. The meaning often changes – sometimes completely – as in these examples:
   • *They* **stopped to talk**. (= they stopped doing something else so that they could talk)
   • *They* **stopped talking**. (= the talking stopped)
   • *I* **didn't remember to email** *you the report*. (= there was no email)
   • *I* **don't remember emailing** *you the report*. (= I may have emailed it to you, but I don't remember)
5 When a verb is followed by a preposition other than *to*, the *-ing* form is usually used:
   • *We* **succeeded in getting** *the loan*.
   • *I'm* **thinking of changing** *my job*.
   When it isn't, the meaning changes:
   • *He* **went on talking** *for over an hour!* (= he wouldn't shut up)
   • *He* **went on to talk** *about profits*. (= he changed the subject)

Study the information on page 89 and complete the following advice on how to produce professional letters and faxes by combining the verbs, prepositions and pronouns in brackets.

a Reply to incoming mail promptly. Don't _____ for more than a couple of days. (put off / write back)

b Always _____ with a proper salutation. (remember / open)

c Don't _____ a subject line. (forget / include)

d _____ a lot of time on social chit-chat at the beginning of the letter. (forget about / spend)

e Most writing experts _____ lots of subheadings and bullet points to make your message clearer. (recommend / use)

f But they don't _____ a lot of old-fashioned formal expressions. (suggest you / use)

g Ideally, you _____ neither too formal nor too friendly. (should / aim / sound)

h You _____ your sentences short and simple. (should / try / keep)

i Some people _____ 10–15 words per sentence. (advise you / not exceed)

j Also _____ long complicated words when short ones will do. (avoid / use)

k If you have a lot of information, _____ a separate document. (consider / enclose)

l Beware the spell check! You really _____ all your mistakes. (can't / trust it / pick up)

m Grammar checks are even worse. You'll certainly _____ on them. (regret / rely)

n If you _____ your whole message into less than 200 words, you've done well. (can / manage / get)

o Reread before you send. _____ your own letter – what impression would it give? (imagine / receive)

p _____ a difficult letter several times before you send it. (think about / redraft)

Phrase bank: Letter-writing expressions

You have been given responsibility for writing to a very good customer your boss knows personally, but you don't. See what your boss would write below and make what you write a little more formal.

Informal

Dear Nick,

How are things?

I got your letter, thanks.

Sorry I haven't got back to you sooner.

About our phone call the other day, ...

Great to meet you last week!

I'm writing about our contract renewal.

I'm afraid I can't give you a bigger discount.

But how about a higher credit limit?

Let's meet and have a chat about this.

I'll give you a call sometime next week.

I'm putting in a copy of our new catalogue.

If you need any help, just let me know.

See you at the conference!

Let's talk soon.

Best wishes, Tony

Formal

Dear Mr Salzmann,

a (hope / well) _____

b (thank / letter of / 12 January _____

c (apologies / not replying) _____

d (Further to / conversation / last Friday) _____

e (pleasure / meeting) _____

f (writing / regard) _____

g (unfortunately / unable / increase) _____

h (what / can do / offer) _____

i (perhaps / meet / discuss) _____

j (in touch) _____

k (enclose) _____

l (any further assistance / please do contact) _____

m (look forward / meeting / again) _____

n (look forward / hearing) _____

o (Yours) _____

15 Solving problems

What's your 'top tip' for problem-solving?

1 How good are you at problem-solving? Where and when do you get your best ideas? Complete the following phrases and tick those that are true for you.

| bath | book | course | court | daydreaming | desk | sleep |
| holiday | meetings | morning | music | night | shower | work |

a first thing in the _____
b in the middle of the _____
c travelling to and from _____
d on _____
e at my _____
f lying in a nice hot _____
g while I'm taking a _____
h listening to _____
i on the golf _____
j on the tennis _____
k after a good _____
l relaxing with a good _____
m in problem-solving _____
n while I'm _____!

2 Compare the phrases you ticked in 1 with a partner.

3 There is a Japanese expression: *None of us is as smart as all of us.* Following this idea, one American company regularly posts questions on a bulletin board and invites its staff to brainstorm suggestions. Read the bulletin board notice on the right.

Work with a partner. Think of as many ways as possible your company could save money. Then compare your ideas with the rest of the group.

4 🔘 **2.31** Listen to the first idea the company awarded a $100 bonus to.

5 Work in groups to solve some problems three real companies faced. Speaker A see page 132. Speaker B see page 136. Speaker C see page 138.

6 🔘 **2.32–2.34** Listen and compare each company's solution with yours. What do you think of the real solutions?

Today's question:

In what ways, big or small, could this company save money?

Write your suggestions below. $100 bonus for all suggestions we adopt.

Suggestions

1 Problem-solving meetings should start with clear objectives and end with clear actions. Look at the problems and objectives in the table. Complete the suggestions in column 3 with the phrases (a–j).

a to shift production to somewhere like South-East Asia
b to sell it direct online
c delay the new product launch
d offered it on a sale or return basis
e encrypting our most confidential information
f sell it off at a discount
g raising prices
h we involved the police
i bought the company out
j just manufacture our own components

	What's the problem?	What's our objective?	What action can we take?
1	We can't get retail outlets to stock our new product.	to get access to the customer	What if we _____? Another option would be _____.
2	Our sole supplier is about to go bankrupt!	to get the supplies we need	Supposing we _____? Alternatively, we could _____.
3	Rising labour costs are reducing profits.	to maintain our profit margins	How about _____? The answer could be _____.
4	Old unsold stock is starting to pile up in the warehouses.	to create space for new product	Why don't we _____? Couldn't we just _____?
5	Someone in the company is passing on information to the competition!	to protect our competitive advantage	What about _____? Maybe it's time _____.

2 2.35–2.39 Listen to extracts from the meetings in 1 and check your answers.

3 2.35–2.39 Listen again and answer the following questions.

Extract 1 Which of the two suggestions is better received?
Extract 2 What will happen if a solution isn't found?
Extract 3 Why isn't a price increase an option?
Extract 4 How is product development affecting the stock situation?
Extract 5 What do you think the last speaker means when he says 'Perhaps we can even turn the situation to our advantage'?

4 Go back and underline the five most useful collocations in 1 (e.g. *retail outlet*, *stock a product*, *labour costs*). What are the equivalent expressions in your own language?

5 Complete the sentences. They were all in the extracts in 2.

| 'd been + wouldn't be | 'd discounted + wouldn't have | 'd known + could have |
| would have + 'd thought | wouldn't have + 'd priced | |

a We _____ this problem if we _____ the product more sensibly in the first place.

b If we _____ this was going to happen, we _____ had our own production plant up and running by now.

c If we _____ able to get the unions to accept a lower pay offer, John, we _____ considering outsourcing to Asia.

d If we _____ it sooner, we _____ had to be so generous.

e I _____ called the police in already if I _____ it would do any good.

Which of the sentences above refer:
1 to the past and present? ☐ ☐ ☐
2 only to the past? ☐ ☐

Problem-solving techniques

1 Do you have a special procedure for dealing with more complex problems? Complete the checklist below using the verbs in the boxes.

a–d

| brainstorm | define | review | select |

e–l

| assign | break | criticize | draw up | eliminate | explore | invite | restate |

Step One: (a) _____ the basic problem

(e) _____ the problem down into parts
(f) _____ the problem as a challenge

Step Two: (b) _____ ideas

(g) _____ everyone to speak
(h) _____ nothing at this stage

Step Three: (c) _____ your ideas so far

(i) _____ the possibilities of each idea
(j) _____ impractical suggestions

Step Four: (d) _____ the best solution

(k) _____ an action plan
(l) _____ different tasks to different people

2 The following sentences were used in a problem-solving meeting. Decide at which step in 1 each sentence was used.

1 Now, what we need are as many ideas as possible. ☐
2 How could we make this idea work? ☐
3 On balance, I think we should go with this idea. ☐
4 Let's think about what we can do, instead of what we can't. ☐
5 I'd like to hear what you all have to say. ☐
6 Okay, basically, the problem is this. ☐

7 Okay, let's see what we've got so far. ☐
8 I think we'll have to reject this idea for now. ☐
9 Now, how do we implement this? ☐
10 Okay, that's a nice idea. ☐
11 Joanne, can I leave the details to you? ☐
12 I think there are three main aspects to the problem. ☐

Everyday problems

1 Work in groups. What sort of everyday problems do you face at work? Write down on separate slips of paper two or three of the toughest problems you have to deal with. Be specific.

2 Swap papers with another group. Read out the problems one by one and discuss with your group how they could be solved. Write down any suggestions on the back of the papers.

3 Return the papers to their original owners. Was any of the advice useful?

Creativity

1 How important is creativity in problem-solving? Work in groups. Each group reads a different piece of advice (paragraph 1, 2 or 3) on how to solve problems creatively.

2 Form groups with people who read different paragraphs. Give each other a summary of what you read. Which is the best advice? Do you know of other companies which successfully use these methods?

HOW TO SOLVE PROBLEMS

① CHANGE YOUR PERSPECTIVE

A lot of problems can be solved simply by looking at them in a different way. Try problem reversal. Don't ask how you can sell more of your products. Ask how you could sell fewer and see where that idea takes you. Perhaps you could create a totally new market where exclusivity was more important than sales volume. As marketing and communications specialist Ros Jay points out: 'Many companies have done well out of problem reversal. Businesses like Apple Computers® have looked at the market and, instead of saying: "How can we compete with all these big players?", have asked themselves: "What can we do that all these other companies aren't doing?" One of IBM's most famous advertising slogans was 'Think'. Apple's was 'Think different'.

② BE PLAYFUL

Must work always feel like work? John Quelch, Dean of the London School of Business, asks: 'How many times a day does the average five-year-old laugh? Answer: 150. How many times a day does the average 45-year-old executive laugh? Answer: five. Who is having more fun? Who is, therefore, likely to be more creative? Need we ask?' At ?What If!, a London-based innovation consultancy, they've worked out that most people get their best ideas away from the office, so they've made the office look like home, complete with armchairs, kitchen and even table football. ?What If! is now a £3 million company whose clients include PepsiCo, ICI and British Airways, so they must be doing something right.

③ MAKE CONNECTIONS

Jonas Ridderstråle and Kjell Nordström of the Stockholm School of Economics have put forward the idea that 'as everything that ever will be invented has been invented, the only way forward is to combine what is already there'. So we get 'email', 'edu-tainment', 'TV dinners', 'distance-learning' and 'bio-tech'. Sometimes the combinations are impossible. Yamaha, for example, hasn't yet worked out a way to combine motorbikes with musical instruments – perhaps it will. But Jake Burton had more success when he gave up his job on Wall Street in 1977 to pioneer a new sport. Bringing together two quite separate things – snow and surfboards – he developed the modern snowboard. Today there are nearly four million snowboarders breaking their limbs all over the world in the name of fun!

A problem-solving meeting

1 Work in groups. Group A see below. Group B see page 132. Choose a chairperson. Using the procedure on page 93, hold a meeting to solve the problem.

- Read paragraph one. What else do you know about this business?
- Read paragraph two. What's your immediate response to the problem?
- Read paragraph three. It should give you some extra ideas on how to solve the problem.
- Conduct a problem-solving meeting with your group.
- Summarize the problem and your solutions for the other group or groups. Find out if they agree with you.

A marketing problem at
SONY ERICSSON

The joint venture

The Sony® Corporation is one of the world's biggest multinational conglomerates and an almost permanent member of the Fortune Global 100. A pioneer in electronic goods manufacture, it is perhaps most famous for the Walkman® as well as the compact disc and Blu-Ray video format, both of which it co-developed. The telecoms powerhouse Ericsson is among Sweden's most successful companies and also a leading innovator, having invented Bluetooth™ wireless technology. Back in 2001, these two corporate giants shook up the mobile phone industry when they came together to launch a new joint venture called Sony Ericsson Mobile Communications.

The challenge

For Sony, a marginal player in the mobile market at that time, the joint venture was chiefly an exercise in diversification. For Ericsson, which was already the third biggest mobile phone manufacturer in the world, it was an attempt to strengthen its position following the dotcom and technology industry crash of 2000. In a nutshell, the Sony Ericsson strategy was to leverage both companies' innovative expertise and release the first ever mobiles with built-in digital cameras and colour screens. But, although the new venture's multimedia product line was revolutionary, in an overcrowded market in the middle of a recession customer response was disappointing. For a time, Ericsson's market share actually declined and in 2002, they announced that they might even have to pull out of mobile phone manufacture altogether if sales didn't pick up. Conventional advertising seemed to have had little effect. The marketing team at Sony Ericsson needed to come up with a truly original campaign if they were ever going to boost sales and challenge Nokia for market leadership in the highly competitive mobile phone market.

The opportunity

You're not paying attention. Nobody is. These days, there's so much marketing hype it's impossible to take it all in. It's estimated that we all see around 3,000 advertising messages every day from billboards to T-shirts, bumper stickers to animated banner ads, and the net result is that we take no notice at all. Particularly in sophisticated luxury goods markets, straight advertising just doesn't work anymore. What does seem to work is word of mouth – either face to face or online. Busy people, especially, don't like their lives being interrupted by stupid commercials. But that doesn't mean they can't be persuaded, as Sony Ericsson discovered.

In company interviews
Units 13–15

2 2.40–2.41 Listen to find out what the companies actually did. Were your suggestions similar? Is there anything in the case studies which is relevant to your own line of business?

15 Solving problems

People and products

1 Decide whether the adjectives below can be used to describe people (staff), products or both. Tick the correct boxes.

		staff	products
a	best-selling	☐	☐
b	efficient	☐	☐
c	high-quality	☐	☐
d	well-qualified	☐	☐
e	household	☐	☐
f	dedicated	☐	☐
g	unique	☐	☐
h	luxury	☐	☐
i	loyal	☐	☐
j	permanent	☐	☐
k	part-time	☐	☐
l	reliable	☐	☐

The workforce

2 Match the verbs and verb phrases in the box to those below which have a similar meaning.

> dismiss   down tools   inspire   instruct   lay off
> motivate   quit   recruit   relocate   resign
> take industrial action   take on   teach   transfer

hire
a _____
b _____

move
c _____
d _____

fire
e _____
f _____

go on strike
g _____
h _____

train
i _____
j _____

leave
k _____
l _____

encourage
m _____
n _____

3 The adjectives below can all be used to describe people in a company. Change each adjective into its opposite by adding *un-*, *in-*, *im-*, *ir-* or *dis-*.

a ____reliable
b ____flexible
c ____organized
d ____patient
e ____responsible
f ____creative
g ____consistent
h ____inspiring
i ____committed
j ____practical
k ____articulate
l ____honest
m ____rational
n ____decisive
o ____supportive
p ____competent
q ____assertive
r ____sociable
s ____considerate
t ____competitive

4 Complete the following staff appraisals using an appropriate positive or negative adjective from 3.

a Laura's a real ideas person. She's exceptionally _____.

b Brian can only do things his way. He's a bit _____.

c Max is always there to give people a hand when they need it. He's really very _____.

d With Olaf, it's just one mistake after another. He's completely _____.

e Greta tends to take no notice of other people's needs. She's rather _____.

f Richard's office looks like a bomb hit it – papers everywhere! He's totally _____.

g With Miyumi, the job always comes first. She's totally _____.

h Sam can never make up his mind about anything. He's extremely _____.

i Callum really knows how to motivate his staff. He's incredibly _____.

j You can never depend on Leo to do what he's supposed to do. He's totally _____.

k Elena meets all her targets month after month. She's incredibly _____.

l Jeanette too often allows her personal life to interfere with her work. She's rather _____.

m Eric always has to be the best at everything. He's extremely _____.

n Gareth tends to keep himself to himself. He's a bit _____.

The production line

5 Match the verbs and verb phrases in the box to those below which mean the opposite.

> go out of   halt   reduce   reintroduce
> scale down   withdraw

go into   ⟷   a _____
start   ⟷   b _____ production
step up   ⟷   c _____
launch   ⟷   d _____
discontinue   ⟷   e _____ a product
boost   ⟷   f _____ productivity

6 Complete the following sentences using appropriate words and phrases from 5.

a We always _____ new products in January at the annual trade fair.

b We'll need to _____ production to keep up with demand.

c A staff incentive scheme helped us to _____ productivity.

d We had to _____ production completely until we'd found the fault.

e There were some complaints about the product, so we had to _____ it to make the necessary modifications. We'll _____ it next month.

Grammar

Conditionals (past reference)

You can use *if* to speculate about the likely effects of things being different in the past. You often use this type of conditional to talk about regrets and make accusations.

- *If we **hadn't invested** so heavily in dotcoms, we'd **have** saved ourselves a fortune!* (1) (but we invested heavily and we didn't save a fortune)
- *You **could have got** an interview with that company if only you'd **taken** my advice.* (2) (but you didn't get an interview because you didn't take my advice)
- *If our lawyers **hadn't spotted** that mistake in the contract, we'd **be** in a real mess!* (3) (but they spotted it and so we are not in a real mess)
- *If you'd **told** me about it sooner, I **might have been able to** do something.* (4) (but you didn't tell me sooner so I couldn't do anything)
- *He **might** never **have been able to** start his own business if his father **hadn't helped** him.* (5) (but he started his own business because his father helped him)
- *If she'd **taken** her studies more seriously, she **wouldn't be** flipping burgers at McDonald's®.* (6) (but she didn't take her studies seriously and now she's working at McDonald's)

1 Study the information above and answer the questions.

a What grammatical tense is used in the *if*-clause of all the examples?

b What modal verbs are used in the main clause?

c What tenses follow the modal verbs in the examples?

d Which sentences directly refer to the effects of the past on the present?

e Which sentences directly refer to the effects of the past on the more recent past?

2 Complete the conversation with the pairs of words in the box.

could + tried	done + have	hadn't + wouldn't
have + known	promised + would	would + could

Two colleagues are having an argument.

A All I'm saying is, if you'd (a) _____ something about it sooner, we could _____ prevented this whole nightmare from happening.

B I know, I know. And I (b) _____ have if I _____ have, but I couldn't.

A You (c) _____ have if you'd _____.

B Maybe if I hadn't already (d) _____, I _____ be able to put them all off.

A Well, anyway, it's too late now. You know, I'd never (e) _____ asked you to organize these visits if I'd _____ you weren't clear about it.

B Well, if you (f) _____ said you wanted us to get involved in the local community more, I probably _____ have had the idea in the first place.

A I mean, what were you thinking of? You've organized factory tours for three infant schools and the Bulgarian Embassy all on the same morning!

Which example above does not contain the Past Perfect?

Phrase bank: Problem-solving

Match each of the four stages of a problem-solving meeting (a–d) to two things you might say (1–8).

a Defining the problem

b Brainstorming ideas

c Reviewing ideas

d Selecting the solution

1 Okay, let's see what we've got so far.
2 On balance, I think we should go with …
3 I think there are three main aspects to the problem.
4 I think we'll have to reject this idea for now.
5 I'd like to hear what you all have to say.
6 Now, how do we implement this?
7 Okay, basically the problem is this.
8 Let's keep the ideas coming.

a ☐☐ b ☐☐ c ☐☐ d ☐☐

Brainstorming

Complete the brainstorming phrases (a–j) with the words in the box. For two of the phrases there are two possibilities with a difference in meaning. What's the difference?

sell it online	selling it online	sold it online	to sell it online

a What if we _____?
b Another option would be _____.
c Supposing we _____?
d Alternatively, we could _____.
e How about _____?
f The answer could be _____.
g Why don't we _____?
h Couldn't we just _____?
i What about _____?
j Maybe it's time _____.

16 Collaboration

"This collaboration would work better if you kept your ideas to yourself."

Learning objectives: Unit 16

People skills Working in a team; Fluency: Problem-solving team meetings
Reading Creating team spirit
Listening A project problem

1 How much of your job involves teamwork?

0% ⟵—————————————⟶ 100%

2 Have you ever been teamed up with anyone like either of the people in the cartoon? What happened? What's the most productive team you've ever worked with?

3 Imagine you're putting together a project team. All the people on your shortlist have the right expertise and skills. So what personal qualities are you looking for? Compare ideas with your group.

4 Now complete the sentences (a–g) with the words in the box. Did you have similar ideas about the ideal team-player in 3? Do you know anyone with all these qualities?

| committed | constructive | co-operative | engaged | flexible | reliable | supportive |

The ideal team-player is:

a _____ – they get the job done to a consistent standard.
b _____ – they have a positive attitude and look for solutions.
c _____ – they really care about the success of the project.
d _____ – they treat everyone with respect and are willing to help.
e _____ – they can adapt to changing needs and circumstances.
f _____ – they take an active role in meetings and discussions.
g _____ – they work well with others and do what's asked of them.

Playing as a team

They say T.E.A.M. stands for 'together everyone achieves more', but we've all worked in teams where the reality was very different! Certainly, when 'the whole is greater than the sum of the parts', synergy is created which can produce terrific results. But teams that lack collaborative skills are likely to disintegrate into a battle of egos and conflicting priorities. And it's hard to reach your goals when everyone has their own agenda and is fighting over who gets the credit!

To avoid the typical arguments and points-scoring of many project meetings, executive coach Carol Kinsey Goman suggests using what she calls the P.P.R. technique. Here's how it works. Whenever someone shares an idea, the first thing you do is mention the 'positives' or what you like about it. This creates a climate of collaboration. Next come 'possibilities' – here you talk about how their idea could be applied, extended or perhaps combined with someone else's idea. Finally, if you have any 'reservations', make sure you leave these till last and focus less on the reservations themselves than how they might be overcome. Don't say: 'This won't work.' Ask instead: 'How could we make this work?' Remember, a team is a group of people who work hard to make each other look good!

5 How do you create team spirit in a meeting? Read the article and answer the questions.
a Without looking back at the article, can you remember what T.E.A.M. and P.P.R. stand for?
b How far do you agree with T.E.A.M.? What are the pros and cons of working in teams?
c What does *synergy* mean?
d What kind of ego battles and 'points-scoring' can go on in team meetings?
e Which cultures (or types of business culture) do you think are best at promoting teamwork?
f What do you think of the P.P.R. approach to creating a collaborative atmosphere in meetings?

6 2.42 Listen to a project team discussing a problem with a project they are running with a client, KNP. Choose the option (a–d) which best summarizes the problem.

KNP …

a wants to have more involvement in decision-making so they don't lose control of the project.

b is changing decisions agreed in meetings and so the project is falling behind schedule.

c is taking too long to respond to proposals with the result that the project is no longer on schedule.

d wants to set up a website so that everyone involved in the project can keep track of progress.

7 2.42 Listen again and note down the following:

a Elaine's idea: _____

b Rolf's 'positives': _____
_____

c Rolf's 'possibilities': _____
_____
_____

d Rolf's 'reservations': _____
_____

8 Form teams to brainstorm solutions to the business problems below. Take turns to be the facilitator – one for each problem. Use the draft agenda to structure your meetings.

Step 1 The facilitator should open and close the meeting, encourage full participation, write down all the ideas generated on a flipchart or whiteboard, and discourage evaluation or criticism of the ideas at this stage.

Step 2 The facilitator should now lead the discussion-and-evaluation stage. Team members give their reactions to each other's ideas in a constructive and supportive way using the P.P.R. technique. Some of the expressions you heard in 6 may help.

a You own a chain of supermarkets. Every week, hundreds of shopping carts are stolen.

b You sell jewellery online. But customers typically like to try on items before they buy.

c You manage a customer helpline. Staff turnover is high, so you keep losing good people.

Positives	Possibilities	Reservations
I really like your idea of … -ing …	And if we did that, we could also …	The only thing is, I'm not sure if we could …
What I especially like about it is …	Perhaps another thing we could do is …	And I'm also a bit worried about …
And it would certainly solve the problem of …	If we combined your idea with X's idea …	How do you think we could manage that?

Agenda

1 Welcome the group.

2 Outline the purpose of the meeting and get the team to define the problem.

3 Invite team members to take a few minutes to note down their ideas individually. Make sure they take the logistical and budgetary constraints into account.

4 Throw the meeting open for discussion by getting the team to share their ideas. Emphasize that they should use the P.P.R. technique.

5 Take a vote on the best idea or combination of ideas.

6 Discuss how your solution will be implemented and who will be responsible for what.

Tricky conversations

1 Heather Sherwood is a sales representative for Flow Information Systems (FIS).
Read some of her recent emails and answer the questions.

a What do you think Heather agreed with Alan before the meeting they just had?

b Why is she angry with him now?

c The subject title of Anton's email is 'Thanks!' But why might Heather not be so happy
to receive it?

d Do you think Anton mentioned to Gabrielle that it was Heather who originally
produced the figures?

e Why is Heather annoyed that Tony hasn't finished the budget report?

f How do you think Tony will react to having Kelly help him finish it?

What were you DOING?

To: a.sugarman@fis.com

Alan

I've just got back to my office and I'm still furious.
You made me look like a complete IDIOT in that
meeting with Gabrielle. You were supposed to back
me up! You know we can't work within our present
budget. So what happened? I notice you left for
lunch very quickly afterwards and your mobile's off.
We need to talk this afternoon, so call me the minute
you read this email.

Heather

Thanks!

To: h.sherwood@fis.com

Hi Heather

I passed on that idea we were discussing the other
day to Gabrielle – about setting up a dedicated FIS
website for each of our major clients. She LOVED it
– especially when I showed her those figures you'd
put together. I had to revise them a bit, but they
were really useful. Anyway, I'll take it from here. No
need for you to be involved. Just wanted to thank
you for your input.

Anton

Budget report?

To: a.kennedy@fis.com

Hi Tony

I'm concerned that the budget report I asked you to complete by last week still isn't ready yet.
I've just come out of a meeting with Gabrielle and if I'd had that report, it would have made my
life a lot easier! Anyway, Gabrielle has asked to see a copy by Friday, so if you can't get it done,
I'm sorry, but I'm going to have to bring in Kelly to help you finish it. I know you've put a lot of
work into it, but it can't be helped. Meet me in my office at 3.30 and we'll go through it.

Heather

---

2 How would you advise Heather to deal with Alan, Anton and Tony when she meets
them face to face?

In company in action

3 Now watch video D1 to see the three conversations between Heather and her colleagues and match them to what she's doing wrong (a–c).

Conversation 1

Conversation 2

Conversation 3

a She lets her personal involvement with the issue take over.

b She doesn't try to understand the situation from the other person's point of view and forces them to accept hers.

c Instead of discussing the problem, she spends too much time blaming the other person for what went wrong.

4 Read the article on handling difficult conversations and decide which tips might have helped Heather in each situation.

Handling Difficult Conversations in the Workplace

If you work in an office environment, you know difficult conversations are a fact of life. Breaking bad news, getting people to keep their promises, complaining about a colleague's behaviour or disagreeing with the boss – most of us would rather avoid conversations like these. But, according to Douglas Stone, Bruce Patton and Sheila Heen of the Harvard Negotiation Project, avoidance is never the answer. Delivering a difficult message, they say, is like 'throwing a hand grenade'. Whatever you do, it's going to cause damage. And not having the conversation is like 'hanging on to a hand grenade once you've pulled the pin'! Typically, say the Harvard team, three things happen in a difficult conversation and you must be sure to guard against them.

1. A lot of time and energy can be wasted arguing about who did what, who should have done what, who didn't do what they said they'd do and who's to blame. But this simply puts everyone on the defensive and guarantees that the problem will not be resolved. So try not to get into the 'blame game'. Focus on the solution.

2. Inside our heads we have an internal voice which expresses our feelings. Sometimes this voice is so loud; we can't hear what's being said. Of course, our feelings shouldn't be silenced, but they must be kept under control. And if you're thinking 'what rubbish, I don't have an internal voice', that's your internal voice speaking!

3. Many of us identify personally with our position in a disagreement. To accept that the other person could be right may affect our self-image in ways they cannot imagine. So be sure to find out what really matters to them. And don't confuse intention with effect – they may not have meant to make you feel the way you do.

5 What do you think Heather should do next time she discusses the situations with Alan, Anton and Tony? How could she have been more diplomatic in her earlier conversations?

In company in action

6 The following day Heather catches up with Alan, Anton and Tony again. This time their conversations are more constructive. Watch video D2 and compare the solutions they come up with to the ones you thought of in 5.

7 You're about to have two difficult conversations with your partner!

Speaker A: Turn to page 133.

Speaker B: Turn to page 141.

8 Now evaluate your performance using the feedback form on page 128.

17 Eating out

Why do you think business lunches are so popular?

Learning objectives: Unit 17

Business communication skills
Describing restaurants; Doing a quiz on table manners and etiquette; Describing typical dishes from your country; Roleplay: Doing business over lunch
Listening A conversation in a restaurant; Conversations over lunch
Vocabulary Food and drink
Grammar The passive
Phrase bank Eating out

1 Work with a partner and discuss the following questions.

a Is lunch an important meal for you?

b Do you ever have business lunches?

c Which of the following are you most likely to say to a foreign colleague visiting your country?

I thought you might like to try some of our local cuisine.
I thought we could just grab a quick pizza or something.
I thought we'd just work through lunch and eat later.

2 What kinds of restaurants do you like? Add the phrases in the box to the diagram below to make 12 useful expressions.

> a fantastic view of the city   a superb menu   a very pleasant atmosphere
> does an excellent lasagne   down the road   five minutes from here
> I sometimes go   round the corner   specializes in fish   they know me
> you can get fresh oysters   you might like

There's a	really nice pretty good great new	place	just	a _____ b _____ c _____
			which	d _____ e _____ f _____
			where	g _____ h _____ i _____
			with	j _____ k _____ l _____

3 Do you have a favourite place where you take clients and colleagues? If so, tell a partner about it.

4 Look at the buffet in the photo. How many of the dishes can you name? Imagine you are about to help yourself to some food. Discuss the food with a partner. Use the phrases and expressions below to help you.

Mm, that looks nice! What is it?

Could you pass me one of those ...?

Looks like some kind of ..., only ...

I think I might try a bit of that.

So, what are you going to have?

Hmm. I don't fancy it. It looks a bit ...

I'm not sure. How about you?

Hmm, I wonder what's in it?

I quite like the look of this ...

Hmm? Oh, sure. Here you are.

Who said it?

1 The following things were said during a business lunch. Who do you think probably said them – the host, the guest or could it be either? Write *H*, *G* or *E* next to each sentence.

a Nice place. Do you come here often?

b Now, what would you like to drink?

c I'll just see if our table's ready.

d This is their standard menu.

e It all looks very good.

f And those are the specials.

g Let me know if you want me to explain anything.

h So, what do you recommend?

i Well, they do a great lasagne.

j Is there anything you don't eat?

k I'm allergic to mussels.

l You could try the lamb. That's very good here.

m That sounds nice.

n Shall we order a bottle of the house red?

o Could we order some mineral water, too?

p This is absolutely delicious. How's yours?

q Now, how about a dessert?

r Better not. I'm on a diet.

s I'll get this.

t No, no, I insist. You're my guest.

2 2.43 Now listen and compare your answers with the conversation in the restaurant. The man is the host.

Table manners

1 In Russia, they sit down at parties. In China, the most important guest is seated facing the door. In Japan, a tip is not expected; in France, it is an insult not to leave one. How culturally aware are you at the table? Try the quiz below. <u>Underline</u> the correct information.

CROSS-CULTURAL QUIZ

a In **Greece** / **Finland**, people frequently stop for lunch at 11.30 in the morning.

b In **Switzerland** / **Brazil**, it's common to be up to two hours late for a party.

c In **Portugal** / **the USA**, a business lunch can last up to three and half hours.

d In **Japan** / **Russia**, the soup is often eaten at the end of the meal.

e In **France** / **Britain**, cheese is normally served after the dessert.

f In **American** / **German** restaurants, you may be asked if you want a bag for the food you can't eat.

g In **Arab** / **Asian** countries, you must wait for your host to serve you the main meat dish.

h In **Mexico** / **Belgium**, you should keep both hands on the dinner table where they can be seen.

i At a **Turkish** / **Chinese** dinner table, it is extremely impolite to say how hungry you are.

j The **Japanese** / **British** sometimes need to be offered more food three times before they will accept.

k **American** / **Latin** executives like to be invited to your home for dinner.

l In **Belgium** / **Spain**, an 11 o'clock dinner is quite normal.

m In **Asian** / **Arab** countries, food is usually eaten with just three fingers of the right hand.

n In **Poland** / **Japan**, you should keep filling other guests' glasses until they turn them over.

o In **African** / **Asian** countries, it is the host who decides when the guests should leave.

Check your answers on page 134.

2 Find seven examples of the passive in the quiz in 1.

*… the soup **is** often **eaten** …*

Sticky situations

2.44–2.46 Listen to business people from different countries chatting over lunch and answer the questions.

Conversation 1

a What is Hiro worried about?

b Hiro uses different expressions to stop his colleague choosing the fugu. Complete them.

   1 It's rather

   _____

   2 It's a little

   _____

   3 You may

   _____

   4 I think you'd

   _____

   5 Really, I think you should

   _____

c What does David say when he decides to change his mind?

Conversation 2

a What is Hans's problem?

b The Spaniards use different expressions to encourage Hans to try the squid. Complete them.

   1 We thought you might

   _____

   2 You'll

   _____

   3 You'll really

   _____

   4 This is something

   _____

   5 It's really

   _____

c What does Hans say when he refuses the Spaniards' offer?

Conversation 3

a Why does Louise have a problem choosing what to eat?

b Jean-Claude and Louise mention lots of different cooking methods. Complete them.

   1 fr_____   **4** gr_____

   2 bo_____   **5** ba_____

   3 ro_____

c Complete these extracts from the conversation.

   1 … nothing made _____ pastry.

   2 … nothing cooked _____ oil.

   3 It comes _____ potatoes and fresh vegetables.

d Have you ever had lunch with anyone like Louise?

The business lunch

Showing interest:
Nice place. Do you come here a lot?
It all looks delicious.

Changing the subject:
By the way, I wanted to talk to you about my business idea.
Anyway, getting back to this idea of mine.
So, what do you think about the idea?

Work with a partner. You are going to talk business over lunch. Speaker A see page 132. Speaker B see below.

Your partner (Speaker A) is a good friend from abroad, whom you've also worked with in the past. You are visiting their city for a few days and they have invited you out for a nice lunch.

You called them about a week ago and mentioned a business idea you'd like to discuss with them over lunch. If they are interested, you'd like them to be involved, so prepare a short business plan to help you describe your idea. You should include:

- an outline of your basic idea (one or two sentences)
- why you think it has great business potential (have at least one good reason!)
- how you'd like your friend to be involved (time, money, expertise, contacts)
- how you see the idea developing in the future.

Make sure you get a chance to talk business over lunch, but don't be a bore and talk about nothing else! Be a good guest. Show interest in the restaurant and the food. (Remember, you're a foreigner and don't know about the cuisine!) Try to keep the conversation moving.

If the lunch goes well, offer to pay!

BASIC BUSINESS IDEA:

Why it has great potential:

How my partner could help:

Future of the business:

17 Eating out

Vocabulary

Food and drink

What's it like?

1 What do the adjectives (a–n) describe? Choose nouns in the boxes.

| dish | fish | lunch | meat | salad | steak | vegetables |

a   heavy/light/late/three-course   _____

b   fillet/rare/medium/well-done   _____

c   green/side/Waldorf/fruit   _____

d   fried/raw/smoked/freshly-caught   _____

e   roast/tough/tender/juicy   _____

f   fresh/frozen/seasonal/mixed   _____

g   traditional/exotic/local/vegetarian   _____

| bread | cheese | coffee | dessert | food | fruit | water |

h   rich/spicy/plain/fast   _____

i   dried/tropical/ripe/tinned   _____

j   crusty/stale/garlic/wholemeal   _____

k   strong/mild/blue/cream   _____

l   fattening/refreshing/light/chocolatey   _____

m   still/sparkling/bottled/tap   _____

n   white/strong/instant/black   _____

You can often turn a food noun into an adjective by adding -y.
  • containing lots of salt = *salty*
  • containing lots of sugar = *sugary*

2 Find five more food adjectives ending in -y in the lists in 1.

3 How would you describe a dish with lots of:
  • oil?   • fruit?   • taste?
  • fat?   • pepper?   • nuts?

What would you like to order?

4 Complete the the restaurant orders with the words in the box.

| bottle | fish | sauce | tart |

a   I'd like the steak with the peppercorn _____, please.

b   Could we also have a _____ of still water for the table?

c   Does the _____ come with any side dishes?

d   I'll have the chocolate _____ for dessert.

5 Use the words in the box to create questions that may be asked when eating out in a café or restaurant.

contains nuts	recommend
glass of water	side dishes
hot or cold	the bill
house special	the menu

Grammar

The passive

You form the passive with the appropriate tense of the verb *to be* + past participle:
  • *The components for Ford ™cars **are manufactured** in 15 different countries.*
  • *In Spain, dinner often **isn't eaten** until ten or eleven in the evening.*
  • *Steve Jobs was **re-appointed** head of Apple Computers® in 1997.*
  • *When **was** the euro first **introduced**?*
  • *As an exporter of computer software, the USA **has been overtaken** by the Republic of Ireland.*

You can also use the passive with modal verbs:

*A   How soon **will** the project **be completed**?*

*B   Well, it **must be finished** by the end of the year.*

*A   Yes, but **can** it **be speeded up**, do you think?*

*B   Well, we'**d have to be given** a bigger budget.*

*A   I think that **could be arranged**.*

You use the passive when it is unimportant or obvious who or what does something. It is, therefore, common to use the passive to talk about **processes** and **procedures**.

1 Look at these two examples and answer the questions.

Active:

These days, email has largely superseded the fax machine.

Passive:

These days, the fax machine has been largely superseded by email.

a   What's the subject of the first sentence?

b   What's the subject of the second sentence?

c   In the second sentence, what word comes before the performer of the action?

d   Which of the sentences are you more likely to hear in a conversation about fax machines?

In both examples above, our attention is focused on the subject of the sentence. You use the passive when you're more interested in the subject than the performer of the action.

2 Complete the article with the correct passive form of the verbs in brackets.

Lloyd's: Insuring the famous and the bizarre

Virtually anything (a) _____ (can / insure) at Lloyd's. In fact, over the last hundred years London's most celebrated insurance company (b) _____ (ask) to issue some of the most bizarre policies ever! Here are just a few.

Car insurance is big business these days. But the very first car (c) _____ (insure) at Lloyd's (d) _____ (cover) by a marine policy. Cars were such a novelty in those days, motor policies (e) _____ (write) on the basis that cars were just ships that sailed on the land!

Actors have always been paranoid. Hollywood film idol, Betty Grable, was so worried her famous legs (f) _____ (might / injure) during filming, they (g) _____ (insure) by Lloyd's for a million dollars.

Multimillionaire rock stars worry too. Bob Dylan, Eric Clapton, Elton John, Rod Stewart and the Rolling Stones have all insured their voices. Bruce Springsteen's (h) _____ (believe) to be worth £3.5 million.

Food critic and gourmet Egon Ronay ran a different risk. Obviously, his career (i) _____ (would / destroy) if he was ever to lose his sense of taste. So a Lloyd's policy for £250,000 (j) _____ (take out) to protect him against waking up one day not knowing a haggis from a hamburger.

Insuring works of art is nothing new, but the laughter (k) _____ (could / hear) all over the city when a grain of rice with a portrait of the Queen and the Duke of Edinburgh engraved on it (l) _____ (estimate) to be worth $20,000. The question is: worth $20,000 to whom?

A few years ago, a killer whale called Namu (m) _____ (capture) off the Canadian coast and (n) _____ (drag) to Seattle for display in an aquarium. The captors insured themselves for $8,000 against Namu (o) _____ (rescue) by other whales! Unfortunately, he wasn't.

One rather confident comedy theatre group insured itself against the risk of a member of the audience dying laughing. So far, however, the insurance (p) _____ (not / claim) …

Phrase bank: Eating out

Label the groups of phrases and expressions (a–h) according to their purpose.

> Avoiding disasters   Being a good host
> Complimenting your host   Describing dishes
> Fighting over the bill   Ordering the meal
> Recommending dishes   Talking shop

a _____
Nice place. Do you come here often?
It was a good choice of restaurant.
It all looks delicious.

b _____
It's basically a fish pie.
It comes with a salad.
It's cooked in wine.

c _____
If you like seafood, you'll love it.
The lamb's very good here.
You could try the goulash.

d _____
It's a bit unusual – you may not like it.
Is there anything you don't eat?
Maybe you should try something else.

e _____
I'll just see if our table's ready.
Shall we have another bottle?
Is everything all right?

f _____
I'm going to have the steak. Rare, please.
I'd like the vegetarian lasagne.
Could we have a bottle of sparkling water?

g _____
About this business idea of mine.
As I was saying, we should have a meeting.
Going back to what we were talking about.

h _____
Let me get this. My treat.
This one's on me. You paid last time.
I insist … Okay, let's split it, then.

18 Telecommunications

1 How is a video- or audio-conference different from a face-to-face meeting? Do you agree with Kate Harper?

2 Look at the advertisements below for web conferencing company Connect. What advantages of web conferencing are the ads referring to? Think about your work–life balance, your department's travel budget and your company's 'carbon footprint'.

How often do you hold 'virtual meetings'? Do you prefer them to face-to-face meetings?

Learning objectives: Unit 18

Business communication skills
Discussing teleconferencing;
Holding a short teleconference;
Fluency: Dealing with emails and voicemail messages
Listening A teleconference
Reading An email exchange
Vocabulary Managing a project
Grammar Reporting
Phrase bank Teleconferencing

SimplyConnect

... and stop your business travel costing the earth

SimplyConnect

... and kiss goodbye to so much business travel

3 Read these two short reports. How do they support or contradict the messages in the advertisements?

A new report from the American Consumer Institute has calculated that the world will save roughly one billion tons of carbon in the next ten years by operating on the Internet. The trends break down like this:

E-commerce will reduce carbon emissions by 200 million tons.

Telecommuting will prevent 250 million tons of emissions from reduced driving.

Teleconferencing could prevent 200 million tons of emissions (if it replaces 10% of face-to-face meetings).

A recent survey conducted at Hygenica Inc. has suggested that travelling for business is one of the top five perks of working for the company. Despite a small proportion (10%) of respondents stating that they found travelling more stressful than coming to the office, the majority (over 80%) actually enjoy spending time away from home.

Over 50% said that the opportunity to travel and visit new, exciting places was the number one reason they enjoyed business travel. In fact, many admitted to combining travel for work with travel for pleasure, planning work trips to coincide with holidays or arranging meetings in destinations they've always wanted to visit. Over 30% stated that the weather of the destination country had an impact on the planning of a work trip.

4 Do any of the statistics in the reports surprise you?

5 Is teleconferencing the future? What sort of meetings (if any) do you think absolutely have to be face to face?

appraisal interviews   complex negotiations   crisis meetings   job interviews
multinational team briefings   new product demonstrations   project meeting updates
routine decision-making   sales presentations   team-building sessions

Teleconference: a project meeting

Ritterberger is a large and successful construction company based in Essen, Germany. At the moment it is building a marina complex in Dubai, managing a multinational team of engineers, and skilled and semi-skilled workers from Germany, Poland and Pakistan. But the project has been hit by a series of problems and is now running three months behind schedule. The client, Dubai entrepreneur Ali Al-Fulani, is unhappy with progress and demanding that penalty clauses in the contract be enforced if solutions cannot be found.

1 🔘 **2.47–2.48** Ritterberger CEO Peter Kessler has set up a teleconference to clarify the situation. Read the email attachment below to see who will be participating and what the main items on the agenda are. Then listen to the meeting and answer the questions.

RITTERBERGER GMBH

AUDIO-CONFERENCE, TUE 29 NOV, 9.00–10.30 (CET)

Participants:

Peter Kessler (CEO, Ritterberger, Essen)

Jarek Gorsky (Chief engineer, Ritterberger, Warsaw)

Ernst Neumann (Project director, Ritterberger, Dubai)

Karim Ibadulla (Foreman, Pakistani team, Dubai)

Feliks Nowakowski (Foreman, Polish team, Dubai)

Sulaiman Al-Fahim (Site manager, Dubai)

Agenda:

1 Supply hold-ups

2 Communication problems

3 Specification changes

Extract 1

a Where is Sulaiman Al-Fahim?

b Why is Jarek Gorsky at the meeting?

c What's the situation with Ali Al-Fulani?

Extract 2

a What is the communication problem?

b What's the situation at the seaports?

c What is Karim's point about the client?

d What is Peter Kessler's conclusion?

2 Complete the teleconferencing expressions you just heard with the words in the box.

agenda	agreed	come	covered	finish	finished	getting
hear	inputs	interrupt	introduce	item	join	leave	meeting
minimum	objectives	recap	skip	started	time	waiting

a Sorry, I had a bit of a problem _____ through.

b We're just _____ for Sulaiman.

c Let's go ahead and start. Welcome to the _____.

d Did you all get a copy of the _____?

e Before we start, let me _____ Jarek Gorsky.

f I've asked him to _____ us today because …

g All right, then, let's get _____.

h As you can see, we have several _____ today.

i I'd like to be _____ by 10.30, if that's okay.

j Can we keep our _____ quite short?

k And let's also try to keep interruptions to a _____.

l Sorry to _____, but …

m I suggest we _____ item one on our agenda until …

n Let's move straight on to _____ two.

o So just to _____ on what we've said.

p So, are we all _____ that …?

q Sorry, Sulaiman, I can't _____ you very well.

r Could I just _____ in here?

s Right, we're running short of _____.

t Ernst, Jarek, can I _____ that with you?

u I think we've _____ everything for now.

v We'll have to _____ there.

3 After the teleconference, Ernst circulated notes to the engineering team on what had been discussed. Put his notes in the correct order. Some have been done for you.

1	Peter Kessler opened the meeting and informed us that
	join us later. He then introduced
	might have to be renegotiated. Ernst and Jarek agreed to
5	that the main objective of the meeting was to get the Dubai Project back
	we skip item one on the agenda until Sulaiman could join us and went on
	have another look at overall logistics and to report back to Peter. Another teleconference
	to outline the communication problems the two work teams had
15	to bring this to the client's attention and that the contract with Al-Fulani
	joined the meeting at this point and described
	Sulaiman had gone to Port Rashid to check on deliveries and would
	the situation at the ports as serious. He explained that
12	nothing was moving and that our backup supplies were insufficient to cope with
	been having. Peter recommended onsite training as a possible solution. Sulaiman
	the present situation. Karim reminded us that
	on schedule. Ernst suggested that
	Jarek Gorsky, Ritterman's new chief engineer in Warsaw, and emphasized
	constant changes to the building plan were also a major problem. Peter promised
18	was scheduled for next week.

4 Work in a group. You're going to hold a short teleconference. Turn to page 133 for instructions.

An urgent matter

1 A management consultancy is putting together a proposal for a major new client, pharmaceutical giant, Hoechst. Put the following emails between two of their consultants in the correct order. Read all the emails first – A and H are in the right place.

A ☐ *1*

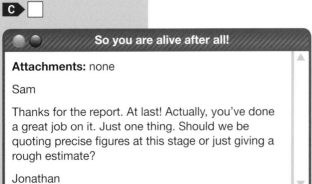

Hoechst report – progress?

Attachments: none

Sam

This is just a quick reminder to let you know that the Hoechst report was due yesterday.

Email me if you're having problems.

Jonathan

B ☐

Costing for Hoechst

Attachments: none

I see your point. Estimates would give us more room to negotiate on fees, but I think the client will appreciate that we've fully itemized all the costs.

Sam

C ☐

So you are alive after all!

Attachments: none

Sam

Thanks for the report. At last! Actually, you've done a great job on it. Just one thing. Should we be quoting precise figures at this stage or just giving a rough estimate?

Jonathan

D ☐

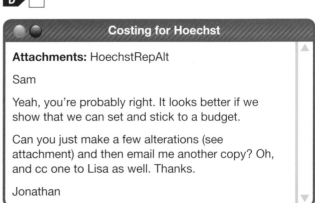

Costing for Hoechst

Attachments: HoechstRepAlt

Sam

Yeah, you're probably right. It looks better if we show that we can set and stick to a budget.

Can you just make a few alterations (see attachment) and then email me another copy? Oh, and cc one to Lisa as well. Thanks.

Jonathan

☐

Hoechst report

Attachments: HoechstRep, CostBrkdn

Jonathan

Sorry for the delay in getting back to you. Our server's been down again. I'm sending a first draft of the report as an attachment together with a detailed breakdown of costs for the whole project. Could you have a look at them and tell me if there's anything you want changing?

Sam

 ☐

HELLO?

Attachments: none

SAM!

Haven't you received my previous two emails? This is getting urgent. I've tried to phone, but you're never in. Look, I'm under a lot of pressure from head office to get this proposal in on schedule. Don't let me down, Sam.

Jonathan

 ☐

Hoechst report – update please

Attachments: none

Sam

Just had a call from Lisa. She wants to know what the hold-up is with the Hoechst report. Did you get my last email? Please let me know what the position is asap.

Jonathan

 8

Revised Hoechst Report

Attachments: HoechstRep2, ConJoke

Jonathan

Here's the revised version of the report. Only two days late in the end; sorry about that. By the way, I found a joke on the Internet the other day that might appeal to your sense of humour; you could use it in your presentation to Hoechst:

Why are they using consultants instead of rats in laboratory experiments these days? See attachment for answer :)

Sam

---

2 What do you think the punch line to Sam's joke is? See page 133 for the answer.

3 Match the words and phrases to make 14 complete expressions. If you need to, refer to the emails you read in 1, where they all appeared in the same order as here.

a	this is just	if you're having	problems
b	the report	to negotiate	costs
c	email me	was due	reminder
d	room	itemized	on fees
e	fully	a quick	yesterday
f	quote	the delay in	estimate
g	give	precise	report as an attachment
h	set and	a rough	getting back to you
i	sorry for	breakdown of costs	figures
j	send a	first draft of the	for the project
k	a detailed	proposal in	a budget
l	be under	stick to	head office
m	get a	pressure from	position is asap
n	let me	know what the	on schedule

Dealing with messages

1 Work in groups to produce a short profile of a company, a department in that company and an executive who works in that department. Invent the whole thing or use the names of real people and companies if you prefer.

PROFILE

Name of company:

Location:

Main business activity:

Department:

Name of executive:

Position in company:

2 Prepare five email messages and (if you can) five voicemail messages that the executive you invented might receive on a typical (or not so typical) working day. Keep each message fairly short. Include personal ones if you like.

Message ideas:

good news	an apology	a rumour
bad news	an offer	an invitation
a reprimand	a complaint	a request
an ultimatum	a crisis	

3 When you are ready, write out your email messages or print them off on a computer. Record your voicemail messages.

4 Swap your profile, voicemail messages and emails with another group.

5 Read and listen to the messages the other group gave you and decide how you are going to respond to each. Classify the messages as 'important', 'urgent', 'postpone', 'delegate' or 'bin'.

6 Write replies to the messages and return them to the group you swapped with.

7 Report back to the class on how you dealt with the messages you received.

18 Telecommunications

Managing a project

Look at the following extracts from emails written by members of an international project team. The last word in each expression has been switched with another. Switch them back. The first one has been done for you.

a This is just a quick **deadline**. ←
b Email me if you're having **costs**.
c I can't quote you a precise **schedule**.
d Can you give me a rough **report**?
e We're working to a very tight **figure**.
f I've attached a detailed breakdown of **problems**.
g We need to stick to our **teleconference**.
h Let me know if there's going to be a **loop**.
i We're in danger of missing our **reminder**.
j Let's set up a **budget**.
k Thanks for the situation **estimate**.
l Keep me in the **delay**.

Reporting

In business, it is important to be able to report accurately what people said in meetings, on the phone and in private conversation. Occasionally, we repeat the exact words someone used, but usually it is sufficient to report the basic message.

Original statement: *There's no way I'm going to accept cuts.*
Direct speech: *He said: 'There's no way I'm going to accept cuts.'* (1)
Reported speech: *He says there's no way he's going to accept cuts.* (2)
He said there was no way he was going to accept cuts. (3)
Reporting verb: *He refused to accept cuts.* (4)

1 Study the information above and answer the questions. Which expression would you use to:

a quote exactly what the speaker said in a meeting?
b report exactly what the speaker said in a meeting?
c summarize the general idea?
d tell someone in the meeting what the speaker just said?

NB When the reporting verb is in the past, you often put the reported speech in the past too:

I'm under a lot of pressure.
Reported speech: *He said he **was** under a lot of pressure.*

2 Change the statements below into reported speech.

a Fritz: I'm ready.
   Fritz said he was ready.
b Akio: I'm going to wait and see.
c Claire: I've had enough.
d Philippe: I must be going.
e Maria: I'll be in touch.
f Sergio: I just can't face it.

Reporting the general idea of what someone said (e.g. offering, inviting, complaining, thanking, suggesting) is often more useful than reporting their exact words. To do this, you can use the verbs *say*, *tell* and *ask*, as well as many other verbs. It is important to learn which prepositions, objects and verb forms follow these reporting verbs.

3 Decide how the following sentences (a–j) were later reported (1–10). Write your answers in the boxes.

a Don't forget to do it.
b Have you done it?
c Could you do it, please?
d It was you who did it!
e Why don't you do it?
f Would you like me to do it?
g I'm not doing it!
h Sorry, I did it.
i I'm sorry I did it.
j I didn't do it.

1 She suggested I do it.
2 He regretted doing it.
3 She apologized for doing it.
4 He denied doing it.
5 She reminded me to do it.
6 He refused to do it.
7 She asked me to do it.
8 He accused me of doing it.
9 She asked me if I'd done it.
10 He offered to do it.

a ☐ b ☐ c ☐ d ☐ e ☐ f ☐ g ☐ h ☐ i ☐ j ☐

4 Do you have a favourite line from a movie? Read the following collection of quotes from some of the 20th century's most famous films. Report each one using a combination of reporting verbs and reported speech. Use the words in brackets to help you. There are different possibilities.

a *Bond, James Bond.* Sean Connery, *Dr No* (1962)
   (say / name) _____
b *Play it, Sam.* Humphrey Bogart, *Casablanca* (1942)
   (ask / Sam) _____
c *Are you talking to me?* Robert De Niro, *Taxi Driver* (1976)
   (ask / me) _____
d *Frankly, my dear, I don't give a damn.* Clark Gable, *Gone with the Wind* (1939) (inform / her)
   _____
e *Come up and see me some time.* Mae West, *Goin' to Town* (1935) (invite / me) _____
f *Hang on, lads. I've got a great idea.* Michael Caine, *The Italian Job* (1969)
   (tell / us) _____
g *What have the Romans ever done for us?* John Cleese, *The Life of Brian* (1979)
   (want / know) _____
h *Go ahead. Make my day.* Clint Eastwood, *Dirty Harry* (1971)
   (invite) _____

5 The human resources department of a medium-sized company is deciding how much money to allocate to training. Read the following short extract from their meeting.

Gerry Okay, now, about our training budget for next year. What does everybody think?

Anna Well, I think we really must spend more on advanced IT skills training.

Ingmar Hmm, I'm not so sure that's what's needed. In fact, it's basic computer skills that most of our people still lack.

Gerry Yes, I think so too. But isn't this really a recruitment problem? I think we should require all new recruits to be computer literate before we employ them.

Anna Now, just a minute. We're forgetting that these are our entry-level staff we're talking about.

Ingmar And?

Anna Well, if you look at the salaries we're paying new recruits, you'll see that we simply don't pay them enough to expect computer skills. IT training is our responsibility.

Gerry Well, if we don't change our recruitment policy, we'll have to spend a fortune on training.

Anna Actually, the current cost of training is negligible, Gerry. That's why I say we should be spending more.

Now complete a report of the meeting with the verbs in the boxes.

a–e

doubted	insisted	invited	pointed out	raised

f–j

agreed	came in	reminded	suggested	wondered

k–o

added	assured	explained	recommended	warned

Report

Gerry (a) _____ the issue of the training budget and (b) _____ comments from the group. Anna (c) _____ that we spend more on advanced IT skills, but Ingmar (d) _____ that was what was needed. He (e) _____ that it was basic computer skills that most of our personnel lack. Gerry (f) _____ and (g) _____ if it wasn't a recruitment problem. He (h) _____ we make computer literacy a requirement for employment. Anna (i) _____ at this point and (j) _____ everyone that we were talking about entry-level staff. She (k) _____ that we didn't pay sufficient to expect computer skills and (l) _____ that IT training was the company's responsibility. Gerry (m) _____ us that if we didn't change our recruitment policy, we'd have to spend a fortune on training, but Anna (n) _____ him the current cost of training was negligible and (o) _____ we spend more.

Phrase bank: Teleconferencing

Label the teleconferencing expressions below according to their function.

closing   handling the technology   interrupting
managing the agenda   managing the discussion
opening   time-keeping

a _____ Welcome to the meeting.
Did everyone get a copy of the agenda?
Let's get started.

b _____ As you can see, we have several objectives today.
Let's skip item two.
Let's move on to item three.

c _____ Could I just come in here?
I just want to say one thing.
Sorry to interrupt, but …

d _____ Can you check your Internet connection?
I think your mic is on mute.
Sorry, we can't hear you very well.

e _____ So, just to recap on what we've said.
So, are we all agreed that …?
Any comments on that?

f _____ I'd like to be finished by 10.30.
Right, we're running short of time.
We'll have to speed up, I'm afraid.

g _____ I think we've covered everything for now.
We'll have to stop it there, I'm afraid.
We'll have to finish there. Thanks, everybody.

19 Negotiating

What skills does a good negotiator need?

1 William Ury is co-author of the world's most famous book on negotiating, *Getting to Yes*. Read the following extract from his best-selling sequel, *Getting Past No* and answer the questions.

a Which of the situations remind you of something that's happened to you? Compare experiences with a partner.

b What would you say in response to each of the people in the text?

> Daily life is full of negotiations that can drive you crazy. Over breakfast, you get into an argument with your spouse about buying a new car. You think it's time, but your spouse says: 'Don't be ridiculous! You know we can't afford it right now.'
>
> A morning meeting with your boss. You present him with a carefully prepared proposal for a new project, but he interrupts you after a minute and says: 'We already tried that and it didn't work. Next item.'
>
> During your lunch hour, you try to return a defective toaster-oven, but the salesperson refuses to refund your money because you don't have the sales slip: 'It's store policy.'
>
> In the evening, you need to return some phone calls, but the line is tied up by your 13-year-old daughter. Exasperated, you ask her to get off the phone. She yells: 'Why don't you get me my own phone line? All my friends have them.'

2 Work with a partner. Decide who's who in the following short negotiations. In each case, you have just three minutes to reach a deal if you can. When you've finished negotiating, compare your results with others in the class.

Situation 1:
The favour

Negotiator A: You have been working extremely hard lately, doing a lot of overtime, and are really looking forward to a relaxing weekend at the beach with friends. It's been raining for weeks, but the forecast for Saturday is for sunshine all day. You can't wait!

Negotiator B: You were supposed to be doing some overtime on Saturday morning and then having a barbecue at your house in the afternoon to celebrate the installation of your new swimming pool! But your favourite grandmother has been taken very ill and you'd really like to fly out and visit her for the weekend. Your boss has said it's okay if you can find someone else to do the overtime.

Situation 2:
The unwanted gift

Negotiator A: You bought a digital camera for a friend's birthday last week, but, rather embarrassingly, someone else gave them a much better one! Take it back to the department store where you bought it and ask for your money back, so you can buy them something else. Unfortunately, you can't find the receipt, but you still have the box which clearly has the store's price label on it.

Negotiator B: You are the manager of the camera department at a large department store. It's company policy not to give refunds on returned products, but you do give gift vouchers to the value of the returned goods, which can be used throughout the store, provided the customer has their receipt. At the moment your store has a massive sale on.

Situation 3:
The mobile phone

Negotiator A: You are the parent of a seven-year-old who has been asking you for months to buy them a mobile phone so they can talk to and SMS their friends. You think they are a bit young to have their own phone, and have heard all sorts of stories about children spending a fortune on calls and buying expensive music downloads. Try to dissuade them.

Negotiator B: You are a seven-year-old child but very intelligent for your age! All your friends at school have mobile phones and you'd like one too. You know your parents are not keen on the idea. But SMS messages are very cheap and having a phone is a very good security measure for kids. Try to persuade your father/mother that it's a good investment.

3 Complete the following sentence in not more than five words: 'A good negotiator ...'. Compare sentences with other people in the class.

4 🔘 **2.49–2.51** Listen to three business people sharing their views on how to negotiate and answer the questions below.

a Put the following stages in a negotiation into the order Speaker 1 mentions them.

have lunch	☐
agree on a procedure	☐
bargain	☐
close	☐
create rapport	☐
set out proposals	☐
agree terms	☐
celebrate	☐
listen and take notes	☐
make counter-proposals	☐

b Speaker 2 refers to the following acronyms. What do they mean?

OP   TP   WAP   FBP   BATNA

c According to Speaker 3, why doesn't 'win–win' usually work?

d Complete the five pieces of advice Speaker 3 offers.
1 Don't get pe_____.
2 Don't agree to an_____ until you've discussed ev_____.
3 Don't make any co_____ without asking for something in re_____.
4 Ask lots of qu_____.
5 Don't gi_____ in to pr_____.

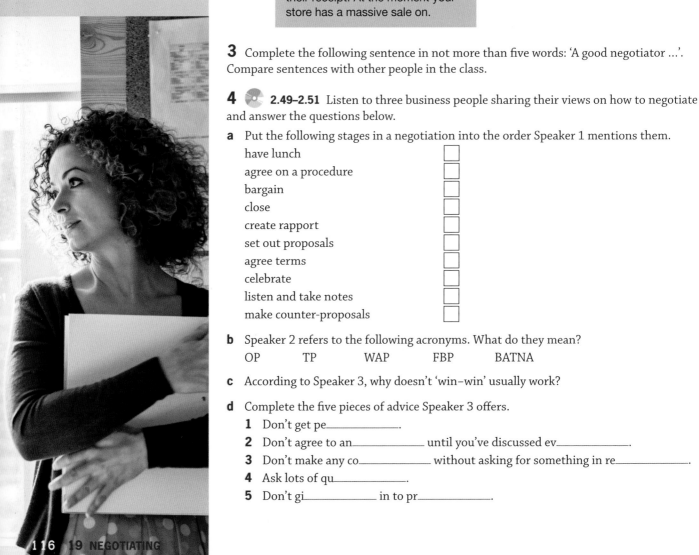

Directness

1 Read the joke. Is there a lesson to be learned from it?

Two priests were so addicted to smoking that they desperately needed to puff on cigarettes even while they prayed. Both developed guilty consciences and decided to ask their superior for permission to smoke.

The first asked if it was okay to smoke while he was praying. Permission was denied. The second priest asked if he was allowed to pray while he was smoking. His superior found his dedication admirable and immediately granted his request.

2 How direct you want to be in a negotiation is a matter of both cultural background and personal choice. On which side of the line below would you place people from your own culture? How about you personally?

prefer the diplomatic approach ⟵————————————⟶ prefer straight talking

3 Find someone in your group who put themselves on the other side of the line from you. Try to persuade each other that your side is better.

4 The following thoughts passed through the minds of two negotiators during a negotiation. Use the words and phrases in brackets to reproduce what they actually said.

a That's impossible.

(unfortunately / would not / possible) _____

b We can't go higher than seven per cent.

(would find / quite difficult) _____

c We won't accept less than $5 a unit.

(afraid / not in a position / this stage) _____

d You'll have to pay more if you want that.

(may / slightly) _____

e We need a commitment from you now.

(would / some kind) _____

f We should spend more time looking for a compromise here.

(shouldn't / little?) _____

g It would be a good idea to agree on a price before we go any further.

(wouldn't / better?) _____

h We hoped you'd pay a deposit today.

(were hoping / able) _____

i It will be difficult to get my boss to agree to this.

(might not / very easy) _____

j That's as far as we can go.

(think / about / the moment) _____

5 What do the negotiators do to make their statements more diplomatic? Do you prefer the direct or diplomatic versions?

The language of negotiations

1 🔘 **2.52** Listen to an extract from a negotiation and complete the notes.

2 Work with a partner. Use the notes you took in 1 to prepare to continue the negotiation. When you're ready, see if you can reach an agreement!

3 🔘 **2.53** Listen to another negotiation extract and complete the notes.

4 Do you think you've just listened to a win–win negotiation?

Mammoth Construction plc

Schumann Tender
Our original bid: 7.8M euros
Client counter-offer: _____ euros
Project to be completed within _____
Plant to be operational by _____
Our revised bid:
_____ euros in advance
_____ euros mid-contract
_____ euros on completion
TOTAL: _____ euros
Schedule overrun penalty: _____ euros per week

Smart Move plc *The communication skills specialists*

Telesales training (2-day seminar)
No. seminars: _____ over _____ month period
No. trainers: _____
_____ to be approved
Max. no. participants per seminar: _____
Full fee: £_____
Discount: _____ % = £_____
Final fee: £_____
_____ % non-refundable deposit = £_____

5 You heard most of the following expressions in the negotiations you just listened to, but some letters are missing from the final words. When you have completed them, the letters down the middle spell out some good advice for a negotiator.

a Perhaps we should begin by outlining our initial …

b Can I make a …

c What if we offered you an …

d Let me get this quite …

e Would you be willing to accept a …

f I'm afraid this doesn't really solve our …

g We may be in a position to revise our …

h I think that's about as far as we can go at this …

i Are these terms broadly …

j Let me just check I understand you …

k I'm afraid we could only accept this on one …

l What sort of figure are we talking …

m Could you give us an idea of what you're looking …

n What sort of timescale are we looking …

o We'd like to see some movement on …

p Can we just run through the main points once …

q At the moment, we do not see this as a viable …

r We seem to be nearing …

s Well, that's it. I think we've earned ourselves a …

The transfer

1 Footballers are today's rock stars and some of the most spectacular negotiations lead to multimillion dollar packages for the world's top players. Match the collocations below and read the article.

a	current market	industry	**d**	stock market	coverage	**g**	blue-chip	brand
b	corporate	value	**e**	media	outlets	**h**	sponsorship	deal
c	money-making	image	**f**	merchandising	flotation	**i**	strong	company

BUSINESS GOALS

A recent news report tells the story of an anthropologist who discovered a lost tribe in the Amazon. Their way of life had hardly changed since the Stone Age and they had never seen a car or met a foreigner. What shocked her most about the natives, however, was not their strange social customs or mysterious religious rituals, but the fact that several of them were wearing Manchester United football shirts!

Whether or not that report is true, what is certain is that Manchester United stopped being just a famous football team several years ago and became a highly successful multinational corporation. The words 'football' and 'club' were officially dropped from the players' badges in 2000 in an effort to strengthen corporate image. With successful London and New York stock market flotations in 1991 and 2012, and a current market value of over $2.3 billion, Manchester United is as much a triumph of the media as of great soccer.

Since 1993, the club has won – to date – twelve League titles, four League Cups, eleven FA Cups, one UEFA Cup Winners' Cup, two UEFA Champions' League Cups, one UEFA Super Cup, one Intercontinental Cup and one FIFA™ Club World Cup. But it was the media coverage of the 1990 World Cup and the arrival of SkyTV in 1993 that really transformed the game into the money-making industry it is today. 'Top clubs have grown on the back of television contracts,' says Richard Baldwin of accountants Deloitte & Touche. Teams like Bayern Munich, Arsenal, Real Madrid and AC Milan turn profits many blue-chip companies would envy.

'It's an oil well,' says Manchester United's former head of merchandising. He should know. The team's megastore at Old Trafford, which stocks 1,500 different items, is constantly packed, and merchandising outlets as far away as Singapore, Hong Kong and Sydney attract thousands of fans who couldn't even tell you where Manchester is on a map. 'United look and behave very much like a traditional business from a corporate point of view,' says financial analyst Nigel Hawkins. 'They have a strong brand and they have worked to maximize it by bringing in good people.'

They certainly have. One sponsorship deal alone – with Vodafone – netted Manchester £36 million and American insurance group AIG just paid £56.5 million for a similar four-year deal. What's in it for the sponsors? Clearly, the glamour and glory of being part of the ManU legend. And let's face it, not even Vodafone has its logo in the Amazon rainforest!

2 With a partner, choose a word or phrase from each of the five paragraphs of the article to write a paragraph heading. Compare choices with the rest of your class.

3 Do you support a football team? Find someone who doesn't and try to persuade them to go to a match with you.

In company interviews
Units 17–19

4 🔘 2.54 You are going to work in two teams to negotiate an international transfer deal. First, listen to a brief description of how such deals are put together and take notes. When you're ready, Team 1 see page 134. Team 2 see page 138.

19 Negotiating

Negotiations

Conducting negotiations

1 Complete the collocations by writing the nouns and noun phrases in the right-hand boxes. They are all things you might do during a negotiation.

a breakthrough	a deadlock	options
pressure	terms	time out

reach	(a)	negotiate	(d)
break		agree	

look for	(b)	apply	(e)
make		give in to	

call	(c)	generate	(f)
take		weigh up	

Sales negotiations

2 The following things were said in a sales negotiation. Who do you think probably said them – the buyer, the seller or could it be either? Write *B*, *S* or *E*.

a What kind of a guarantee can you give us? ☐

b Would that be a regular order? ☐

c Is that your best price? ☐

d There are no hidden extras. ☐

e I'm afraid it's not really what we're looking for. ☐

f Would you like to have the product on a trial basis? ☐

g What sort of quantity were you thinking of? ☐

h How flexible can you be on delivery times? ☐

i I'd like to think it over. ☐

j I can't be any fairer than that. ☐

k What immediate benefits could we expect to see? ☐

l Supposing we were to offer you deferred payment? ☐

m We'll match any price you've been quoted. ☐

n What sort of discount could you offer us on that? ☐

o Could we rely on you to meet all our deadlines? ☐

p Now, we'll just need to sort out one or two details. ☐

q So, if you'd just like to sign here. ☐

3 The following collocations all appeared in the negotiation in 2. Try to find the other half of each one in under 90 seconds!

a a regular _____

b _____ benefits

c offer _____

d _____ a guarantee

e delivery _____

f _____ deadlines

g quote a _____

h _____ extras

i deferred _____

j _____ the details

k match a _____

l a _____ basis

Language of diplomacy

Your choice of language can have a powerful effect on the outcome of a negotiation. Compare the following:

We reject your offer. → *I'm afraid at this point we would be unable to accept your offer.*

The use of softeners (*I'm afraid*), restrictive phrases (*at this point*), modal verbs (*would*) and rephrased negatives (*unable to accept*) in the second sentence make the rejection sound more acceptable.

Look at the following ways of making what you say in a negotiation more diplomatic:

1 **Modals:** *would, could, may, might*
   - *This is a problem.* → *This **would** be a problem.*
   - *Of course, there's a disadvantage to this.* → *Of course, there **could** be a disadvantage to this.*

   In both examples above, the speaker sounds less direct, but in the first example, the basic message doesn't change. *This would be a problem* still means it is a problem! But it sounds better.

2 **Qualifiers:** *slight, a bit, rather, a few, etc*
   - *There may be a delay.* → *There may be a **slight** delay.*
   - *We're disappointed with the discount on offer.* → *We're **rather** disappointed with the discount on offer.*

   Qualifiers soften the impact of bad news, but don't actually change it.

3 **Rephrased negatives 1:** *not very, totally, completely +* positive adjective
   - *We're unhappy with this arrangement.* → *We're **not very happy** with this arrangement.*
   - *I'm unconvinced.* → *I'm **not totally convinced**.*

   Using positive adjectives makes you sound more positive – even when you use them in the negative!

4 **Rephrased negatives 2:** *unable, not able, not in a position to*
   - *We can't go any higher than 7%.* → *We're **unable to** go any higher than 7%.*
   - *We won't accept anything less.* → *We're **not in a position to** accept anything less.*

   Try to avoid using *can't* and *won't*. They make you sound powerless and obstructive.

5 **Negative question forms:** *shouldn't we …?, wouldn't you …?* etc
   - *We should be working together on this.* → ***Shouldn't we** be working together on this?*
   - *You'd be taking an enormous risk.* → ***Wouldn't you** be taking an enormous risk?*

   Negative question forms are incredibly powerful in negotiations. Questions sound more tentative than statements and also more persuasive. Use them to make suggestions and give warnings.

6 **Comparatives:** *-er, more, less*
- *We're looking for something cheap.* ➔ *We're looking for something **cheaper**.*
- *Would you be willing to consider this?* ➔ *Would you be **more willing** to consider this?*

The use of comparatives makes what you say sound more negotiable.

7 **Softeners:** *unfortunately, I'm afraid, to be honest, with respect,* etc
- *This doesn't meet our needs.* ➔ ***Unfortunately**, this doesn't meet our needs.*
- *You don't quite understand.* ➔ ***With respect**, you don't quite understand.*

Softeners at the beginning of a statement signal bad news. *With respect* is a particularly bad sign!

8 **Restrictive phrases:** *at the moment, at this stage, so far,* etc
- *That's our position.* ➔ *That's our position **at the moment**.*
- *I don't think we can go any further.* ➔ *I don't think we can go any further **at this stage**.*

Using a restrictive phrase does not exclude the possibility of future movement.

9 **The passive:** *it was understood, it was assumed,* etc
- *You said you were ready to sign.* ➔ ***It was understood** you were ready to sign.*
- *We thought you had accepted these terms.* ➔ ***It was assumed** you had accepted these terms.*

By avoiding the use of statements beginning *You said …* and *We thought …* and using passive forms instead, you depersonalize the situation and reduce the amount of personal responsibility or blame.

10 **The -ing form:** *were aiming, had been hoping*
- *We aimed to reach agreement by today.* ➔ *We **were aiming** to reach agreement by today.*
- *We had hoped to see some movement on price.* ➔ *We **had been hoping** to see some movement on price.*

Using the Past Continuous keeps your options open – you were aiming to reach agreement and still are. The Past Perfect Continuous closes the door a little more – you've stopped hoping, but could be persuaded to hope again.

Study the information above and make the direct remarks below more diplomatic using the words in brackets to help you.

a This is too expensive. (unfortunately / would)

b We're not interested in your economy model. (would / less)

c It will be difficult to sell the idea to my boss. (unfortunately / may / very easy)

d We should be near a decision by now. (shouldn't / a bit nearer?)

e We can't pay straight away. (afraid / might not / able)

f I won't make any promises. (not / position / this stage)

g This is difficult for us to accept. (would / a little / the moment)

h You said you wanted immediate delivery. (understood)

i We hoped you would provide after-sales service. (honest / hoping)

j Our discussions have been unproductive. (not very / so far)

k A fixed interest rate would be a good idea. (wouldn't / better?)

l We had aimed to get further than this this morning. (aiming / slightly)

Phrase bank: Negotiating

Complete the six stages of a negotiation (a–f) with the verbs in the box.
Then match each to two things you might say.

agree	check	create	enter	put	work

a _____ rapport

b _____ a procedure

c _____ forward proposals

d _____ the facts

e _____ the bargaining phase

f _____ out the details

1 So what you're saying is this …
2 Thank you all for coming.
3 We'd like to see some movement on price.
4 Great, I think that's everything.
5 I'm afraid we could only accept this on one condition.
6 Perhaps we could begin by outlining our initial position.
7 Okay, let's just tie up a few loose ends.
8 What we're looking for here is this …
9 Would you like to set out your requirements first?
10 Ideally, we'd like to see …
11 We're looking forward to a productive meeting.
12 Let me just check I understand you correctly.

a ☐☐ b ☐☐ c ☐☐ d ☐☐ e ☐☐ f ☐☐

Assertiveness

Learning objectives: Unit 20

People skills Dos and don'ts of being assertive; Roleplay: Being assertive
Reading Hofstede's power distance
Listening Asserting yourself

1 Do you know anyone like the man in the cartoon? Why is it that some people get walked all over at work, while others seem to get their own way?

"You must assert yourself more."

2 Complete the situations with the words in the box. Have you ever been in similar situations? How did you react?

down (x2)   in (x2)   off   on (x2)   under

a   Your boss shoots _____ your great idea at a meeting and moves straight _____ to the next item on the agenda without giving you a chance to elaborate.

b   _____ pressure to meet a deadline, you find the rest of your team are letting you _____ by not doing their share of the work.

c   In the staff canteen, a group of people push _____ front of you _____ the queue – again!

d   You're asked to take _____ a lot of extra work and are often expected to stay late at the office to finish _____ urgent business – even if it disrupts your social life.

3 Read the short article below. What does the author say about assertiveness and culture? Do you agree?

Power Distance

How much does the freedom to assert yourself depend on the culture you work within? A great deal, according to intercultural expert Geert Hofstede. In his landmark book *Culture's Consequences*, Hofstede talks about what he calls 'power distance' in different countries. Power distance, he explains, measures the willingness of less powerful members of an organization to accept the unequal distribution of power. So a large power distance score means a lot of inequality is accepted and subordinates generally follow directives without question. And a small score means subordinates feel freer to query directives and take the initiative. Scores vary a lot from country to country. But not all companies are typical of their national culture. Multinationals, for example, tend to reflect the culture of the parent company rather than those of the countries they are located in, creating all kinds of intercultural problems in the process.

4 Where would you place these countries on Hofstede's Power Distance scale? How about your own a) country and b) company? Check your answers on page 127.

Argentina   Germany   Japan   New Zealand   UAE   USA

Austria (11)   _____ (35)   _____ (49)   France (68)   Malaysia (104)

Small Power Distance ←————————————————————————→ Large Power Distance

_____ (22)   _____ (40)   _____ (54)   _____ (80)

THE BULLDOZER
(aggressive)

THE DOORMAT
(passive)

THE PRIMA DONNA
(manipulative)

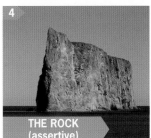

THE ROCK
(assertive)

5 Communication styles can be divided into four basic types. With a partner, match the character traits to the type you think they describe. The first one has been done for you.

is open and honest	☐	stands firm	☐	uses sarcasm	*4*
avoids conflict at all costs	☐	gives in too easily	☐	hides their true feelings	☐
uses emotional blackmail	☐	plays the victim	☐	disregards your feelings	☐
loses their cool	☐	pulls rank	☐	tries to get you on their side	☐
keeps their cool	☐	is respectful	☐	shows empathy	☐

6 What are the pros and cons of each communication style? Is your own style different when speaking English?

7 🔘 2.55–2.57 Listen to three versions of the same conversation and answer the questions.

Version 1

a What communication styles from 5 are the speakers using? Give some examples of their behaviour.

b How good a listener is Carmen? Does she at any point sympathize with Lars's position?

c Lars uses the words *sorry* and *but* quite a lot. What effect does this have?

d Carmen uses verbs of obligation (*should, have to*) to pressure Lars. How effective is this?

Version 2

a What communication styles are the speakers using? Give some examples of their behaviour.

b Which of the following tactics does Carmen use: flattery, bullying, blackmail? Do they work?

c Lars is quite sarcastic at times and makes some sweeping generalizations. How helpful is this?

d How successful is the outcome of the conversation?

Version 3

a What communication styles are the speakers using? Give some examples of their behaviour.

b Can you remember any expressions the speakers used to show empathy and understanding?

c Carmen uses specific *I*-statements to describe her feelings (*I'd really like*; *I would prefer it*; *Naturally, I'm disappointed*) and Lars politely repeats his objection. How effective is this?

d How successful is the outcome of the conversation?

8 Using what you've learned from the conversations you listened to, divide the following advice on being assertive into Dos and Don'ts by deleting where applicable:

a *Do / Don't* say *Yes, but …*

b *Do / Don't* say *Yes, and …*

c *Do / Don't* be specific about what you want.

d *Do / Don't* apologize by saying things like *Look, I'm sorry, but …*

e *Do / Don't* generalize by saying things like *You always …* or *You never …*

f *Do / Don't* accept any valid criticisms in principle, but stand your ground.

g *Do / Don't* reflect what the other person is saying using expressions like *It sounds like you …*

h *Do / Don't* use a lot of *I*-statements such as *I'm not happy about …*, *I'm disappointed that … or When you …, I feel …*

i *Do / Don't* say *You should …* or *You have to …*

j *Do / Don't* say *I'd prefer it if you …*

k *Do / Don't* empathize using expressions like *I appreciate that you're …*

l *Do / Don't* validate your relationship with the other person by saying things like *I think we both need to …*

9 Work with a partner to practise being assertive in different situations. Speaker A see page 131. Speaker B see page 136.

The difficult customer

1 Heather Sherwood, sales representative for FIS, received this email from her manager, Anton Vega. Read the email and answer the questions.

a Do you think Louis Lagrange is Heather's 'favourite client'? Why? / Why not?

b What is the KKM bid? Why is it important to FIS right now?

c Why has Anton chosen Heather to negotiate with Lagrange?

d What instructions does Anton give Heather? What problems does he foresee?

e Why has he cc'd Alan into the email? Could he have another motive for wanting him at the meeting?

KKM bid

To: h.sherwood@fis.com
Cc: a.sugarman@fis.com

Hi Heather

Got a call from your favourite client this morning – Louis Lagrange! Seems KKM are inviting bids for their new management information system and he'd like FIS to join the bidding. Now I know what you think about Louis, but this would be a major contract for us. I've attached a list of KKM's basic requirements. You're more familiar with their business than anyone else here, so I'd like you to put together a preliminary proposal and then fix an appointment with Louis to negotiate the details sometime next week.

As I say, winning this order would really help our cash flow this quarter, so be prepared to be flexible on price – I'll leave that to your judgement. Just make sure you give our technical department enough time to do the job. For something of this scale, I'd say we'd need a lead time of at least 6–8 weeks. We both know how Louis likes to push for fast delivery, so please be firm on that.

BTW I'm cc'ing Alan on this in case you want to take him along to the meeting – strength in numbers!

Anton

---

2 Write Heather's reply to Anton – accept the assignment, thank him for his advice and reassure him that you can deal with Lagrange without Alan's assistance.

In company
in action

3 Watch video E1 to see the meeting between Heather and Louis Lagrange the following week. Then discuss the comments below with a partner. Which, if any, do you agree with?

a Lagrange's demand was perfectly reasonable. Heather should have been more flexible.

b Lagrange was overly aggressive and probably bluffing. Heather should have called his bluff and walked away from the negotiating table.

c Lagrange and Heather should have offered to meet each other halfway.

d Heather missed an opportunity to find a creative solution to the problem.

4 Read the article on interest-based negotiation and complete the summary that follows.

Uncovering Interests in Negotiations

The biggest mistake inexperienced negotiators make is to think that negotiation is all about getting what you want. But it isn't. It's about satisfying each other's interests. What do we mean by this? Well, the term negotiators use to describe wants is 'positions'. So when I tell you that I want a 12% discount, that's my position. And when you tell me that you don't want to give me a discount, that's your position. Of course, by taking up positions like this, we usually end up settling for a compromise – say, a 6% discount, halfway between zero and twelve. But a compromise is an agreement that satisfies nobody!

To avoid this outcome, good negotiators instead try to find out what interests lie behind their counterpart's position – in other words, the reason they want what they want. And to do this, they ask a lot of questions. In fact, according to leading negotiation training company Huthwaite International, good negotiators ask twice as many questions as average ones. And of all the questions good negotiators ask, the most valuable is 'Why?' For example, 'Why can't you offer me a discount?' Ask that question and you may discover that your counterpart is only authorized to offer discounts to regular customers – so already you can see a possible solution to your problem. And a solution, unlike a compromise, is an agreement that satisfies both parties.

SUMMARY

a In a negotiation, positions are what you _____, whereas interests are why you _____.

b Taking up positions often leads to a _____, which _____.

c Uncovering interests, on the other hand, can lead to finding a _____ which _____.

d The best way to uncover interests is to _____ – good negotiators ask _____ as many as _____.

e On hearing your counterpart's position in a negotiation, the most important _____ to ask is: _____?

5 If Heather had read the article you've just read, how do you think she might have handled the negotiation with Lagrange differently?

In company in action

6 Now watch video E2 to see how the negotiation might have gone if Heather had taken the advice in 4 and answer the questions.

a Is Lagrange's initial approach any different this time?

b What does Heather do differently?

c How is Heather able to satisfy Lagrange's main interests?

d Before agreeing to consider Heather's offer on the lead time, what concession does Lagrange ask for? Does he get it?

7 Work with a partner to practise dealing with difficult demands.

Speaker A: Turn to page 135.
Speaker B: Turn to page 141.

8 Now evaluate your performance using the feedback form on page 138.

Additional material

01 Making contacts
Conference advice (p6, ex5)
Speaker A

One way to stand out at conferences, even if you're a bit shy, is to wear one subtle but interesting thing. It could be an unusual tie, watch or piece of jewellery, or just a flower in your lapel. You'll be surprised how many people comment on it and it's a great way to start a conversation! Don't be afraid to hand out your business cards. I always run out by the second day. So take plenty! Eat in the conference centre. Don't be put off by long lunch queues – they're a great place to meet people. As for which presentations you should attend, the best way to make sure you're keeping up with the latest trends is by going to all the big talks by the industry leaders. Find out who the stars (and bores) are before you go. BTW, don't be embarrassed about walking out of boring presentations halfway through. Your boss isn't paying you to waste your time. Hate to disappoint you, but 80% of the talks will be BORING. Don't be tempted to do the tourist stuff. You don't have time. You can always go back there on holiday. And avoid the hotel bar in the evenings. Find a nice quiet place to relax at the end of what will feel like very long days. Oh, and don't forget to pack comfortable shoes – you're going to do a lot of walking! Hope this is some help. Good luck!

Posted by Angelina Wasserman at 4.23 pm on 4 October

03 Keeping track
World records quiz answers (p23, ex7)

a   Exxon Mobil
b   the Nokia 1100
c   the Toyota Corolla
d   KLM
e   Google
f   Louis Vuitton
g   the Banca Monte dei Paschi di Siena
h   the electric light bulb
i   Ireland
j   Sweden
k   Liechtenstein
l   1,400 years

Scenario B Meetings on the go
(p53, ex9)

Work with a partner. Using all the information you gathered watching the previous conversations, hold the conversation Alan might now have with Heather, following his talk with Anton. You can play the two characters as yourselves (Alan/Alana, Heather/Heath) and feel free to employ your own strategies to reach a successful outcome, but try not to change the basic facts of the situation.

08 Influence
(p51, ex8)
Speaker A
Situation 1 (↓)

You run an industrial design company and urgently need one of your designers, Speaker B, to check a product design brief for a deluxe espresso coffee maker which is three weeks behind schedule. Although this brief was not originally their responsibility, the person whose responsibility it was has left the company suddenly, all your other designers are busy with other projects and the client who sent the brief (a big kitchen appliance manufacturer) needs a preliminary design plan by next Friday at the latest. This is a new client who could become an important customer in the future. You start: *Could I ask you to take a look at this design brief?*

Situation 2 (→)

You work for a construction company in London and were supposed to be entertaining a group of Japanese clients from the Shimamura Company. The plan was that you'd meet them at the airport on Saturday afternoon, take them out to dinner and then on to the West End show *Chicago*, which they expressed an interest in seeing. You'd then be available to show them around London on Sunday if they wanted before the meeting at your offices on Monday. However, you'd forgotten you are due to give a speech at a conference in Paris on Saturday, so there's no way you can make it. When your colleague, Speaker B, comes over to you at the coffee machine, ask them if they'll stand in for you. They've done this before and enjoy the social side of business more than you do, anyway. You start: *Oh, hi. Could I ask you a favour?*

Situation 3 (↑)

You run the marketing department of a small automotive engineering company based in Stuttgart. When your previous boss was in charge, you used to attend the international trade fair every year. However, your current boss, Speaker B – who's very keen to cut costs – put a stop to that three years ago. This year, the trade fair is going to be in Moscow and you really think it's time you made an appearance. All your competitors attend and, if you don't go, you will again be noticeable by your absence. You read an independently commissioned report recently which clearly shows that, on average, attendees see 15% more business in the 24 months following attendance – and small companies like yours seem to benefit the most. You fixed an appointment to speak to your boss about this and give them a copy of the report. You start: *Thanks for agreeing to see me.*

04 Listening

(p27, ex9)

Speakers A and B

1   Prepare to talk about two of the topics below (or you can change the topics to ones you prefer).

The things I like best about my job.

My long- and short-term career plans.

A problem I'm currently having at work.

Some things I'd like to change about my job.

A place I've always wanted to visit.

Something I've always wanted to try.

A person who had a great influence on me.

A personal experience which had a great influence on me.

2   With a partner, alternate the conversation topics, speaking for 1–2 minutes on each. The listener should encourage the speaker and ask for any necessary clarification as they speak, but not make any judgements or comments of their own.

3   When all four topics have been spoken about, both speakers should alternately try to recall and summarize what the other said on each of their topics, asking further questions if necessary. Speakers should confirm or correct the listeners' summaries and elaborate further on their topic if asked to do so.

4   Do the activity again if you like, using the other topics or two new ones of your own.

Scenario A The networking event

(p29, ex9)

FEEDBACK (Self-evaluation)

Making contacts

1   Did you make any useful contacts at the event?
Yes / No / Almost
If so, who did you meet and what arrangements (if any) did you make? _____

2   Do you think you made the most of the opportunities you had? Why / Why not? _____

Maximizing your time

1   In general, how well did you deal with unproductive conversations? Well / OK / Badly

2   Who were the most difficult people to deal with? _____

3   What would you do differently if you had another chance? _____

03 Keeping track

Sorry? (p21, ex3)

Speaker A

1   Read out Part 1 of the article below to your partner. When you read the information in **bold**, cough so they cannot hear!

Your partner should ask you for the exact information they missed. If not, keep reading!

If your partner just says 'Sorry?', reply 'Sorry what?'

A TALE OF TWO BROTHERS (PART 1)

Adidas and Puma are the second and third **biggest** sportswear manufacturers in the world. They're also two of the most profitable and globally recognized brands. But they might never have existed at all if the two brothers who founded them hadn't had a disagreement that lasted over **30** years!

Originally, Adi and Rudi Dassler were partners in the Dassler Brothers Shoe Factory in the small German town of **Herzogenaurach**. By the 1930s, they were already very successful and Dassler running shoes were worn by Jesse Owens, by far the greatest athlete of his day, when he famously won four gold medals at the **1936** Olympics.

Nobody really knows what caused the disagreement between Adi and Rudi, but their relationship steadily grew worse and worse over the years. And in 1947, they finally split up and built their own factories on opposite sides of the river. Adi Dassler called his company Adidas and Rudi called his **Ruda**, but later changed the name to Puma.

Competition between Adidas and Puma eventually became so aggressive that workers from one factory weren't allowed to **mix** with those from the other. But this was a great deal more than just professional rivalry. Even **shops and bars** would refuse to serve you if you were from the wrong side of the river. In fact, employees of the two companies were divided on almost everything – from politics to religion!

2   Now listen to your partner reading out Part 2 of the article. Ask them to clarify anything you don't understand. When you're clear about what the information is, write it down in full. Check each point you clarified with your partner at the end.

20 Assertiveness (p122, ex4)

	Austria (11)	Germany (35)	Argentina (49)	France (68)	Malaysia (104)	
Small Power Distance ←						→ Large Power Distance
	New Zealand (22)	USA (40)	Japan (54)	UAE (80)		

Scenario A The networking event
(p29, ex8)

You're going to practise making business contacts at a networking event. First, write a short profile of yourself in the form below. You can choose to represent FIS, use your own personal information or invent a new character for yourself.

Name:

Company:

Business activity:

Details (years in business, top products and/or services, major clients, plans, etc):

Your job:

Type of contacts you hope to make:

You need to make sure you have a business card to give out; complete the card below:

Work with a partner and decide where the event is being held. When you're ready, practise three or four short conversations with your partner. Take turns to be Speaker A. Make sure you have at least one productive conversation!

Speaker A: You are a good networker who listens well and follows all the networking rules in the article you read earlier. Choose one of the following aims for your conversation:

a   Try to get Speaker B to agree to a business lunch with your CIO.

b   Try to fix an appointment with Speaker B's sales director.

c   Try to convince Speaker B to make your company their new supplier.

Check your partner's profile and start the conversation using the following:

Excuse me? Are you (name) *from* (company)?

Speaker B: You are one of the following:

a   A good networker (You listen well and follow all the networking rules in the article you read earlier.)

b   A time waster (You ask lots of questions, look interested, but are reluctant to agree to anything or fix an appointment to speak later.)

c   An autobiographer (You talk a lot about yourself and your company and try to impress Speaker A but ignore most of what they say; you may be prepared to talk business after you've delivered your 'autobiography'.)

d   An escape artist (You aren't rude, but introduce Speaker A to someone else as quickly as possible so that you can make your escape!)

e   A hard seller (You do your best to sell something to Speaker A – a product, a service, even yourself as a prospective employee or consultant; cut the small talk and get straight to business!)

Scenario D Tricky conversations
(p101, ex8)

FEEDBACK (Self-evaluation)

1   Did you get what you wanted out of the conversation? If not, why not? _____

2   How would you describe the general tone of the conversation?

aggressive   awkward   neutral   constructive   friendly

3   Did you play the 'blame game'? If so, who got the blame for what? _____

4   Did you focus sufficiently on finding a solution to the problem? _____

5   Did you keep your feelings under control? Give a few positive and/or negative examples. _____

6   Did you keep your self-respect or did you feel personally under attack at any point? Give a couple of examples. _____

7   If you could have the conversation again, is there anything you'd do differently? If so, what? _____

07 Making decisions
(p43, ex2)

Whether you wrote *yes* or *no* is unimportant.

If you wrote *it depends* to five or more questions, you are a reflective decision-maker. You like to take your time thinking things through before coming to a final decision. In some jobs, this is a good strategy. But in a world of rapid change be careful you don't take too long to make up your mind!

If you wrote *it depends* to two or fewer questions, you are a reflexive decision-maker. You'd rather think fast and make the wrong decision occasionally than take so long to decide you miss an opportunity. This can be a vital skill for a manager. Just make sure you're right more often than you're wrong!

If you wrote *it depends* to three or four questions, you are a balanced decision-maker. You don't waste time agonizing over simple decisions, but you don't rush decisions that have serious implications either. You seem to be in control of both your head and your heart. But are you so in control you never take a risk?

08 Influence
(p51, ex8)

Speaker B
Situation 1 (↑)

You are a designer for an industrial design company and Speaker A is your boss. As this is your first job since changing careers from engineering to product design, you've had a lot to learn and been kept very busy. On the other hand, you haven't had the in-service training you were promised when you joined the company (three months day release at the local technical college) and, so far, you've only been working on food mixers and electric toasters. You were hoping for something more glamorous such as tablet computers and mobile phones! Speaker A will start.

Situation 2 (→)

You work for a construction company in London and, after a particularly hard week, are really looking forward to the weekend. Your plans for Saturday include dinner with friends at a restaurant followed by the West End show *Chicago*. Then on Sunday, you're watching your son play football for his local Boy Scouts' club team. You were thinking of inviting your friend and colleague Speaker A to join you on Saturday evening, but then you remembered they're giving a conference presentation in Paris. You see them standing by the coffee machine and decide to go over and wish them luck. Speaker A will start.

Situation 3 (↓)

You are the managing director of a small automotive engineering company based in Stuttgart. When you took over from your predecessor three years ago, you quickly realized that the company was wasting a lot of money on marketing trips, and so you cut back on unnecessary foreign travel and attendance at conferences. You know your marketing manager, Speaker A, is not happy about this. You also know that most, if not all, of your competitors usually attend at least the bigger international conferences. But you have never let yourself be very influenced by the competition and you're not convinced that small companies like yours can make much of an impact at conferences. Although you don't really want to discuss the issue again, your marketing manager has requested another meeting about it. Speaker A will start.

09 Small talk
Cultural sensitivity test (p54, ex2)

Speaker A

Work with a partner. You have two intercultural dilemmas and your partner has two different ones. Take turns to describe the dilemmas to each other and discuss what you'd do in each situation. Do you agree on what you *should* do? Is that what you'd both *really* do?

Dilemma 1: You meet a Spanish business contact you haven't seen for ages who wants to stop and chat, but you're running late for an appointment. Do you stay or do you make your excuses and go?

Dilemma 3: A British salesman is giving you a demonstration of a new office product. He seems to like telling a lot of jokes. Do you join in the joke-telling or wait until he gets to the point?

For comments on your answers, see page 140.

12 Impact
(p75, ex9)

An elevator pitch is a short presentation of a new product, service or idea which you could give in the time it takes to ride the elevator from reception to the CEO's office on the top floor. Of course, you don't have to be in an actual elevator to give one – just as well if you don't work in a skyscraper and have a problem keeping things brief!

With your partner, prepare a 2–3 minute presentation to persuade a venture capitalist to fund an idea for a mobile phone or tablet computer app.

EITHER come up with your own idea for a completely new app. (The iPhone App Store alone currently has nearly a million apps, so you'll need to do some research! Your app can serve a real need or just be for fun – some of the most popular apps are pretty bizarre!)

OR use an existing app which you are familiar with.

Before your team present your elevator pitch, you'll need to make sure you've:

- got a solid N.A.B.C. structure – need, approach, benefits, competitors.
- researched any existing competition and worked out how your product surpasses it.
- decided who's going to speak about what – perhaps one of you can concentrate on establishing professional credibility, while the other aims to make an emotional connection.
- incorporated some of the impact techniques you've just studied relating to body language, voice, statistics, stories and humour.
- produced two or three simple visuals (or props) if you need them – and maybe just one S.T.A.R. moment!

Be prepared to answer one or two questions at the end of your pitch.

Some popular apps:

Siri Speak a command and Siri will call you a taxi, confirm a flight or reserve a table for two at nine

Trapster Maps the location of speed cameras, road works and other highway hazards

Fandango Lets you watch movie trailers, read reviews, find a local cinema and book your seat

Shazam 'Listens' to any recorded music, and identifies the song and artist for download

iMapMyRUN+ Keeps track of your daily jog: routes, gradients, speed, calories burned

Flashlight Turns your iPhone's camera flash into a torch

05 Business travel
The nightmare journey (p31)

Speaker A

Work with a partner. In each of the situations below, you are a business traveller. Your partner is the other speaker.

06.00

Business traveller: You didn't get your five o'clock alarm call at your hotel this morning, so you overslept! Now you've missed your taxi to the airport. Your plane leaves in 90 minutes and it's at least half an hour to the airport. Go and complain at the reception desk. Get them to book you another taxi and telephone the airline to say you are on your way. You start: *What happened to my alarm call?*

06.15

Business traveller: Your taxi has finally arrived. Explain that your plane leaves in an hour and a quarter, and that you must be on it. If you miss the Zurich meeting at 11.00, your boss is going to kill you! You thought about taking the Underground, but you have a very heavy bag of product samples to carry. You start: *Heathrow airport. Terminal 5. And please hurry!*

07.00

Business traveller: By some miracle, you have arrived at Heathrow! But your plane leaves in half an hour. You'll have to run! You didn't have time to change any money at the hotel, so you only have three £50 notes and your credit cards. Pay the taxi driver and go!

07.15

Business traveller: You are at check-in with your case of product samples for the Zurich meeting and your hand luggage. Fortunately, the hotel phoned the airline and they were expecting you. Thank goodness you're travelling business class!

07.30

Business traveller: After all the panic to get to the airport, your British Airways flight is going to be delayed for an hour and a half! You wanted to fly Swissair, but they only had economy class seats left. Now there's nothing to do but wait. Luckily, your meeting is three hours away, so you can still just make it.

09.15

Business traveller: You managed to get a seat in economy on the Swissair flight. You're scheduled to arrive in Zurich in an hour, which gives you another 45 minutes to get to your meeting. You might just do it! Suddenly, you hear the following announcement: 'Good morning, ladies and gentlemen. This is your captain speaking. I'm afraid I've just been notified that, due to bad weather over Zurich, we've been diverted to Geneva. I am very sorry for the inconvenience this may cause, and will keep you informed of any further changes to our schedule.' You must call Zurich! Ask a flight attendant if it's okay to use your mobile. You start: *Er, excuse me!*

06 Handling calls
Asking politely (p38, ex3)

Speaker A

Your partner is a colleague at the same level in the company as you.

Call them (they always seem to be very busy!) and ask them to do the following:

Call 1 Organize the itinerary for a visit by some Chinese government officials next week (your partner is much better at this kind of thing than you are).

Call 2 Email you a copy of the Warsaw report. (It's a week late!)

Call 3 Get on to your IT department (the system's down on the whole of the first floor).

How often did you get your partner to do what you want?

You'll receive calls from your partner asking you to do things for them. Respond according to how important and/or urgent it is, and how busy you are.

Call 1 You're doing a cost breakdown for the Budapest contract, but you can't finish it until the Hungarians send you more detailed figures.

Call 2 You keep calling your London office to check the arrangements for the big presentation you and your partner are giving next Friday, but can't get through.

Call 3 You're in the middle of a difficult meeting with a group of union officials who are unhappy about working conditions.

Scenario B Meetings on the go (p53, ex10)

FEEDBACK (Self-evaluation)

Corridor Meetings

1 What was the outcome of your conversation? How satisfied with it are you? _____

2 How constructive was your conversation?
   constructive ←——————————→ confrontational

3 Did you find yourself using any of the influence strategies you've been studying?

flattery ☐	appeal to fairness ☐
threat ☐	emotional pressure ☐
incentive ☐	

4 Which of the following adjectives best described your behaviour?

ineffectual ☐	accommodating ☐
submissive ☐	aggressive ☐
authoritative ☐	disrespectful ☐

5 Did you make any compromises or generate any creative options? If so, what? _____

6 If you could have the conversation again, what (if anything) would you do differently? _____

   Optional: What part did status play in the conversation you had?

13 Being heard
(p79, ex5)

The questionnaire shows what type of 'animal' you are in meetings. First, add up your total number of points.

a	Agree = 0 points	Disagree = 1 point
b	Agree = 1 point	Disagree = 0 points
c	Agree = 1 point	Disagree = 0 points
d	Agree = 0 points	Disagree = 1 point
e	Agree = 0 points	Disagree = 1 point
f	Agree = 1 point	Disagree = 0 points
g	Agree = 1 point	Disagree = 0 points
h	Agree = 1 point	Disagree = 0 points

If you scored:

0–2 points You're a mouse at meetings – shy, quiet; you don't like to be the centre of attention. You make a very good listener, but need to say what you really think more often.

3–4 points You're a fox at meetings – sly, patient; and sudden in your attacks on other people's points of view. You don't say much, preferring to let others give you all the information you need to destroy their arguments.

5–6 points You're a horse at meetings – enthusiastic and full of energy; it takes a strong person to keep you under control. You work very hard to get your ideas across, but will sometimes do as you're told just to keep the peace.

7–8 points You're a bulldog at meetings – loud, proud and fond of the sound of your own voice. People know you always mean what you say, but you need to listen to what they're saying a bit more often.

14 Snail mail (p87)
Could I see you a moment?

Speakers A and B
Situation 1

Speaker A, you are the boss. Your secretary, Speaker B, just gave you this letter to sign. Point out the mistakes in it and tell him/her how to rewrite it. Can you find at least 20 mistakes? Don't sign anything until she/he writes it properly!

Speaker B, defend yourself! You were in a rush when you wrote the letter and can probably correct a lot of it without your boss's help.

Speaker A starts: *Could I see you a moment …?*

You don't need …	ABC = capital letters	? = question mark
That's spelled …	abc = lower case letters	. = full stop/period
That should be …, not …	, = comma	( ) = brackets
With an 's' / without an 's'	' = apostrophe	
ff = double f	Mr, Ms, Dr = abbreviation	

Dezember 3RD

Daer Mister Barghiel.

I'am writing to confirm our apointment on 7 Dec. Off course, I have your adress, but I am wonder if you could to send to me instruction on how to get to your office for that I will be come by my car.

A lot of thanks. I very much am look forward to meet you.

Yours faithlessly,

Situation 2

Repeat the previous activity. This time, Speaker B is the boss and Speaker A is the secretary. Can you find at least 20 mistakes?

Speaker B starts: *Could I see you a moment …?*

7th Mai

Dear Doc Jane Garland,

With referrance to your order (ref NO. 606-1, I am regretting informing you that the the DCS1 is currently out of stock May I suggest you consider to upgrade to the DCS2? When you are interesting, I would be happy to send you detales.

Letting me know if I can to be of any furthest help?

You're sincere,

20 Assertiveness
(p123, ex 9)

Speaker A
Situation 1

You need to hold a one-hour emergency meeting with your team this afternoon (you decide why), but forgot to book the meeting room. When you go to book it at the last minute, you see that Speaker B has it block-booked for the whole afternoon – again! Go and see them in their office to see if they'll free up an hour for you. You start the conversation by knocking on their door and saying: *Hi, have you got a minute?*

Situation 2

You run the Frankfurt office of your company. Your assistant Yvette has been on secondment to the Shanghai office for the past two months. It was your idea that she gain experience overseas, but in her absence your workload has increased (you decide in what way) and, frankly, you are now finding it difficult to cope. Fortunately, Yvette is due back next week, so things should get a bit easier. Now the phone's ringing – it had better not be more work!

Situation 3

You work in the marketing department. When you joined your company four months ago, your boss, Speaker B, gave you the long-term goal of exploring the possibilities of social media. This is an area your company currently does not exploit very well. But, although you've had a few initial ideas (you decide what), your schedule has been so hectic you've had little time to get very far. When you see your boss at the water cooler, you decide to raise the issue.

15 Solving problems
(p91, ex5)

Speaker A

Read the business dilemma below. Then summarize the basic problem to the rest of your group and brainstorm some solutions.

The owner of a Mexican restaurant in San Francisco faced a dilemma. She wanted to advertise, but couldn't afford to pay for space in the local newspaper or for airtime on the local radio station.

17 Eating out
The business lunch (p105)

Showing interest:	Changing the subject:
Sounds interesting.	**So**, let's order, shall we?
Nice idea.	**Anyway**, how do you like the wine?
Tell me more about it.	**By the way**, how's the family?
	Just to change the subject for a moment, have you tried the local speciality?

Speaker A

Your partner (Speaker B) is a good friend from abroad, whom you've also worked with in the past. They are only in town for a few days, so you've invited them out for a really nice lunch.

Think of a local restaurant you like, and prepare a short menu of dishes and a drinks list to explain to your guest. Write the names of the dishes and drinks in your own language. You should include:

- at least one dish which you really like and think everyone should try
- one dish which most people don't like very much and which you don't recommend
- one dish, if you can, which is a little difficult to explain to a foreigner (prepare for this)
- one dish or drink which is a speciality of the region (prepare an appetizing description).

Your partner phoned you a week ago and mentioned a business idea they wanted to talk to you about. Perhaps they will tell you more over lunch, but do your best to be the perfect host and don't just 'talk shop'! Try to keep the conversation moving.

You're the host, so insist on paying!

Menu	
Starters	Desserts
_____	_____
_____	_____
_____	_____
Main courses	Drinks
_____	_____
_____	_____
_____	_____

15 Solving problems
A problem-solving meeting (p95, ex1)

Group B

Using the procedure on page 93, hold a meeting to solve the problem below.

- Read paragraph one. What else do you know about this business?
- Read paragraph two. What's your immediate response to the problem?
- Read paragraph three. It should give you some extra ideas on how to solve the problem.
- Conduct a problem-solving meeting with your group.
- Summarize the problem and your solutions for the other group or groups. Find out if they agree with you.

A downsizing problem at Tata Steel

The company
Tata Steel is a subsidiary of the Tata Group, one of India's most successful multinational conglomerates, operating in seven different business sectors in more than 80 countries. Established in 1907, Tata Steel has manufacturing plants throughout India as well as China, the USA and the UK. In 2006, its acquisition of Anglo-Dutch steel-maker Corus was the largest ever Indian takeover of a foreign company. And in 2012, *Forbes* magazine listed Tata Steel amongst the world's most ethical companies. Today, it is one of the world's top ten steel producers.

The challenge
But in the early 1990s, the outlook for Tata Steel was very different. Faced with an overlarge workforce, outdated facilities at its aging plant in Jamshedpur and a resistance to change throughout the company, there was an urgent need to rationalize. Senior management knew that mass redundancies would have to be a major part of that rationalization. But at Tata Steel, redundancies were practically unheard of. Tata was the major employer in the region and the people who worked there were guaranteed a job for life. After 25 years' service, their children were also guaranteed a job and it was not uncommon for three generations of the same family to be working at the Jamshedpur factory. The result was massive overstaffing. Niroop Mahanty, the head of HR, says: 'At the time, we were so large that we didn't even know how many employees we had!' When, after a three-month audit, they discovered that they were employing 78,000 people, it became obvious that Tata Steel would have to cut its payroll by around 50% over the coming decade if it was to survive.

The opportunity
Indian corporate culture is one of reciprocal obligation between employer and employee. Tata Steel's own website emphasizes that the company 'has always believed that the principle of mutual benefit – between countries, corporations, customers, employees and communities – is the most effective route to profitable and sustainable growth'. Companies that lay off large numbers of workers in times of struggle often find themselves with serious skills shortages when business improves. And Tata Steel's managing director Dr J.J. Irani knew that he would have to reinvent the whole idea of downsizing if he was to reduce the workforce whilst retaining and rewarding the loyalty of his staff.

18 Telecommunications
An urgent matter (p111, ex2)

Answer:
Consultants are more common than rats; the lab technicians get less attached to them and there are things a consultant will do that a rat won't.

18 Telecommunications
Teleconference: a project meeting (p110, ex4)

Work in the largest group possible. You are all human resources directors of different branches of a multinational IT solutions company. You want to send 30 of your staff on a team-building weekend. You've drawn up a shortlist of options. Things you should consider include: the practical training element, the fun factor, safety, cost.

1 Dragon boat racing followed by riverside barbecue and evening firework display

Teams of 15–20 take part in three boat races during this fun-filled, action-packed day! After an initial team-briefing and training session, teams spend the morning practising their rowing technique and working out a winning race strategy. Then it's off to the races! Food, drink and fireworks on the river round off the day.

Venue: Macau, China

Cost: $300

2 'Rock Idol' contest followed by a night on the town in New York

Teams of five form rock bands to take part in a battle-of-the bands contest. After song selection, voice coaching, costume-fitting and rehearsals, it's off to a local karaoke bar to perform in front of a panel of 'expert judges' and a live audience! Then it's dinner and dancing at one of New York's hottest music venues.

Venue: New York, USA

Cost: $250

3 Lapland dog-sledding followed by banquet at mountain lodge and wolf-watch

Teams of three build their own traditional dog sleds from construction plans and materials supplied on site. After a short dog-handling session, they set off with a local expert on a wilderness trail in search of treasure buried deep in the forest. The day ends with a fabulous banquet by roaring fires! Optional night trip to hear the howling wolves!

Venue: Rovaniemi, Finnish Lapland

Cost $300

Note: prices are all per person and do NOT include flights or accommodation.

Choose a chairperson. You have just 15–20 minutes for the teleconference. Try to stick to the following agenda:

1 Open the meeting and explain its objective.
2 Ask participants to briefly introduce themselves.
3 Give each participant a chance to present their preference, but keep inputs short and try to discourage too much interruption.
4 Allow some time for participants to discuss their preferences, but prevent arguments and digressions.
5 Ask each participant to vote for their preferred event and announce the group's final decision. If a clear decision cannot be made, choose the cheapest of the preferred options.
6 Thank participants and close the meeting.

When you are ready, sit in a circle, a metre apart if possible, facing outwards (so that you cannot see the other speakers) and hold your teleconference.

Scenario D Tricky conversations
(p101, ex7)

Speaker A

SITUATION 1 You've been sent by FIS's head office in Seattle, USA, to their subsidiary in London to help Speaker B finish off a long-running project, which needs to be finished in six weeks. You also need to make sure the project meets fairly strict company requirements (decide why this is important). The last project your partner led did not meet the requirements, so you will need to monitor everything this time. Try to be sensitive to Speaker B's needs and expect some resistance, but make sure you get what you were sent for.

You start: [Partner's name]! *Great to meet you at last! I'm* [name]. *You know, this is my first time at the London office.*

SITUATION 2 Six months ago you joined FIS's sales team in Barcelona. Prior to that you worked for InterPharm in Mexico City, where you were their top salesman. In the last six months, you've also risen to become one of FIS's top-performing sales representatives. You are very ambitious and expect to be promoted to sales manager quite soon. Recently, you had a team appraisal and Speaker B, your boss, would like to discuss it with you. You expect there may be a few criticisms from the rest of the sales team because you are better at your job than them and like to do things your own way. Your philosophy is: if I get results, it doesn't matter how I get them. You like taking lots of short holidays because it 'recharges your batteries' and is much more useful than training sessions, which you consider a waste of time. Speaker B will start.

19 Negotiating
The transfer (p119, ex 4)

Negotiating team 1: The player's agents

You represent the interests of _____ (choose or invent a name), young superstar forward / midfielder / defender / goalkeeper who plays for _____ (choose or invent a club). Already a member of his national squad, your client clearly has a brilliant career ahead of him. Your job is to negotiate your client's financial package with the management of Manchester United.

You do not have to reach an agreement with Manchester United. Other top clubs are also very interested in your client. But you do know he particularly wants to play for them, so you have approached them first.

It is in your interests to:

- get a higher than average wage for such a superb player of international status (more than £75,000 per week) – your agent's commission will be calculated on the basis of this!

- go for the shortest contract you can get or one with a very low termination penalty – no more than £500,000 (your client may not be as happy at Manchester as he hoped).

- secure a fair percentage of merchandising profits (maybe 15% – the fans are sure to want to buy products with your client's name on).

But you may need to be flexible on some of these points. Your client has also asked you to try to get:

- a penthouse apartment in central Manchester (he wants to enjoy the nightlife).

- first-class air tickets for his immediate family (eight people) to come and visit him occasionally, plus half a dozen trips home for himself every year.

At present, your client has a £300,000 a year sponsorship deal with Adidas, which he would like to keep.

The negotiation is scheduled to be held at Old Trafford. First, with your team, work out your opening, target and walk-away positions for each of the following points. When the other team is ready, they will invite you into the boardroom. You may take two five-minute time-outs during the meeting, if you need them. Write down any terms you agree to.

	OP	TP	WAP
Basic wage			
Length of contract			
Contract termination fee			
Percentage of merchandising profits			
Accommodation			
Flights home			

Scenario C Morale problems
(p77, ex8)

You are going to produce a 2–3 minute motivation speech. You can either:

a Deliver Anton's speech the way you would have delivered it.

b Think of a time when a team you worked in had morale problems, faced a disappointment or received bad news, and imagine you are addressing that group.

c Present to the team profiled below and invent any extra information you need to.

Team profile:

You work for Zantis Pharmaceuticals, and are the team leader for an R&D team developing a revolutionary and highly cost-effective vaccine for use in the developing world. You are personally very committed to this project, but senior management has recently cut your budget by 30%. This has meant losing two members of your team (Helga and Michael) and increasing the workload for those who remain. A star member of your team (Akiro) is also talking of leaving the company, but you hope to prevent this, at least in the short-term. Morale is very low and the pressure is on to launch the vaccine.

As you prepare, you should consider the following:

- Acknowledge the problems you face, but focus on solutions and goals – don't talk about hopes, talk about intentions and remain realistic but positive.

- Use intrinsic motivators rather than extrinsic ones – you don't have long to build a social relationship with your team, but you can make a start.

- What you say may be less important than how you say it – practise raising and lowering your voice, and pausing in the right places.

- Your body language also has a big effect on your audience – make sure you look sincere and professional, but also try to create some emotional connection with your audience.

- A little bit of humour can go a long way!

17 Eating out
Table manners (p104, ex1)

a	Finland	f	American	k	American
b	Brazil	g	Arab	l	Spain
c	Portugal	h	Mexico	m	Arab
d	Japan	i	Chinese	n	Japan
e	Britain	j	Japanese	o	Asian

05 Business travel
The nightmare journey (p31)

Speaker B

Work with a partner. In each of the situations below, your partner is a business traveller. You are the other speaker.

06.00

Hotel receptionist: You have just come on duty at the Novotel reception desk. Your colleague, who went home five minutes ago, says there has been a problem with the internal telephone system all night. Since you arrived, it's been one complaint after another!

06.15

Taxi driver: You have just picked up someone at the Novotel who wants to go to Heathrow airport. On your way to the hotel, you heard this on the radio: 'Traffic news now, and there's been a major accident on the M25 this morning involving three lorries and eight cars. Police say to expect delays of up to an hour. If you're travelling to Heathrow this morning, you're advised to take the Underground to Paddington station and then the Heathrow Express …'

07.00

Taxi driver: Fortunately, the traffic was not as bad as you expected. But your last two passengers paid you in £50 notes and took nearly all your change – you only have a £10 note and three pound coins. There is a cashpoint machine in the airport terminal if you need it, but another customer is waiting to get into your taxi. You start: *Well, we made it! That's £23, please.*

07.15

Check-in clerk: You are checking in a late business class passenger. Their hand luggage is okay, but their suitcase is well over the 25 kilo limit – 38 kilos! The flight is full and due to depart in 15 minutes. You cannot accept their luggage. You could book it onto a later flight if they pay excess baggage. You start: *I'm sorry, but your case is too heavy.*

07.30

BA representative: You are at Gate 42, Heathrow airport. Flight BA922 to Zurich is delayed and you have a lot of unhappy passengers sitting in the departure lounge. A few have already asked for seats on the 8.30 Swissair flight. You have just received this message on your mobile: 'The plane has serious mechanical problems and cannot leave London today. Another plane is flying out from Zurich, but there will now be a delay of approximately four hours.' You start: *British Airways regrets to announce …*

09.15

Flight attendant: You are the chief steward on Swissair flight 711 from London Heathrow to Zurich. Unfortunately, your flight has just been diverted to Geneva because of bad weather. A lot of passengers are getting angry and insisting they make phone calls. The use of mobile phones is strictly prohibited on aircraft and in-flight phones are only available in business class.

Scenario E The difficult customer
(p125, ex7)

Speaker A

You are the IT director for FreightFlow Inc., a transport and logistics company, and are about to negotiate the purchase of a supply chain management (SCM) system with Speaker B, a senior sales representative from Flow Information Systems (FIS).

- In a previous telephone conversation with Speaker B, you were quoted a software licence fee of $70,000 plus an annual maintenance and support charge of $20,000, making a total of $90,000. This seemed fairly reasonable, although, of course, it was negotiable.

- Unfortunately, a project approved by your assistant director a few days ago (without your knowledge) has absorbed $100,000 of your annual budget. So you now cannot afford to pay any more than $60,000 for the system, including maintenance and support, without going over budget. This puts you in a slightly embarrassing situation, but you have no intention of showing weakness in the negotiation!

- You could consider providing your own maintenance and support if you have to (though this is extremely risky), but you must not in any circumstances exceed your budget. At the same time, upgrading to a modern Cloud-based SCM system is a matter of urgency for your company. There are cheaper systems on the market, but the FIS system is the best.

- You expect FIS to be unhappy with your low offer, so be prepared to ask as many questions as possible to uncover any underlying interests which may help you to reach an agreement. Try to be as flexible as you can, but you must stand firm on price! Nor can you accept an inferior system. If you need to telephone your CEO (your trainer) to get special authorization for a concession, you can.

Good luck!

03 Keeping track
Didn't I say that? (p23, ex8)

Speaker A

1 Read out the following sentences to your partner. Each one contains a silly discrepancy. Can she/he spot it?

a I love Scotland, especially Dublin.

b I always drive German cars. My new Citroën is my favourite.

c I first met Ulrike today. She's one of my closest friends.

d I've nearly given up chocolates. I'm down to ten a day now.

e Let me introduce you to my wife. And then I'll introduce you to her husband.

2 Listen to your partner reading out some sentences. Can you spot the discrepancies? Query any you hear using some of the expressions on page 23.

06 Handling calls
Asking politely (p38, ex3)

Speaker B

Your partner is a colleague at the same level in the company as you.

You'll receive calls from your partner asking you to do things for them. Respond according to how important and/or urgent it is, and how busy you are.

Call 1 You're in the middle of trying to do your quarterly accounts for the third time this week and don't want to be disturbed!

Call 2 You're a few days late with the Warsaw report and need about another day to finish it.

Call 3 You've been having computer problems all day and haven't got any work done.

Call your partner (they always seem to be very busy!) and ask them to do the following.

Call 1 Email you a cost breakdown for the Budapest contract (you need it for a meeting next week).

Call 2 Make sure everything is arranged for the big presentation you and your partner are giving in London next Friday.

Call 3 Set up a meeting with head office to discuss complaints about working conditions at the plant.

How often did you get your partner to do what you want?

15 Solving problems
(p91, ex5)

Speaker B

Read the business dilemma below. Then summarize the basic problem to the rest of your group and brainstorm some solutions.

The manager of a bank in the UK had become alarmed at the number of stolen cheques being cashed. Signatures were simply too easy to forge. Something had to be done.

Scenario C Morale problems
(p77, ex9)

FEEDBACK (Peer-evaluation)

1 Did the presenter focus on solutions more than problems? _____

2 What intrinsic/internal motivators (if any) did the presenter use? _____

3 How would you rate the presenter's delivery of the speech?
Pace ☹ ☺ ☺   Pausing ☹ ☺ ☺   Volume ☹ ☺ ☺

4 What impression did the presenter's body language give? _____

5 Did the presenter use any humour? If so, how successful was it? _____

---

20 Assertiveness
(p123, ex9)

Speaker B

Situation 1

You have the meeting room booked for the whole of this afternoon so you can hold your monthly update meeting with the rest of your team (you decide what you have to discuss). Last time you held the meeting, you found 90 minutes was not long enough to cover everything, so you've scheduled it from two till five this time. First, find out who's knocking on your door.

Situation 2

You run the Shanghai office of your company. For the past two months, you have had an assistant, Yvette, on secondment from the Frankfurt office helping you out. It was her boss's idea that she transferred and, to be honest, it took rather a lot of time to train her, but she's proved to be very creative and efficient. She's due to return to Germany next week, but you really need her to stay on for another four or five weeks to complete an important project (you decide what). Phone the Frankfurt office and see if her boss can spare her for a little longer.

Situation 3

You run the marketing department of your company. When Speaker A joined your department four months ago, you gave them the long-term goal of exploring the possibilities of social media. This is an area your company currently does not exploit very well. You're rather sceptical about social marketing (you decide why), but your boss is very keen and now wants a progress report on his desk in two weeks' time! When you see Speaker A at the water cooler, you decide to find out what progress they're making.

---

05 Business travel
In arrivals (p34, ex3)

Speaker A

It is 9.30 pm. You are in the crowded arrivals area at Newark airport in New York. There has just been a terrible thunderstorm and it is still pouring with rain.

You are picking up a senior colleague who works in your Cologne office. Because of the weather, their flight is two hours late, but your boss told you to 'look after them well' – take them out to a top-class restaurant, maybe a nightclub or two. You have never met them before, so you are holding up a large piece of card with their name written on it.

Your car is just five minutes away in the car park. You have booked a table at Guastavino's, a fabulous restaurant in Manhattan and are looking forward to an enjoyable evening. According to your boss, 'money is no object'. If he can, he's going to join you both later for drinks.

You've been working very hard recently. Tonight you are going to relax and have fun!

09 Small talk
Cultural sensitivity test (p54, ex2)

Speaker B

Work with a partner. You have two intercultural dilemmas and your partner has two different ones. Take turns to describe the dilemmas to each other and discuss what you'd do in each situation. Do you agree on what you *should* do? Is that what you'd both *really* do?

Dilemma 2: Your new American boss organizes a weekend barbecue. You find yourself amongst a lot of people you've never met. Do you join in the fun or leave as early as you can?

Dilemma 4: You are having a pre-negotiation coffee at a potential client's headquarters in Berlin. Do you mingle with the opposing team or stick with your own people?

For comments on your answers, see page 140.

13 Being heard
Hang on a minute! (p80, ex1)

Speaker B

Read the short article below about intercultural business etiquette. In a few minutes, you are going to try to read it aloud to your partner in under a minute, so first check you understand everything and mark places where you can pause for breath!

Your partner is preparing to read a similar article aloud to you. So, when you are both ready, decide who will read first. Read as fast as you can, but try to make sense!

As you listen to your partner read, you should interrupt them as often as possible to clarify anything which isn't absolutely clear. Your objective is to stop them reaching the end of the text in a minute. See who can get further. Good luck!

06 Handling calls
Unexpected phone calls (p40, ex5)

Speaker B

Call 1 You receive the call 09.30 local time.

You are a student of journalism in Paris working for *Cosmopolitan* magazine during your summer vacation. There was no one in the office when the phone rang, so you picked it up. You've never spoken English on the phone before and misunderstand everything Speaker A tells you. After a minute or so, end the call by offering to get someone who speaks better English.

Call 2 You make the call 16.30 local time.

You work in the finance department at Daimler-Chrysler in Stuttgart and are responsible for the management of the company pension scheme. You want to query something with the fund manager at Barclay's Global Mutual Funds in New York, Neil Thomas. It's rather urgent. You finish work at six.

Call 3 You receive the call 15.00 local time.

You work in the sales department of General Accident Insurance, UK. You are holding a meeting in your office to discuss the training programme for your new intake of 25 sales personnel. At first, you have no idea who Speaker A is when she/he calls – probably a sales rep from one of the computer companies you contacted on the Internet the other day. Be civil, but get him/her off the phone.

Call 4 You make the call 10.45 local time.

You work for a small public relations company in Bath, UK. Eighteen months ago you met Speaker A at an international conference in Chicago. He/She works for Burson-Marsteller, the world's biggest PR firm. You got on very well and stayed up till three in the morning. You mentioned you'd love to work for a bigger company and she/he offered to introduce you to his/her boss if you ever came to Boston. You're in Boston at the Logan Airport Hotel. Your mobile number is 751 533 200.

It's said there's a universal language of business, but if so, it's not too clear what it is. Just saying hello can get you off to a bad start, with well-qualified Germans wanting you to call them Herr Doktor Professor and Americans wanting you to just call them Chad or Brianna. Even 'Yes' and 'No' can cause problems. To most of us, a nod is 'Yes' and a shake of the head is 'No'. But in Bulgaria, Greece and Turkey, the opposite is true. In Mexico and Japan, the word 'No' is often avoided altogether. In Monterrey, they may just be anxious not to disappoint. In Nagoya, it's the harmony of the meeting they don't want to disrupt. In Britain, the best route to harmony is thought to be humour. And with bad weather, bad government and bad public transport, they certainly have plenty to joke about. Perhaps there's a cultural universal there, after all. Cultures that have less fun feel the need to be funny.

Interruptometer

You're hopeless!

Learn to be more assertive.

Okay, but avoid doing business in Latin America.

Pretty good. You could be a politician.

Excellent! Nobody else can get a word in.

Scenario E The difficult customer
(p125, ex8)

FEEDBACK (Self-evaluation)

The Deal

1 Did you reach an agreement? Yes / No / Almost
   If so, what did you (almost) agree?
   Total fee: _____
   Maintenance and support
   arrangements: _____
   Payment terms: _____
   Any other conditions: _____

2 Do you think you got the best result you could
   have got? _____

The Process

1 How much did you explore interests as
   opposed to arguing about positions?

   _____

2 What questions did you ask to uncover the
   interests of your counterpart? _____

3 What (if anything) do you think you could have
   done better? _____

4 Compare with your partner: do you agree with
   each other's self-evaluations? _____

15 Solving problems
(p91, ex5)

Speaker C

Read the business dilemma below. Then summarize the basic problem to the rest of your group and brainstorm some solutions.

A company that makes industrial cleaners and sells them by direct mail had an obvious problem – boring product, boring market. The question was: how could they get noticed?

05 Business travel
In arrivals (p34, ex3)

Speaker B

It is 9.30 pm. You are in the crowded arrivals area at Newark airport in New York. There has just been a terrible thunderstorm and it is still pouring with rain.

You have just arrived two hours late after a nightmare flight from Cologne. Normally, you are a good flier, but there was so much turbulence you were almost sick on the plane. You don't know who is meeting you, so you are looking for a sign with your name on it.

To be honest, you don't feel like talking much and would just like to go straight to your hotel, have a shower and go to bed. But maybe you should eat something light first – it's a long day of meetings tomorrow and you want to be on good form.

This is your first time in New York. It's a pity you feel so ill.

19 Negotiating
The transfer (p119, ex4)
Negotiating team 2: Manchester United

You represent the management of Manchester United Football Club and are interested in buying a young superstar *forward / midfielder / defender / goalkeeper (ask Team 1 for his name)* who plays for *(ask Team 1 for the name of his club)*. Your job is to negotiate the financial package on offer.

You do not have to sign this player. There is no shortage of young internationals wanting to play for the world's most famous football club. But he is something special. With the right training, he could become one of the world's top players within the next five years.

It's in your interests to:

- pay no more than the standard wage (already high at £50,000).
- go for a five-year contract with a heavy penalty for early termination – £2 million (you don't want to invest in the development of a player who disappears to another club after just a few seasons).
- pay as low a percentage of merchandising profits as possible (perhaps 8% – you don't know how popular the new player will be with supporters).

But you may need to be flexible on some of these points. You can also offer:

- the use of a £2.5M house with six bedrooms and a swimming pool, in a quiet suburb 12 miles outside Manchester (you already own this property, so it would not incur extra costs).
- three first-class flights home with British Airways.

You understand the player currently has a sponsorship deal with Adidas, which would have to be cancelled. Nike are your current team kit sponsors.

The negotiation is scheduled to be held at Old Trafford. First, with your team, work out your opening, target and walk-away positions for each of the following points. When you are ready, welcome the player's agents into your boardroom. You may take two five-minute time-outs during the meeting, if you need them. Write down any terms you agree to.

	OP	TP	WAP
Basic wage			
Length of contract			
Contract termination fee			
Percentage of merchandising profits			
Accommodation			
Flights home			

under pressure from

03 Keeping track
Sorry? (p21, ex3)
Speaker B

1 Listen to your partner reading out Part 1 of an article. Ask them to clarify anything you don't understand. When you're clear about what the information is, write it down in full. Check each point you clarified with your partner at the end.

2 Now read out Part 2 of the article to your partner. When you read the information in **bold**, cough so they cannot hear!

Your partner should ask you for the exact information they missed. If not, keep reading!

If your partner just says 'Sorry?', reply 'Sorry what?'

A TALE OF TWO BROTHERS (PART 2)

Adidas and Puma are now both large multinationals. But, in terms of the number of employees, Adidas is over **four times** bigger than Puma, with a workforce of **39,000**. Adidas is also the world's leading soccer brand. Celebrity endorsements include David Beckham and tennis champion **Andy Murray**.

Puma, of course, has its own share of celebrity endorsements. Top athletes, such as the fastest man ever, Usain Bolt, wear Puma. So do international rock stars like **Madonna**. Not quite as prominent in soccer as Adidas, Puma has a considerably greater presence in **Formula One**™, where it is the number one producer of driver-wear. Joint ventures with Ferrari and **BMW** have also led to the development of some of Puma's **best-selling shoes**.

Very few **family** businesses break up as dramatically as the Dasslers did. But then very few family businesses are even half as **successful**. And some say that the break-up was actually a good thing because it motivated both brothers to succeed and created twice as many local **job opportunities**!

Adi and Rudi died back in the **1970s** – predictably, they were buried at opposite ends of the town's cemetery! And the Dassler family no longer has control of either company. But relations didn't really improve between the two firms until 21st September 2009 when, to celebrate world peace day, they arranged a **football match** – not between Adidas and Puma, but between the bosses and workers of both factories. To prevent any dispute, both **logos** were on the football!

01 Making contacts
Conference advice (p6, ex5)
Speaker B

One thing I've learned about conferences is always to carry 'useful stuff'. You'd be surprised how many people don't have the right money for the coffee machine or turn up to a talk without a pen. Lending them yours is a great way to start a conversation! But, whatever you do, don't give your business card to everyone you meet or you'll have a mountain of email when you get back! Make a few notes on the back of useful cards and throw away useless ones at the end of each day. Also, use coffee breaks to take notes on what you've learned and who you've met, or you'll forget it all later. It may sound strange, but I'd skip the big presentations. You can network much better at small group sessions where you can talk more easily. A word about audience etiquette. It's very bad manners to walk out of a talk halfway through, even if you're not enjoying it. Think how you'd feel! Make sure you get to see something of Rome while you're there – shouldn't be all work and no play! On the subject of work, remember, the hotel bar is where the real networking gets done. Finally, dress to impress. Best suit, best shoes = best results.

Posted by Gianni Corbucci at 8.06 pm on 7 October

07 Making decisions
The decision-making meeting (p47, ex4)
Plan B

💿 **1.41** If you are unable to reach a decision, perhaps it is because the film series itself needs to be brought into the 21st century. Why not make Bond a woman? You could reverse all the stereotypes and attract a new audience. You know the actress below is interested. Read her profile, then listen to an interview extract.

name and age Diane Fairchild 26	
nationality Anglo-French	
marital status single	
height 1.78 m	
physical pursuits swam for her university, black sash White Crane Kung Fu	
experience Did a law degree at Cambridge before going into acting. A rising star who has become 'hot property' after her huge success in the action thriller *Spider-Web*. Though 'typically British', the Americans love her.	
achievements Won a Golden Palm at the Cannes Film Festival.	
usual fee At least $2 million a film.	
comments Likes to combine serious theatre work with escapist films. Thinks a female Bond is what the 007 series needs.	

09 Small talk
Comments on cultural sensitivity test

Dilemma 1: Business people from Latin and Arab countries tend to have a more flexible, 'polychronic' attitude to time than their 'monochronic' North American and North European counterparts, for whom time really is money. Their 'high-context' culture also places greater emphasis on personal relationships than 'low-context' northerners do.

The message? Try not to be too busy for Brazilians or Italians and don't mess up Americans' tight schedules.

Dilemma 2: Mixing with colleagues out of work-hours is an integral part of business in America where many companies are run like sports teams with the boss as both captain and coach. Elsewhere, there may be a strong dividing line between work and home. The message? In social situations, simply be yourself. Neither do anything that offends you nor that you think may offend your hosts.

Dilemma 3: A good sense of humour is an admired quality in many cultures – notably British, American and most Latin countries – though the type of humour may vary from wordplay to sharp sarcasm to innuendo and even the surreal. In other cultures, however – particularly Germanic ones – humour is not usually considered appropriate in a business context. The message? You don't have to be a comedian with the British, but always smile at their attempts at humour. With Germans or Swiss, leave the jokes for the bar after the meeting.

Dilemma 4: The amount of socializing you do prior to and during a negotiation will depend both on your own and the opposing team's negotiating styles, and where the negotiation is being held. In Japan, for example, the negotiation process is long and relationship-building plays an important part. The same is true of the Middle East. In the USA, things move faster, and their negotiating style tends to be both more informal and adversarial. In Germany, there may be little time for small talk. The message? Follow your opponents' lead, but do all you can to create rapport.

03 Keeping track
Didn't I say that? (p23, ex8)
Speaker B

1 Listen to your partner reading out some sentences. Can you spot the discrepancies? Query any you hear using some of the expressions on page 23.

2 Read out the following sentences to your partner. Each one contains a silly discrepancy. Can she/he spot it?

a I've got three children – one of each.

b We met the French negotiating team at their headquarters in Lisbon.

c I'm worried about this trip to Denmark. For one thing, I don't speak a word of Dutch.

d The managing director must be at least 70. But it's his grandfather who really runs the company.

e I work for a firm called Network Software. We make washing machines, fridges, that kind of thing.

13 Being heard
Hang on a minute! (p80, ex1)
Speaker A

Read the short article below about intercultural business etiquette. In a few minutes, you are going to try to read it aloud to your partner in under a minute, so first check you understand everything and mark places where you can pause for breath!

Your partner is preparing to read a similar article aloud to you. So, when you are both ready, decide who will read first. Read as fast as you can, but try to make sense!

As you listen to your partner read, you should interrupt them as often as possible to clarify anything which isn't absolutely clear. Your objective is to stop them reaching the end of the text in a minute. See who can get further. Good luck!

Do business across cultures, and you'll be faced with a minefield of dos and don'ts. But whose dos should you do? And whose don'ts should you avoid? The Chinese, for example, traditionally enter a room in order of seniority, whereas in Spain the boss will usually make a late entrance. So who enters first in a Spanish–Chinese meeting? In Singapore, strong eye contact is considered aggressive. But, according to Austro–German superstition, you must look people directly in the eye whenever you say 'Cheers' in a bar. If you don't, you'll be unlucky in love for seven years. Is it worth it? And, in these times of globalization and the networked economy, can there really be such a thing as a business lunch when in New York it's all about business and in Paris it's all about lunch? They say 'When in Rome, do as the Romans do.' But what if the Romans are meeting the Koreans in Krakow?

Interruptometer

You're hopeless!

Learn to be more assertive.

Okay, but avoid doing business in Latin America.

Pretty good. You could be a politician.

Excellent! Nobody else can get a word in.

06 Handling calls
Unexpected phone calls (p40, ex5)

Speaker A

Call 1 You make the call 17.30 local time.

You work in the marketing department of Shiseido Cosmetics, Tokyo. Phone the advertising department of *Cosmopolitan* magazine, Paris. You want to speak to either Monique Leblanc or Philippe Roussel about the cost of a full-page advertisement.

Call 2 You receive the call 10.30 local time.

You work for Barclays Global Mutual Funds in New York and deal with corporate investment. Your colleague, Neil Thomas, deals with company pension schemes, but you have no idea where he is. He went out to get a bagel an hour and a half ago, and hasn't been seen since. You're very busy and have to keep putting Speaker B on hold to deal with different problems. Neil's mobile number is 181 650 777.

Call 3 You make the call 15.00 local time.

You are a sales representative for Fujitsu Computers, UK. You're calling Speaker B at General Accident Insurance with a quote for 25 laptops, which they asked for by responding to one of your company's Internet advertisements. You have a range of discounted prices you can offer from $19,000 to $25,000 depending on the model. You could email these, but prefer to phone because it gives you a chance to get an appointment.

Call 4 You receive the call 10.45 local time.

You work for Burson-Marsteller, the world's biggest public relations company, and are based in Boston, USA. In the course of your job, you get to go to a lot of conferences and meet a lot of people. You can't always remember them all, although it's an important part of your job to pretend to do so. You've just got a new boss, who you don't like very much, and are on your way to a meeting with her now.

Scenario E The difficult customer
(p125, ex7)

Speaker B

You are a senior sales representative for Flow Information Systems (FIS) and are about to negotiate the sale of a supply chain management (SCM) system with Speaker A, the IT director for FreightFlow Inc, a transport and logistics company.

- In a previous telephone conversation with Speaker A, you quoted them a software licence fee of $70,000 plus an annual maintenance and support charge of $20,000, making a total of $90,000. They seemed to be fairly happy with this quote and claimed they had the budget for such a sum, although, of course, you expect them to offer a lower figure in the negotiation you are about to have.

- Your company is having a poor end of year and your boss has authorized you to offer up to a 15% discount in order to secure a deal with FreightFlow today, but that's your absolute limit. Your boss would fire you if you offered more!

- For legal reasons, FIS has a policy of only selling software licences with maintenance included and you are not authorized to sell licences without it.

- With authorization to offer such a generous discount, if necessary, you do not expect there to be major problems. But you need to make this sale, so if there are problems, be prepared to ask as many questions as possible to make sure you reach an agreement. If you need to telephone your sales manager (your trainer) to get special authorization for a concession, you can.

Good luck!

Scenario D Tricky conversations
(p101, ex7)

Speaker B

SITUATION 1 You are the team leader for a long-running project at FIS's London office. Speaker B has been sent by head office in Seattle, USA, to help you finish off the project within the next three months. This is not a problem as you are making good progress and should be able to finish in ten weeks. But, to be honest, you don't like head office interfering. The last time this happened, there were all kinds of arguments about meeting company requirements. Speaker A seems nicer than the last person they sent, but you like to do things your own way (decide why this is the best way) and don't need assistance as you have everything under control.

Speaker A will start.

SITUATION 2 You are a sales manager at FIS Barcelona and Speaker A is a star member of your team, even though they've only been with you for six months. Unfortunately, however, 360° feedback has shown that they are not popular with the rest of the team. They don't turn up for in-house training sessions, take time off work whenever they feel like it and, worst of all, do not refer potential clients to colleagues who may be better qualified to deal with their IT requirements. You place great importance on team spirit (you decide why) and want to encourage Speaker A to be more of a team-player in future. Listen carefully to what they have to say, but make it clear you need to see a change in their behaviour. You start: [Partner's name], *do you have a moment? I'd like to have a chat with you about the team appraisals. Let's get a coffee first …*

Listening scripts

01 MAKING CONTACTS

 1.01

Extract 1

Two thousand years ago, it was the home of the ancient Mayan civilization. Today, Cancún is the most popular resort in Mexico; its unspoilt coastline a water sports paradise. With its 426 rooms overlooking the Caribbean, 24-hour room service, express checkout, outdoor pools, residents-only health club and 200 metres of exclusive private beach, the Hilton Cancún is rated among the three best hotels in Latin America. Whether swimming with the dolphins or playing roulette in its own offshore casino, you can be sure of an experience to remember. Or why not take advantage of the Hilton's car rental service and explore the nearby ruins of Chichen Itza? Whatever your company's needs, send them your requirements and they will plan the logistics for you. What's more, if you book on special value dates, you'll get a generous 10 to 30% discount. This year, why not let your annual conference be part of Cancún's 2,000-year-old tradition?

Extract 2

Half an hour from the world's most romantic city and rated by conference organizers the 'hottest' venue in Europe, Disneyland® Paris's corporate clients include American Express, Unilever and MCI. If you think business and *The Lion King* don't mix, the Disney® magic will soon change your mind. With its unique atmosphere and superb fully equipped convention centre for 2,300 people, its 95 meeting rooms and 3,000 square metres of exhibition space, Disney's theme park is sure to be a huge success with both you and your family. As well as fabulous banqueting facilities for over a thousand people, Disney is able to arrange special private events, such as the amazing 'Journey through Time' and the 'Cape Caribbean' adventure or, if you prefer, golf tournaments and team-building activities. Walt Disney's aim was always 'to make people happy' and that aim now extends to corporate hospitality in the cultural heart of Europe.

Extract 3

At 321 metres high, higher than the Eiffel Tower and only 60 metres shorter than the Empire State Building, the magnificent Burj Al Arab is one of the world's tallest and most luxurious hotels. Diamond white by day and a rainbow of colours at night, occupying a central location in Dubai with flight connections to all the major cities of the world, the Burj Al Arab combines the latest technology with the finest traditions of the past. Spacious deluxe suites from 170 to 780 square metres, in-room laptops with Internet access, full conference facilities on the 27th floor, a VIP helipad on the 28th, a golden-domed ballroom and a world-class restaurant with spectacular views across the Arabian Gulf all make this the ultimate business venue. As they say in the Emirates, 'Welcome, honoured guest.'

 1.02

Conversation 1

A Oh, hi, David. How are things? We were just talking about the guy over there.

B Who?

A The big, tall guy in the green tie behind those women. The guy standing at the bar.

B Oh, yeah.

A You know him?

B Yes, that's Karl Schelling.

A Karl who?

B Schelling. He's the new director of R&D at Siemens.

A In Munich?

B Yeah, that's right. Nice guy. I was talking to him last night in the bar.

A Oh, he's at the Hilton?

B Yeah. He was telling me about how he got the job.

A Really?

B Yeah, apparently he was headhunted from Philips. They made him an offer he couldn't refuse. Doubled his salary.

A Headhunted? Don't expect Philips are too happy, then. All that sensitive information.

B Well, no, quite.

A He's presenting, isn't he?

B Yeah, he's on this afternoon. He's talking about data security.

A You're joking.

B No, here he is on the programme: Data Security in the Connected Economy.

1.03

Conversation 2

C Chris, who's that man over there in the light suit?

D You mean the grey suit?

C No, not him! Over there, standing by the entrance. Talking to that woman in black.

D Oh, yes, that's, er, what's-his-name? William Hill. Hall. William Hall, that's it. He's at the Sheraton where I'm staying, actually. He's head of research at Sony® UK. Yes, he's giving a talk on ... where's my programme? ... Ah, yes, here it is. Erm, ... yes, on New Generation Gaming Systems. Ten o'clock on Saturday. I think I'm going to that.

C Mm, sounds interesting. He doesn't look very happy, though, does he?

D Well, no. Neither would you in his position.

C How do you mean?

D Well, this is just a rumour, mind you, but, erm, I've heard they may be moving R&D to Frankfurt.

C Really? Are you sure?

D Well, no, but that's what I heard.

C And he doesn't want to make that move?

D Well, the thing is: I'm not sure they're keeping him on. I think they want a German to lead the team.

C Oh, I see. Well, no wonder he's unhappy ...

 1.04

Conversation 3

E Anne, you know nearly everybody here. Who's that woman in the brown jacket with the long red hair? She's talking to that other woman, the one with the blonde hair.

F Oh, you mean, Irena, Irena Stefanowitz?

E Yes, who is she? I saw her coming out of the Marriott last night with a whole group of people. Going to some dinner party, by the look of it. Sounded like they were speaking Polish.

F Yes, she's a professor at the Warsaw University of Technology. And I think she does quite a lot of consultancy work as well. Amazing speaker. You should go to her talk.

E Really? What's she talking about?

F I think she's doing a session this year on innovation strategies.

E Interesting. You know, I'm going to be working on a project in Krakow next year.

F Krakow? Oh, you'll love it there. Very nice city.

E Yes, if all goes well, there might be a lot more work in Poland.

F Oh, well, in that case, perhaps you should meet Irena. I'm sure she'd be interested in talking to you.

E Yes, perhaps you're right.

F I should warn you, though ...

E What?

F Well, she's quite influential in Warsaw.

E Oh, yes?

F Yes. Let's just say it doesn't pay to get on the wrong side of her. A friend of mine knew her well. They had a bit of a disagreement and his latest project proposal was rejected by the authorities.

E Hmm. Okay, I'll remember that.

F But you must meet her. In fact, why don't I introduce you now?

E Erm, well, okay then ...

 1.05

Conversation 4

G ... So, anyway, that's how it ended up costing me 75 euros just to get from the airport to the hotel!

H Oh, dear. Well, I did warn you about some of those mini-cab drivers.

G Yes, yes, I know. I'll wait in the queue with the rest of you next time … Anyway, let's change the subject … Who's that blonde woman over there?

H Hmm?

G The one in the black dress. Over there, talking to those two guys.

H Which two guys?

G Those two. The woman with her back to us!

H Oh, her! That's Margo Timmerman.

G Ah, so that's Margo Timmerman. I thought so. She still works for Cisco, right?

H Yeah. Heads up their technical department in the Netherlands.

G Isn't she giving the keynote presentation tomorrow morning?

H Yes, she's talking about new server technology or something. Why?

G Hmm, I'd quite like to talk to her if I get the chance. Is she staying at the Marriott, do you know? I might leave her a message.

H Erm, no, she's probably over at the Hyatt. That's where most of the Cisco people are staying.

G Ah, right … Listen, you seem to know her. You couldn't introduce us, could you?

H Er, well, to tell you the truth, I'm really not the best person to ask.

G Oh?

H No. She, er, used to be my boss. You know, years ago. We, er … Well, let's just say we had very different ideas about how to manage a project. And she, er, let me go.

G You mean she fired you!

H Yes, well, all right. Keep your voice down! I wasn't exactly fired …

1.06

Conversation a

A Is this your first visit to Russia?

B Er, yes it is, actually. Fascinating place.

A Yes, isn't it? I come here quite a lot. What do you do, by the way? I see you work for Glaxo.

B How did you know? … Oh, yeah, my badge. Yeah, I'm in R&D. Molecular modelling, to be precise.

A Really? We should talk. Can I get you a drink?

B Er, no thanks. I'm fine.

A Sure?

B Well, just a coffee, then. Thanks. So, what line of business are you in?

1.07

Conversation b

C Hi, Fiona Hunt. Sun Microsystems. Mind if I join you?

D Erm, no. Er, Michael Steele.

C Pleased to meet you, Mike. Try one of these – they're delicious.

D Er, thanks, but I'm allergic to seafood.

C Oh, then try the cheese dips instead. They're really good! Have we met somewhere before? Oslo, perhaps?

D I don't think so.

C Mm. I was sure I recognized you … You're an Aquarius, aren't you? I can tell.

D Well, I don't know. I'm not really into horoscopes, I'm afraid.

C When's your birthday?

D Oh, er, February the 2nd.

C I knew it! A typical Aquarius.

D Er, yes. Geez, is that the time? If you'll excuse me, I have to make a phone call. It's been nice talking to you.

1.08

Conversation c

E I really enjoyed your talk this morning.

F Oh, thanks. Yeah, it went quite well, I think.

E You had some very interesting things to say. I'm Amy Cooper, by the way. Yes, I'd like to talk to you about some of your ideas. My company may be interested in your product. Where are you staying?

F At the Regency.

E I'm at the Hyatt. Why don't we fix up a time to chat over a drink? Here's my card.

F Oh, thanks. I've got mine here … somewhere.

E Don't worry. I know who you are. So, how are you enjoying the conference?

F Well, it's been good so far. More people than ever this year. But, er, isn't this weather awful? Half a metre of snow this morning, I heard.

E Yeah, it gets pretty cold here in Moscow, that's for sure.

F Erm, would you excuse me a moment? I'll be right back.

1.09

Conversation d

G So, how's business?

H Fine. This merger's meant quite a lot of work for us, but, fine.

G Hmm. Well, mergers are often difficult. So, er, what do you think about the strikes in Europe?

H I'm sorry?

G The rail strikes in France. It was in the news again this morning.

H Er, well, I, er …

G I mean, it must affect a company like yours – you being in logistics.

H Er, no, I think you've made a mistake. I'm not in logistics. I work for Audi.

G Audi? Oh, sorry. Thought you were someone else.

H That's okay. Er, if you'll excuse me, I must just go and say hello to someone.

1.10

Conversation e

J I like your watch. An Omega, isn't it?

K Er, well, to be honest, don't tell anyone, but it's a fake.

J No! Well, it looks real to me. Where did you get it?

K Turkey. It cost me 25 dollars.

J Amazing! So, do you know many people here?

K No, not really. It's the first time I've been to one of these conferences.

J Me too. So, what's your hotel like?

K Hmm, pretty comfortable. Nothing special, but it's okay, I suppose.

J Yeah, you're at the Sheraton, aren't you? Last year, they held this thing in Mexico. The Hilton Cancún. Fabulous hotel, they say.

K Cancún! A bit warmer than here, then!

J Oh, yeah. I went there on holiday once. Beautiful place. Can I get you anything from the buffet?

K Oh, that's all right. I'll come with you. I'd like some more of that Beluga caviar before it all goes!

02 MAKING CALLS

1.11

A Hello?

B Hello.

A Hello. Is that Dutch Hydro?

B That's right.

A Can I have the accounts department, please?

B Yes.

A Sorry?

B This is the accounts department.

A Oh, right. Erm, I'd like to speak to Marius Pot, please.

B Yes.

A Sorry?

B That's me.

A Well, why didn't you say so?

B Can I help you?

A I hope so! I'm calling about an invoice I received.

1.12

B Hello, accounts department. Marius Pot speaking.

A Ah, Mr Pot. Just the person I wanted to speak to. I'm calling about an invoice I received.

1.13

A Good morning, Cheney and Broome. Can I help you?

B Yes, please … er, … Just a moment …

A Hello? Are you still there?

B Yes, sorry … erm …

A How can I help you?

B Oh, yes, can I speak to, er, to, er … just a minute … yes, to, er, Catherine Mellor, please?

A Certainly. Who's calling, please?

B Sorry?

A Can I have your name, please?

B Oh, yes, it's Ramón Berenguer … from Genex Ace Pharmaceuticals.

A Thank you. Can I ask the purpose of your call, Mr Berenguer?

B Oh, yes. It's about, er … an invoice.

A Thank you, Mr Berenguer. Putting you through now.

1.14

A Good morning, Cheney and Broome. Can I help you?

B Er, yes. This is Ramón Berenguer from Genex Ace Pharmaceuticals. Can I speak to Catherine Mellor, please?

A Certainly, Mr Berenguer. Can I ask the purpose of your call?

B It's about an invoice.

A Putting you through now.

 1.15

a Can I help you?

b Can I ask who's calling?

c Can you spell that, please?

d Can I give her a message?

e Can you tell him I called?

f Can you read that back to me?

g Can you speak up, please?

h Can you tell me when she'll be back?

i Can you get back to me within the hour?

j Can you ask her to call me back?

k Can I get back to you on that?

l Can I leave a message?

 1.16

Message 1

Hello. This is Cheryl. I phoned you about five times yesterday, but you weren't in. Anyway, I corrected those figures you faxed me. Okay, speak to you later.

Message 2

Hi, Peter. Anne here. I wanted to talk to you about the project meeting tomorrow, but you're obviously not there. The good news is we finished phase one on time. As I explained, I may be a little late for the meeting. So just go ahead and start without me. I'll join you at about ten.

Message 3

Er, this is Zoltán. Just to let you know, I started the report this morning and just emailed you the first part. Oh, I included the quarterly accounts in the report, too. Let me know what you think.

Message 4

Mr Carter. It's Philip Heath. I talked to our stock control manager about the Venezuelan consignment and he says we despatched the goods a week ago. The shipping agent says they delivered them this morning. So, problem solved!

Message 5

Hello, Mr Carter. This is Ryan Hope from SilverStar. I called you a couple of weeks ago about an estimate for a contract in Malaysia. Erm, we discussed my client's requirements and, well, I expected to hear from you last week. Could you give me a call on 01865 555959 as soon as possible, please?

Message 6

Pete. It's me. Sorry, mate, I tried everything, but head office say we can't have any more time. They say they waited six months for the preliminary report, another six months for the feasibility study and now they want to see some results. Anyway, I booked the conference room for three tomorrow. Give me a call when you get in. We need to talk.

 1.17

Message A

Hi, it's Seiji. Listen, the negotiations here in Nagoya are going pretty well, but we seem to be deadlocked on price. Can you authorize me to offer them a 14% discount on 50,000 units? I think that should do it.

Message B

Hi, it's Jim. Listen, I'm in a bit of a panic. I'm at the Expo in Dublin and, you won't believe this, but I've lost the memory stick with my entire presentation on it! Could you email over my PowerPoint slides as attachments as soon as possible? Thanks!

Message C

Hi. Tony here. I'm still stuck in a meeting at head office. Are you making progress with the conference arrangements? Please make sure you contact the speakers to confirm their attendance. Cheers.

Message D

Hi, Kate here. I'm with the people from InfoTag in Seattle and they're querying our invoice for the third quarter. Can you ask someone in accounts to check the figures and reinvoice them if necessary? Thanks.

Message E

Hello, this is Alicia. This is urgent. I really need a copy of the Turin report from you by tomorrow afternoon at the latest. Call me straight back if you're having problems.

Message F

Hi there, this is Mike. Listen, I've got an appointment over at your offices on Friday. Do you want to meet up? Maybe go for a coffee or something? Oh, by the way, Ian sends his regards. Catch you later. Bye.

 1.18

Call 1

A Hello. This is Patterson Meats, Sylvia Wright's office. Thank you for calling. I'm afraid I'm not able to take your call right now, but if you'd like to leave a message, please do so after the tone and I'll get back to you as soon as I can.

B Hello, Sylvia. It's Tim Curtis from the Sydney office. I just wanted to know how the meeting with the people from Temco Supermarkets went. This is a really good chance for us to start exporting to Britain. I hope their visit was a success. Er, give me a ring when you get in, would you? Bye now.

 1.19

Call 2

A Hello. Tim Curtis.

B Hi, Tim. It's Sylvia here. I got your message.

A Sylvia, hi. So, how did it go?

B It went pretty well, I think. They sent three people in the end.

A Three? Well, that's a good sign.

B Yeah, there was Bill Andrews, head of meat purchasing. I think you met him when you went to the UK last month.

A That's right. He seemed pretty interested when I spoke to him then.

B Yeah, he asked me a lot of questions about our quality control.

A Uh huh. I thought he might. I hope you told him he's got no worries there.

B I certainly did.

A Good. So who else came? Er, did Stephanie Hughes come?

B Er, they sent Jonathan Powell from their marketing department instead and Melanie Burns, who's in charge of imported produce.

A Oh, right. I didn't meet them in London. So, did you show them the processing plant?

B I did. There wasn't time to do a tour of the factory, but I showed them the packing department and the freezer units. Then we gave the presentation – Ian and I – and took them out to dinner afterwards.

A Great. Did they say when they'd let us know? I mean, do you think they'll place an order or not?

B Well, it's too early to say. But I think they were quite impressed.

A Hmm.

B They said they'd be in touch in the next couple of days or so. They were a bit worried at first about British customers accepting our product. Although they do sell other exotic meats already. Ostrich, for example, and that's quite popular.

A Erm, excuse me for a moment, Sylvia ... Sorry about that. I just had to sign for something. Where were we? Oh, yeah, they were worried about UK customers accepting our product, you say?

B Well, I don't think it's a problem. Er, you know what the Brits are like – animal lovers and all that. They weren't sure if people would accept kangaroo meat as an alternative to beef.

A Kangaroos are too cute and lovable to eat, huh?

B Well, something like that. But I told them they're not exactly endangered. There are twice as many kangaroos in Australia as there are Australians. Kangaroo's been on the menu here for years. They agreed it tastes good and, as I said to them, it's a really healthy option – ten times less fat than a beef steak and no chance of getting mad cow disease!

03 KEEPING TRACK

 1.20

Extract a

A The problem is money.

B Sorry, what did you say?

A The problem is money.

B Oh, as usual.

Extract b

A We have to reach a decision by next week.

B Sorry, when did you say?

A Next week.

B Oh, I see.

Extract c

A An upgrade will cost $3,000.

B Sorry, how much did you say?

A Three thousand dollars, at least.

B Oh, as much as that?

Extract d

A Ildikó Dudás spoke to me about it yesterday.

B Sorry, who did you say?

A Ildikó Dudás – from the Budapest office.

B Oh, yes, of course.

Extract e

A The company is based in Taipei.

B Sorry, where did you say?

A In Taipei.

B Oh, really?

Extract f

A The whole project might take 18 months.

B Sorry, how long did you say?

A Eighteen months.

B Oh, as long as that?

💿 1.21

A Okay, so, just to give you a summary of the sales figures for last month.

B Last month? Don't you mean this month?

A No, I mean last month. This month's figures aren't ready yet, are they?

B Oh, no, of course not. Sorry.

A So, overall, sales for last month are up again – by 2.6%, in fact, which is pretty good.

C Er, 2.6%? Shouldn't that be 6.2?

A Yeah, up by 6.2%. Didn't I say that?

C No, you said 2.6.

A Oh, … right. Well, you know what I mean. So, anyway, the thing is, we're getting the best results in Denmark and Norway – 30,000 units.

C Thirty thousand? That doesn't sound right to me. Thirteen thousand surely?

A No, the figures are here – Denmark and Norway: 30,000 units.

B Denmark and Norway? Are you sure? That can't be right. Sales have never been good in Scandinavia.

A That's just the point. Sales in Scandinavia are usually terrible, but they were excellent in June.

C June? Isn't it July we're talking about?

A July! Yes, of course, July! If you'd just let me finish! What I want to know is if we could sell our product in Scandinavia in June, …

C July.

A … in July, then why can't we sell it there every month?

B Good point. Have you spoken to John about it?

A John? You mean Jim.

B Jim, yes. Whoever's in charge of Northern Europe these days.

A Jim Munroe. I couldn't. He had to fly to Scotland. His mother's ill apparently.

C There must be some mistake.

A Hmm?

C Well, I saw Jim this morning as I was coming in – on his way to play golf, by the look of it.

A What? Are you sure? Wait till I see him!

💿 1.22

A So, welcome to Tokyo, Matt. It's good to have you on the team.

B Thanks, Sally. It's good to be here.

A I think you're going to enjoy your three months here, Matt. Now, this is Sharon Hall. She's the person you'll mostly be working with on the project.

C Hi, Matt.

B Hi … Sorry, I didn't catch your name.

C Sharon. Sharon Hall.

B Hi, Sharon.

A Sharon's in charge of our corporate loan department. She's sorting out an office for you at the moment. You'll probably be working over at Empire House.

B Sorry, where did you say?

C Empire House. It's our office building on the other side of town.

B Oh, okay.

A Don't worry, I'll take you over there later. Now, you and Sharon will be reporting directly to Daniel Cash, our VP for corporate finance.

B Sorry, who?

C Daniel Cash.

B Oh, right. And he's the vice-president for …?

A Corporate finance. I thought you two had met? Anyway, Daniel's had to rush off to a meeting, but he told me to say he'd meet you both at two tomorrow.

B Sorry, I don't understand. I thought the whole team was meeting tomorrow at nine?

A We were. But, er, something came up. Anyway, Sharon can fill you in on most of it. Sharon?

C Yes, you'll have two assistants working with you, Matt. Janet White and Robin Sellers.

B Okay, Janet White and Robin …?

C Sellers. Janet's our top mergers and acquisitions specialist. I think you two will get on well. She'll be helping you with your research. And Robin's your interpreter. He's very familiar with business procedures here – as well as being fluent in Japanese, of course.

B Sorry, I'm not with you. Interpreter? What do I need an interpreter for? I thought I was just here as an advisor.

A Erm … The situation's changed a little since we last spoke, Matt. We'd now like you to lead the negotiations with the Sapporo Bank. In fact, that will be your main responsibility.

B I don't quite see what you mean, Sally. Erm, I'm no negotiator, especially not for a takeover as big as this. I'm the guy with the pocket calculator. I just make sure the figures add up.

C Oh, come on, Matt. You're too modest. We know your track record. Janet can take care of the figures. We want you to lead the first round of negotiations on the 13th.

B You mean the 30th, right? The 13th is next week.

A That's right. We've scheduled the first meeting for next Wednesday. Janet will be able to brief you before then. This is your big chance. I'm counting on you, Matt. I know you won't let me down.

04 LISTENING

💿 1.23

Extract a

A James, do you have a minute? … James?

B Oh, hi, Ingrid … Er, sorry, what was that?

A Well, it's just that I need to have a word with you about the quarterlies. But if you're busy, I can come back later.

B Yeah, okay … I mean no, no, that's fine … Sorry, what was it you wanted to talk to me about?

A The quarterlies, James. Only the meeting's on Friday, and I still haven't received figures from Hugh and Alison … James?

B Yes, yes, I'm listening! Erm, so Alison still hasn't sent you her figures?

A No, she hasn't, but I'm dealing with that. It's Hugh I'm having problems with.

B Hugh? I thought we were talking about Alison.

A And Hugh, James! This is the third time now he's been late with his quarterlies. I keep sending him reminders and he keeps ignoring them! I thought you might talk to him.

B Hmm, would you like me to talk to him?

A That's what I just … Look, James, you're obviously in the middle of something else. I think I'd better talk to you later when you can give me your undivided attention!

B Sorry, Ingrid, sorry! … Okay, where were we?

Extract b

A Tim, we really need to talk about your team's expense claims. Frankly, they're getting out of control. I don't how to put this, but some of these restaurant bills are just ridic …

B Nicole, we've discussed this before and, as I've told you …

A Tim, could I just finish what I was saying?

B There's no need, Nicole. We have this same conversation just about every month, don't we?

A But your team's total expenses are now almost twice as much as everyone else's! You know we have a set budget for …

B Nicole, let me stop you right there. My team has far more client contact than anyone else's! So it's hardly surprising we're spending more on meals and entertaining, now is it? And I might remind you that we are also bringing in a lot more business than any other team.

A If you'd just let me finish …

B No, let me finish, Nicole! I have repeatedly asked for expense budgets to be performance-related and you have repeatedly blocked that idea because …

A Whoa, now wait a minute! I haven't blocked anything. As a matter of fact, …

Extract c

A Now, then, Mr Hepburn. There are obviously one or two details we still need to sort out, but, in principle, I think, er …

B … we've got a deal?

A Well, yes, I think so.

B Splendid! So if you'll just sign here.

A Erm, yes, of course, in just a moment. Now, as you know, reliability …

B … is a major concern for you. Yes, I know that. And, let me assure you, you have no worries there. You'll be one of our priority customers! I'll see you get the very best service.

A Er, yes, well, that's good to know. It has been quite a few years since we last did business with you. Must be at least …

B … six years, as a matter of fact. I checked in our computer records.

A Six years? Is it really that long? Well, anyway, you'll understand I just want to make sure …

B … you don't end up with the wrong consignment like you did last time!

A I'm sorry?

B The wrong consignment. We sent you the wrong consignment. And then it took us weeks to get the right one to you because of an administrative error. Rest assured, Ms de Vries, that won't happen again. We've got a completely new order system now. One hundred per cent efficient!

A Erm, well, actually, I'd forgotten all about that consignment … I was going to say we need to make sure you're able to shorten your delivery times whenever our stocks run low.

B Ah.

A But now you mention it, that delay we had six years ago did cause us all kinds of problems … In fact, now I think of it, it was something of a nightmare. Erm, maybe I need to have another look at your proposal, Mr Hepburn, and get back to you on it in a couple of weeks.

B Oh …

 1.24

Extract 1

A Ian, I think it's time we had a chat about training.

B Sure, Sally. What's on your mind?

A Well, I've been looking at our annual spend on T&D and, frankly, it's pretty high.

B Hmm, are you saying we've run over budget on that?

A Well, no, we're still within budget – just. Don't worry. We keep a tight control on that. But when you look at the percentage of employees receiving

training each year, it's only about 20% of them. For what we're spending, that doesn't seem very cost effective.

B Do you mean we should be shopping around for cheaper training?

A Well, that's certainly one thing we could do to save money. But I think it's more a question of efficiency.

B What do you mean by 'efficiency'?

A Well, look at this. Last year, we ran three separate time-management courses for three separate units in Italy. Couldn't we have put all those people on just one course?

B Sorry, I'm not quite with you. Aren't there limits on the number of participants to get the maximum benefit?

A Well, yes, of course, but most of these courses weren't even fully attended.

B Oh, right.

A So why don't we centralize training?

B Centralize? How do you mean exactly? Don't we use freelancers for training?

A Yes, but if we offered all training from the most central office in each country we operate in, we could combine courses, save money and actually train more people.

B Mm, I see what you're saying …

 1.25

Extract 2

A Amund! Come on in. How's it going?

B Oh, fine, Louise, fine. I'm pretty busy at the moment with the Expo arrangements. But it's all going well.

A Oh, the Expo. Yes, of course. It's going well, you say?

B Well, yes, I think so.

A Great, great! Well now, you said you had an idea you wanted to run past me.

B Er, yes. Well, you know how normally we give out hundreds of business cards at these events?

A Uh huh.

B And then people just lose them, throw them away or forget who it was that gave them to them in the first place!

A Uh huh, go on.

B Well, I found this company that produces fairly inexpensive digital business cards that look just like an ordinary business card, but you can put them into the CD drive of your computer and they contain all this multimedia content.

A Really? Multimedia business cards, you say?

B Yeah. I mean, you can put slideshows, animations, audio, video, everything on them – a full company presentation, client testimonials, commercials, show-reels, the lot.

A Oh, that's interesting. Video and slideshows would be great.

B Exactly. I mean, we are a media company, after all. Shouldn't our business cards be a little more high-tech than a piece of cardboard?

A Right, I'm with you. Good point. So how much are these cards?

B Well, if we order a thousand, it works out at less than a euro per card. I mean that would be a fortune for a normal business card, I know. But this is the sort of thing people will make sure they don't throw away because they'll want to see what's on it. What do you think?

A Hmm, nice idea. I like it. Of course, we'd have to put the content together.

B No problem. Leave that to me.

A Okay, then, let's give them a try. Order a thousand and we'll see what the response is …

 1.26

Extract 3

A Maria, are you busy? I need to talk to you about Jeanne.

B Problem?

A Well, you remember how she blew up at last week's kick-off meeting?

B How will I ever forget? Have you spoken to her about that?

A I have, but I'm afraid it didn't do much good. Seems like there's just a lot of bad chemistry between her and the rest of the team.

B Hmm.

A Anyway, I've given the situation some thought. And I've decided to pull her off the project altogether.

B Oh, really? Do you think that's wise? I mean, how is that going to affect our timeline? Jeanne's the most experienced person we've got working on this.

A I know, but I'm thinking of bringing Martin in to take over her role.

B Martin? Yes, he's good. But wouldn't that mean taking him off the Minerva project?

A It would, but, to be honest, I think he's rather wasted on that.

B Oh, why do you say that?

A Well, Minerva's not really a priority right now, is it? And I think we could use Martin better on this. Besides, Martin thinks the whole project should be targeted much more towards the Latin American market. And, frankly, I agree with him.

B Latin America? Are you sure? Do you have figures for that?

A I do, as a matter of fact. I'll email them over to you.

B Okay, fine. Just one question: what are you going to do about Jeanne?

A Oh, don't worry about that. Leave Jeanne to me.

 1.27

Extract 4

A So, Grant, how are people in your unit reacting to these new structural changes to the company?

B Well, we've had a lot of mixed reactions, to be honest. It's not been easy.

A So what you're saying is you're getting some push-back from your people.

B Well, some resistance certainly. But, I mean, that's normal when you're implementing change on a scale like this. It's really a question of keeping people informed, managing their expectations, you know...

A Hmm, it sounds like you think we should be having more information-sharing meetings.

B Yes, that's right. I think it's important to be open and honest about what's happening and how it will affect people at all levels of the company.

A In other words, show people that we have nothing to hide, that we're not doing anything behind their backs. We want to involve them.

B Right.

A Okay, so the way you see it is we need more openness, more transparency. I think I'd go along with that. Does anyone else have any views on this? Yeah, Alicia.

C Well, I agree with a lot of what Grant says, but I also think we need to deal better with people's fears. We need to be preventing rumours flying around; showing people that, in many ways, it's business as usual.

A So, for you, it's a question of restoring some stability. Yes, that's a good point. Okay, well, thanks for your input, everybody. I think it's good to be discussing these issues at this stage ...

05 BUSINESS TRAVEL

1.28

Conversation 1

A Excuse me. Is there somewhere I could send a fax from?

B Certainly, sir. There's a business centre on the third floor.

Conversation 2

A Did you pack your bags yourself, sir?

B Well, no, my wife ... Oh, er, I mean, yes. Yes, of course.

Conversation 3

A Could I ask you to open your luggage, please, madam?

B Oh, ... all right. Will this take long? Only someone's meeting me.

Conversation 4

A Window or aisle?

B Er, window, please. But not near an emergency exit, if possible. You can't put the seats back.

Conversation 5

A This is your captain speaking. We're now at our cruising altitude of 11,000 metres, making good time and just passing over the Costa Brava.

B Oh, look. There it is. Full of British tourists.

Conversation 6

A Can you tell me what time you stop serving dinner?

B Half past ten, madam. Are you a resident? I can reserve you a table if you like.

Conversation 7

A Er, Heathrow airport, please. Terminal 1. I'm in a bit of a hurry.

B Well, I'll do what I can, sir. But the traffic's terrible this morning. Some sort of accident it said on the radio. Might be quicker taking the Tube.

Conversation 8

A British Airways regrets to announce the late departure of flight BA761 to Buenos Aires. This is due to the late arrival of the plane from Argentina. Estimated departure time is now 15.10.

B Oh, here we go again!

Conversation 9

A This is your captain speaking again. We're in for some turbulence, I'm afraid. So, for your own safety, would you please return to your seats and make sure your seatbelt is fastened while the 'fasten seatbelt' sign remains on. Thank you.

B Erm, excuse me. You're sitting on my seatbelt. Thanks.

Conversation 10

A I'm sorry, but this bag is too heavy to take on as hand luggage. You're only allowed six kilos. You'll have to check it in, I'm afraid, sir.

B But I've got my computer and everything in there. And gifts for my family.

Conversation 11

A I'm afraid I'll have to check your hand luggage too, madam. Could you open this side pocket? And, er, would you mind not smoking, please?

B Oh, I'm sorry. I didn't realize.

Conversation 12

A Have you got anything smaller, sir? Don't think I can change a twenty.

B Uh? Oh, just a minute. I'll see.

Conversation 13

A There has been a change to the schedule for flight BA761 to Buenos Aires. This flight will now depart from Gate 59. Would all passengers travelling to Buenos Aires please go to gate 59.

B Gate 50-what?

Conversation 14

A Right. That's fine, thank you, madam. You can go through now.

B What! You've just unpacked everything in my suitcase! How am I supposed to go through like this?

Conversation 15

A Could you switch off your laptop now, please, sir? We're about to land.

B Uh? Oh, yes, of course.

Conversation 16

A Here you are. Keep the change.

B Oh, thank you very much, madam. Have a good flight.

Conversation 17

A Excuse me. Erm, do you think I could have an alarm call at half past six tomorrow morning?

B Certainly, madam. Could I have your room number, please?

Conversation 18

A Good afternoon, ladies and gentlemen. Flight BA761 to Buenos Aires is now ready for boarding. Would you please have your passports and boarding cards ready for inspection.

B And about time too!

1.29

Conversation 1

A Excuse me, could you tell me where the rest room is?

B Certainly, sir. There's one just across the lobby, by the elevators.

A Thank you.

B You're welcome.

Conversation 2

A That's five quid, please.

B Erm, I've only got a ten, I'm afraid.

A That's fine. So that's five pounds I owe you. Just a minute.

B By the way, could you tell me which way's the nearest Underground?

Conversation 3

A Excuse me, am I going the right way for the shopping mall?

B Er, no. Erm, you need to go back the way you came till you come to a big drugstore.

A Uh huh.

B Turn left, then take a right at the parking lot and the mall's right in front of you.

A Thanks.

B Have a nice day!

Conversation 4

A Day return, please.

B To the City?

A Yes, please ... Oh, no!

B Is there a problem?

A I've just realized I left my briefcase with my wallet in the boot of that taxi!

Conversation 5

A Your bill, madam.

B Oh, thank you. Er, who do I make the cheque out to?

A Er, just Webster's will be fine. Did you enjoy your meal?

B Er, yes ... Everything was ... fine. Er, is there a chemist's nearby, do you happen to know?

Conversation 6

A Which way you headed, ma'am?

B Er, Liberty Street.

A That's quite a few blocks from here. Can I call you a cab?

B Won't that be expensive? Maybe I should take the subway.

A I wouldn't at this time of night. Cab'll probably only cost you five or six bucks.

Conversation 7

A One way or round trip?

B Er, one way, please. Is there a cart I could use for my baggage?

A Sure. They're over by the phone booths. You'll need two quarters.

B Oh, then could you change this for me?

Conversation 8

A Erm, excuse me. I'm looking for a gas station.

B Oh, right. A petrol station. I think there's one at the next roundabout.

A Pardon me? ... Oh, you mean a traffic circle. Great. Thanks a lot.

B No problem.

 1.30

Conversation 1

A Hello. You must be waiting for me.

B Mr de Jong?

A That's right.

B How do you do, sir. Let me take those for you. Did you have a good flight?

A Not bad, not bad. It's even colder here than Cape Town, though. And we're having our winter.

B Oh, yes. It's rained all week, I'm afraid. Always does for Wimbledon.

A Hmm? Oh, the tennis. Actually, I was expecting to meet Mr Hill.

B Yes, sir. I'm afraid Mr Hill had to go to a meeting. He sends his apologies. He said to take you straight to your hotel, give you a chance to freshen up and he'll meet you in a couple of hours or so.

A Oh, right. Fine.

B You must be tired after your long flight.

A Oh, not too bad. Luckily, I managed to get some sleep on the plane.

 1.31

Conversation 2

C Greg! I'm over here ...

D Caroline! Good to see you again! Wow, it's crowded here. I nearly missed you.

C I know. Didn't you see me waving? So, how are things?

D Fine, fine. Susan sends her love.

C How is she?

D Very well. Congratulations, by the way.

C Hmm?

D On your promotion.

C Oh, that. Yeah, well, if you work for the same company long enough ... Now, my car's just five minutes away. Let me help you with your bags.

D Oh, that's all right. Well, maybe the really heavy one.

C Now, I thought we could get some lunch first, and then go back to the office and do some work. Oh, you're staying with us, by the way. David's dying to meet you.

D Sounds good to me. David, yes. A new job and a new husband. So, how's married life?

 1.32

Conversation 3

E Miss Sheridan?

F Yes, you must be Alan Hayes.

E That's right.

F Hello. Thanks for coming to meet me.

E Not at all. We thought it would be quicker. This way you can meet the whole team this afternoon. We thought you might just want to relax this evening.

F Oh, yes. Probably.

E So, how's business?

F Couldn't be better. So we're all set for the meeting tomorrow?

E We certainly are. Martin sends his regards, by the way.

F How is he?

E He's fine. So, how was your flight?

F Oh, pretty good. I got upgraded.

E Lucky you! That never seems to happen to me.

F Mm. It certainly makes a difference. I could get used to it.

E Well, now, we'll go straight to the office if that's okay with you. I'd like you to meet Graham Banks. He's the head of our legal department.

F Yes, I think I spoke to him on the phone.

E Oh, yes, of course. Now, let's see if we can get a taxi ...

 1.33

Conversation 4

G Mr Okada?

H Er, yes.

G Hello. Welcome to London. I'm Sharon Miller.

H Er, from Sabre Holdings?

G That's right. I'm the head of the M&A department – Mergers and Acquisitions.

H I see. I was expecting ... Never mind. So, Miss Miller. Pleased to meet you.

G Pleased to meet you, Mr Okada. Now, I've got a taxi waiting outside. So why don't we let the driver take those bags of yours?

H Oh, thank you very much.

G We'll drop your things off at the hotel. We booked you into the Savoy. I hope that's okay. I think you'll be comfortable there.

H Yes, that will be fine.

G Great. Then I thought we could meet up with my assistant Geri King and get some lunch.

H Gerry King? I don't think I know him.

G Her, actually. No, she's just joined us. She's got a lot of questions she'd like to ask you.

H Yes, of course. I wonder ... It was a very long flight ... Do you think I could go to my hotel first?

G Yeah, sure. We booked a table for 1.30, but that's okay.

H I am a little tired and I need to freshen up.

G Of course. We'll check you into your hotel and then meet in, say, three quarters of an hour?

06 HANDLING CALLS

 1.34

Call 1

A Allo!

B Oh, hello. Do you speak English?

A Er, ... yes, a little. Can I help you?

B This is Anne Cook from *What Car?* magazine.

A I'm sorry?

B Anne Cook. *What Car?*

A What car?

B Yes, that's right.

A You want a car?

B No, no, sorry. I work for *What Car?* I'm a journalist. Er, can you put me through to Yves Dupont?

A I'm afraid I don't understand. Can you speak more slowly, please?

B Yes, I'd like to speak to Yves Dupont, if he's available.

A Ah ... One moment, please. I'll get someone who speaks better English.

B Thank you!

 1.35

Call 2

A Hola ...

B Hello. Is that Joaquín Fuentes?

A Er ... Yes, speaking.

B Joaquín. It's Geoff White.

A Geoff White?

B NetWorth Systems? We spoke last week.

A Oh, yes. I'm sorry. Geoff, of course.

B Er, yes. Anyway, I'm calling about those prices you wanted, ...

A Oh, yes ... Listen, Geoff, I'm afraid I can't talk right now. I'm in a meeting.

B Oh, I see.

A Yeah. Can you call me back – say, in an hour?

B Erm, yeah, sure ... No problem.

A Okay, I'll speak to you later ... No, wait, could you just email me the figures instead?

B Erm, yeah, yeah, sure.

A Thanks a lot.

B I'll do that right away.

A Great. Thanks for calling.

B Yeah, bye.

A Bye.

 1.36

Call 3

C Jim, can you get that?

A Uh? Oh, okay ... Yeah?

B Hello? Is that Western Securities?

A Uh huh. What can I do for you?

B This is Laura Como from Tricolor. I'd like to speak to Karl Lesonsky, please. It's about a pension fund.

A Just a minute. Anybody seen Karl? ... He's not here.

B Do you know when he'll be back?

A No idea. He's usually in by now. Probably taken a long lunch.

B Oh, I see. Well, perhaps you can help. Who am I speaking to?

A Er, Jim Savage. But, er, ... Oh, just a minute ... Er, hello Ms Como?

B Yes!

A Look, I don't normally deal with pensions. I think you'd better wait till Karl gets back.

B Well, when will that be?

A I really don't know.

B Well, that's helpful.

A Okay. Look, give me ten minutes. I'll see if I can reach him on his cellphone.

B No, don't bother. I'll call back later.

 1.37

Call 4

A José Senna.

B Ah, Mr Senna. Hello. I'm sorry to bother you. Your secretary gave me your mobile number.

A Er, that's okay … Can I ask who's calling?

B Oh, I'm sorry. This is Nigel Waters. We met at the Expo in São Paulo last year.

A Oh, yes, Mr Waters. How are you?

B Fine, fine. You said if I was ever in Rio you'd introduce me to your boss? Remember?

A Oh, … Yes. Um, so you're here in Rio?

B That's right.

A Erm, well, it's a bit difficult right now. I'm on my way to a meeting. But … er, leave it with me. I'll see what I can do.

B Right.

A Can you give me a contact number?

B Oh, yes, I'm staying …

A Just a minute, where's my organizer? … Okay.

B Yes, I'm staying at the Mirador in Copacabana. It's 548 8950, er, room 314.

A 3-1-4 … Okay. I'll try to make the arrangements. Don't worry, I'll sort something out.

B Great.

A And, er … Oh, the traffic's moving. Look, I'll get back to you tomorrow. Okay?

B I can't hear you very well.

A No, the signal's breaking up. Speak to you tomorrow.

B Okay, fine. I'll wait to hear from you then. Bye.

07 MAKING DECISIONS

 1.38

A Welcome to the *In Company* Business Podcast. This week: the art of decision-making …

B In business, is it better to make good decisions or better to make lots of decisions? Peter Kindersley, the founder of Dorling Kindersley Books, is in no doubt. 'It doesn't matter,' he says, 'if the decision you make is right or wrong. What matters is that you make it and don't waste your company's time. If you make the decision, you begin to distinguish the good from the bad.' But Michael Begeman, who runs the Meeting Network at 3M®, takes a different view. He claims that 'not all successful meetings end with a decision'. 'Decisions,' he says, 'are the Valium of meetings.' People think, 'Great, we've finally made a decision. Now we don't have to worry about that issue any more.'

So who's right? Does decisiveness lead to good decision-making? Or is the best decision sometimes no decision?

The answer is partly cultural. In countries like the United States, for example, the ability to make speedy decisions is valued because decisions tend to lead to action. And, as America is an action-oriented culture, being seen to be actively doing something is an important part of a manager's job. In Japan, on the other hand, managers may prefer to gradually build up agreement among their colleagues until the right course of action simply emerges – without a conscious decision ever having been made. By contrast, in France the decision-making procedure is very different from both the American and Japanese approaches. For the French, a long process of logical debate generally precedes all important decisions – some of which, as Begeman recommended, may never be made!

How do you make your decisions – by logically analyzing all the available data or by trusting your gut instinct? Research done by Daniel Goleman, the originator of Emotional Intelligence, shows that highly successful decision-makers do both. But according to Dan Ariely, a psychology professor at Duke University, much of our decision-making is actually highly irrational. For instance, it was noticed some time ago that culturally similar countries varied considerably in their willingness to donate their bodily organs after their death. In Austria, for example, organ donation is 100%, whereas in Germany it's only 12. In Sweden, it's 86%, but in Denmark only 4. How do we explain this dramatic difference? In fact, it turned out to be the result not of culture, but of the way the organ donation questionnaire was worded. In Germany and Denmark, people were asked to tick the box if they wanted to participate in the organ donation program. Most didn't tick it, and so didn't participate. In Austria and Sweden, however, people were asked to tick the box if they didn't want to participate in the organ donation program. Again, most didn't tick it, but by deciding not to tick it, they ended up participating!

So it seems like, given the choice, most of us are more comfortable not doing than doing. Maybe that's why in 1999, George Bell – the former CEO of web portal Excite – turned down the opportunity to buy a start-up search engine company because the asking price of $750,000 just seemed too high. The search engine, of course, was Google, with a current market value of $250 billion – a 330,000-fold increase since Bell decided not to buy it!

 1.39

A Thanks for coming, everybody. Okay, let's get down to business. As you know, we're here to talk about the relocation to the UK and I'd like to hear what you have to say. Now, the plan is to make the final move in January, but that's a busy month for us. So, what do you think?

B Can I just stop you there for a moment, Elke? This relocation idea – I mean, it's ridiculous. I don't think anyone here actually wants to go and live in Britain.

A With respect, you don't quite seem to understand, Erich. The decision has already been taken.

B Sorry, I don't quite see what you mean. I thought we were here to discuss this.

A No, perhaps I didn't make myself clear. We are relocating to Cambridge in November. That's been decided …

B So why are we having this meeting?

A If I could just finish what I was saying. What we are discussing today is how to implement the decision. This affects our Scandinavian office too, you know. There's a lot to talk about. Now …

C Can I just come in here?

A Yes, what is it, Axel?

C Well, I can see why we should have a branch in the UK instead of Scandinavia. We do most of our business there. But we're a German company. Head office should be here in Germany, surely.

A I'm afraid that's completely out of the question. The decision to relocate makes good logistic and economic sense. We're still a fairly small business. Having branches in different countries is just not an option.

B I totally disagree. Our market is Northern Europe and Germany is at the heart of Northern Europe.

A Yes, but 70% of our market is in the UK. Look, perhaps we can come back to this later. I can see some of you are not happy about it and I agree with you up to a point, but I am not in a position to change company policy. Okay, let's move on. How are we going to handle administration during the relocation? Does anyone have any suggestions? How about using the Stockholm office while we move from Bremen to Cambridge? Kjell?

D Well, to be honest, Elke, we feel very much the same as our German colleagues here. We think the decision to close down the Bremen and Stockholm offices is a mistake.

A I see …

C Look, maybe we should take a short break, Elke. I think one or two of us would like to have a word with you – in private if that's okay.

A Right. Well, sorry everybody. We'll have to break off here, I'm afraid. Axel, Kjell, Erich, I'll see you in my office …

 1.40

Interview 1

A So, Peter, how do you see the Bond role?

B Well, Richard, I think playing Bond is really about getting the balance right.

A The balance?

B Yes. I mean, on one level, Bond is a fairly predictable superhero. He travels the world, meets beautiful women, drives fast cars, has a joke for every dangerous situation he finds himself in, gets captured by the bad guy, but always wins through in the end. I mean, that's fine. That's an important part of the Bond formula. It's what people come to the cinema to see.

A Right.

B But for us to care about the character, I think he has to give us some surprises. We have to see behind his superhero mask from time to time. We have to see the man behind the legend – and struggling to live up to the legend. We have to see some small signs of weakness. I think we have to believe that this time Bond just might not make it.

Interview 2

A Well, Sam, you're an American. Is that going to be a problem for you playing Bond?

C No, I don't think so. And I've been working on my English accent. How's this? 'The name's Bond. James Bond.'

A Not bad.

C But actually, Richard, ... er ... I don't see why Bond has to be British. I mean, Bond's just whatever you want him to be. The music, the stunts, the bad guys, ... they're not what make the film. Humour is the important thing. Because if Bond isn't funny, then it's just a silly film with lots of explosions and car chases, and exotic women who get killed just after they meet Bond. Bond isn't Batman. He's not a psychologically damaged superhero. He's an old-fashioned adventurer like Indiana Jones. And he has to keep his sense of fun.

Interview 3

A Now, Jon, how do you see yourself playing the part of Bond?

D Well, firstly, Richard, I'd make sure Bond looks dangerous. Because that's what Bond is, first and foremost – a killer. He has a licence to kill. Everything else – the women, the cars, the gadgets – are just perks of the job.

A You don't think that's a bit ... um, two-dimensional?

D Come on, Richard, this is Bond we're talking about! I think people need to believe in the actor playing Bond, believe that he's really capable of violence, even does his own stunts. Of course, people expect the special effects, the exotic locations and the glamour, but that's no good unless Bond looks like he really means business. So I'd just play Bond as me, Richard. That's all I ever do anyway!

Interview 4

A Charles, you've wanted the Bond part for a long time. How would you play him?

E Well, Richard, we've seen a lot of different versions of the Bond character now, haven't we? The assassin, the chauvinist, the lover, the comedian, the mixed-up loner.

A I guess so.

E And each time a new actor takes over, the story gets updated – newer gadgets, more current issues.

A Yes, that's right.

E I actually think it might be time to stop those endless revisions and go back to the world of the original novels.

A You mean set the movies in the 1960s again?

E Yes, why not? I mean, that's where Bond really belongs. And I think by putting Bond back in the 60s, you avoid the problem of trying to reinvent him in every film.

A Hmm.

E Look, when you ask people who the best Bond actor was, who do they generally choose?

A Well, different people have different preferences, but generally, I suppose most people would say the classic James Bond was Sean Connery.

E Exactly. Now why is that? I'd say it's because his Bond was true to the time. And that's what I'd like to recreate.

 1.41

A Diane, this would be quite a professional challenge for you, taking over as Bond. Would people accept a woman in the part, do you think?

F Well, frankly, no, I don't think they would, Richard. It'd be like having a woman play Superman. And what are you going to call her? Jane Bond? It would be ridiculous. But ... erm ... I don't really see myself becoming Bond ... so much as replacing him. I think you've got to begin again really. Maybe have James finally killed off in one of those spectacular opening sequences before you introduce the new female character. Now, Bond is a pretty hard act to follow after 50 years, so, obviously, my character has to be larger than life and twice as dangerous! The great thing would be you could do all the old sexist jokes in reverse and nobody would complain. But ... erm ... I think the secret of a female Bond is, she's got to have style and a wicked sense of humour or everyone will just hate her for getting James's job.

08 INFLUENCE

 1.42

Conversation a

Édouard, could I ask you to take a look at this design brief? I realize you already have a lot of work on this week, but it's absolutely essential that we get back to the client on this by Friday. And I think you may find it an interesting change from what you normally do. Can I leave it with you?

Conversation b

John, about my request to take some unpaid leave – I was wondering if you had a moment to talk about it. Only, I know how you like to encourage your trainers to gain some outside experience and I think this is a really great

opportunity to do that. You said yourself we need to make savings and with business a little slow this quarter I thought it might be a good time for me to do something like this.

Conversation c

Pam, could I ask you a favour? We've got the people from Shimamura coming over next week, and I'm supposed to be taking them out to dinner and a show, you know. But something's come up and I was wondering if you could take care of it. I know I already owe you one for standing in for me last time! But, to be honest, you're much better at this sort of thing than me, anyway. Would you mind? All the arrangements are made. It's just a case of turning up.

Conversation d

Simone, thanks for agreeing to see me. I wanted to talk to you about the Moscow trade fair. I really think we should attend this year. I mean, just about everybody who's anybody is going to be there – all our competitors, for sure. Now, I know you're worried about the cost, but have a look at this report I just received. It's completely independent, by the way. And it shows the financial benefits of attending the conference over a 24-month period. Pretty impressive. So, I wondered if you could think about it, please. I'll leave the report with you ...

Conversation e

Er, Rafael? Listen, mate, I've got a bit of a problem and I was hoping you might be able to help me out. You remember a couple of weeks ago I took the Morelli account off your hands because you were busy with the Brazilians? Yeah, well, now it seems they want me to do a full audit of their whole business and it's going to mean an enormous amount of work I wasn't expecting. So I was wondering if you'd run the induction session for me again. You said how much you enjoyed it last time. And it would be a real help to me if you could.

Conversation f

Heather, I've been wanting to have a word with you. I'd like you to lead the negotiations with GMK. I was very pleased with the way you handled the Korean deal and I think you're ready to take on a bit more responsibility. What do you say? Do you think you're up to it?

09 SMALL TALK

 2.01

Extract a

A Er, how do you do. I'm Tom Pearson, Export Manager, Falcon Petroleum.

B How do you do, Mr Pearson. I am Sakamoto, Assistant Director of International Investments, Mizoguchi Bank. Please sit here opposite the door. You'll be next to Usami-san.

A Oh, okay. I sit here, right?

B That's right. Have you tried green tea before, Mr Pearson?

A Er, yes, I have. I had it last time I was here. I like it very much.

2.02

Extract b

A Good morning, everyone. I'd like to introduce you all to Dr Alan Winter, who's come over from the Atlanta office to spend a few days at our research centre. Welcome to Berlin, Dr Winter.

B Thank you very much, Wolfgang. It was kind of you to invite me.

A Okay, let's get down to business, shall we?

 2.03

Extract c

A … And then Juventus scored the winner. It was an incredible goal! Did you see the Lazio game last night, Miss Sterling?

B Yes, I did. Wasn't it a great match? One of the best I've ever seen. But then, there's nothing like Italian football.

A So, you like football, then?

B Oh, yeah. I love it. In fact, my father was a professional footballer.

A Really?

B Yes. He wasn't a superstar or anything, but he, er, played for Leeds.

A Leeds United?

B Yes, that's right.

A They were a great team in the 70s, weren't they?

B Yeah, that's when he played for them.

A Amazing. Wait till I tell Luigi. Our new partner's father played for Leeds United, ha!

B Where is Luigi, by the way?

A Oh, he'll be here soon. He's never the first to arrive, not Luigi …

 2.04

Extract d

A Rain stopped play again yesterday, I see.

B Sorry?

A The cricket. They cancelled the match.

B Oh, they didn't! Well, we certainly haven't seen much cricket this summer.

A No. Chocolate biscuit?

B Oh, have we got chocolate ones? Business must be good.

C Right, everyone. Er, I suppose we'd better get started …

 2.05

Extract e

A Right, shall we start? First of all, this is Catherine Anderson from London. I think this is your first time in Finland, isn't it, Catherine? Or have you been here before?

B Actually, I came here on holiday once, but that was a long time ago.

A Well, we hope you enjoy your stay with us. Now there's fresh coffee if you'd like some before we begin …

 2.06

Extract f

A Okay, you guys. Thanks for coming. Now, to business … Oh, did you all get coffee?

B Hey, wait up. I've got a great one here.

C Oh no, it's one of Marty's jokes.

B See, there's this guy George goes for a job, right? And it's a really cool job. Right here in New York. Big money. So, anyway, he takes a test, like an aptitude test, you know, him and this woman. There's two of them. And they have to take a test to get the job.

C Yeah, yeah, so …?

B So they both get exactly the same score on the test, George and the woman – 99%.

C Uh huh.

B So George goes into the interviewer's office. And the interviewer says, 'Well, you both got one question wrong on the test, but I'm sorry, we're giving the job to the other candidate.' So George says, 'Hey, that's not fair! How come she gets the job?' And the interviewer says, 'Well, on question 27, the question you both got wrong, she wrote "I don't know" and you wrote "Neither do I".'

C That's a terrible joke, Marty.

B No, you see, he copied her test, right?

A Marty, we've heard the joke before. It's ancient. Okay, everybody, time to work.

B I thought it was funny.

 2.07

Extract g

A As you know, Albert, I'm the last person to talk about other people's private lives. If the president of France himself wants to have an affair, I don't care. I mean, this is not the United States.

B Yes, quite.

A What I do worry about is what's going on between our vice-president and our head of finance.

B They're having an affair?

A Haven't you heard? I thought everybody knew.

B No! No one ever tells me anything.

A I mean, it's not the affair I care about. It's how it affects our meetings. Haven't you noticed?

B Noticed what?

A How they always agree on everything.

B Well, now you mention it …

10 EMAIL

 2.08

Erm, well, being cc-ed on every little thing drives me nuts. I'd say 60% of the messages I get have nothing to do with me.

What I can't stand is all the junk, the stupid jokes, all the meaning-of-life stuff that seems to fill my inbox. All those things, you know, like, 'Send this to ten more people or a disaster will hit your city.' I mean, come on!

I think all the silly stuff is quite cool, actually. The jokes, the slideshows. I mean, it's just a way of keeping in touch. It's not meant to be taken seriously!

The really neat thing is that you can go back through your emails and see what's been said. You have a permanent record

of every discussion. Which is really useful sometimes.

What really annoys me are those little smiley things, emoticons. Just childish.

I'm a big fan of email. You leave a voicemail, nobody gets back to you. You send an email, it always gets through. I think people are better about answering their email than their phone.

People expecting an instant reply – that really bugs me. I mean, okay, so you sent me an email. Like I'm supposed to drop everything and answer it?

Well, I'm not crazy about 15-paragraph emails. Or those 20-megabyte attachments that take an hour to download. When do these people get any work done?

I read somewhere that 20% of email gets read by the boss, which is kind of scary. I'm not keen on the idea that Big Brother is watching me!

 2.09

Message 1

Hi Koichi, it's Sarah Greenwood here. There's been a change of plan. Peter and I were hoping to arrive in Nagoya on Monday. That's not going to be possible now, I'm afraid, because I have to be in Edinburgh that day. So, we're aiming to get there by Wednesday, but that should still give us plenty of time to get organized before the presentation.

 2.10

Message 2

Hi Koichi, it's Sarah again. Peter and I were planning to stay at the Radisson, because it's near, but apparently there's a conference next week and it's already fully booked. Sorry, I was going to email you about this yesterday. Could you find us somewhere else? Thanks very much.

 2.11

Message 3

Hi Koichi, it's me again. Just one more thing, sorry. We're intending to keep the presentation itself quite short – about 45 minutes – to allow plenty of time for questions and we're going to use PowerPoint, so we're going to need a projector and screen, if you can organize that. Thanks, see you on Wednesday.

11 PRESENTING

 2.12

Extract a

They tried it. They liked it. So they bought it.

Extract b

They tried it. They liked it. So they bought it.

Extract c

We can never be the biggest, but we can be the best.

Extract d

We can never be the biggest, but we can be the best.

Extract e

Did you know that the whole thing was absolutely free?

Extract f

Did you know that the whole thing was absolutely free?

 2.13

The first thing I figured out / and learned / sometimes the hard way / about entrepreneurship / is that the core / the essence of entrepreneurship / is about making meaning / many many people / start companies to make money / the quick flip / the dotcom phenomenon / and I have noticed / in both the companies that I have started / and funded / and been associated with / that those companies / that are fundamentally founded to change the world / to make the world a better place / to make meaning / are the companies that make a difference / they are the companies to succeed / my naïve and romantic belief / is that if you make meaning / you'll probably make money / but if you set out / to make money / you will probably not make meaning / and you won't / make / money.

 2.14

Part A

A Okay, this brings us on to the next item on our agenda this morning, which is online business. Now, I know some of you are concerned about the recent performance of E-Stock, our online subsidiary. So I've asked Gary Cale, our new head of e-business, to bring us up to date. Over to you, Gary.

B Thanks, Michelle. To start off, then, I know you have all seen the figures up to the last quarter – disappointing to say the least. Nine months ago, when we first went online, we were getting over 250,000 hits a day. Three months ago, when I joined this company, we were getting just 60,000 and it was obvious we were failing to attract sufficient customers to our website. So, what was going wrong? In a word, technology. The problem was not the service we were offering, but the website itself.

 2.15

Part B

Now, three things make a good website. First, access to the website must be fast. The slow access speed of our website meant people were getting bored waiting for pages to load and simply going somewhere else. Second, a good website must be easy to use. Ours was so complicated, customers sometimes didn't know if they were buying or selling! And third, a good website must have excellent search engines. Ours didn't. To give you an example of what I mean, a fault we hadn't noticed in the programming caused 1,500 people to invest in a company that didn't even exist. Yes, embarrassing. I'm glad I wasn't here to take the blame for that one! Okay, to move on. Greenbaum-Danson is unquestionably one of the world's leading financial services companies. We're the biggest, oldest and most respected firm in

the business. But to succeed in online stock trading, to succeed in any area of e-business, you need a first-class website. So, creating a first-class website was our first priority. The next thing was Internet advertising, winning back the customer confidence we'd lost. That's a longer job, but we're making progress. The final thing, and this always takes time in e-business, will be to actually make a profit. Well, we can dream!

 2.16

Part C

Have a look at this. It's a graph showing the number of trades our customers make per day on our website. As you can see, the figure was fluctuating for the first three months and then fell sharply to bottom out at just 10,000 trades a day. For a company of our size, that wasn't too impressive. But look. We're up to nearly 40,000 trades now, our highest ever, and still rising.

Okay, I'm going to break off in a minute and take questions. So, to sum up. One, improvements in our website have led to more hits and increased trading. Two, advertising on the Internet will help us win back customers. Three, profits will follow. E-trading in stocks is the future. In the US alone, it's the way a quarter of the public choose to buy their shares. This is the information age and the Internet is the ultimate information provider. I'm reminded of what banker Walter Wriston once said: 'Information about money is becoming more valuable than money itself.' Thank you.

12 IMPACT

 2.17

Speaker 1

Of course, everyone in this room is an experienced IT professional. I myself have been in the personal computer business for about 15 years now. And I was fortunate enough to be part of the team at Apple® that developed the first iPhone and iPad. So I guess you could say I've learned quite a bit about portable and mobile devices.

 2.18

Speaker 2

Okay, so much for the product specs. What about the sales prospects? Now, I know what you're thinking. You're thinking how can there be a market for such a niche product? So let me reassure you that we've carried out extensive market research and the figures are very, very promising. You'll find a full breakdown in your product information pack, but let me just share with you some of the most exciting results.

 2.19

Speaker 3

So that's the Orion 7. Let me tell you, this revolutionary new product is going to be huge! As we've seen, the technology behind it is absolutely cutting-edge and we've made several radical changes to the functionality

and design of the old Orion 6. This is the product that's not only going to destroy the competition – it's going to totally transform the industry!

 2.20

Speaker 4

Now, in this country we all tend to think that the unemployment situation has gotten out of control. But here's something that might surprise you. Did you know that right now, right here in the USA, there are three million unfilled jobs? Three million genuine job openings! Those are the latest figures just posted. What's more, those jobs are only being filled half as fast as in previous recessions. We don't have a job shortage, ladies and gentlemen, so much as a skills shortage! And that's where we come in …

 2.21

Speaker 5

Talking of the failure rate of start-up companies, that reminds me of the joke about the entrepreneur who goes to his bank manager and asks her: 'How do I start a small business?' 'Simple,' says the bank manager. 'Buy a big one and wait!'

 2.22

Speaker 6

Okay, so those are the key product benefits. And that was the first thing I wanted to talk to you about this morning. Now, let's see how we measure up against our main competitors. Well, in terms of overall performance, there really is no comparison. Frankly, the Zamira leaves the competition standing. And when it comes to compatibility – well, as you can see, the figures speak for themselves.

 2.23

Speaker 7

Now, the text-flow process itself is quite complex. So we've broken it down into three simpler stages. Have a look at this. This diagram shows you how text and images from the original digital source reconfigure themselves to fit the screen of your tablet or mobile. As you can see, …

 2.24

Speaker 8

You ask how Leo and I started our business. And I can tell you exactly how. Seven years ago, I was getting bored at the company I was working for and applied for another job. Now, the firm I was applying to had hired a recruitment agency to do the interviewing and guess who the interviewer was? That's right – Leo! He said: 'If you want my honest opinion, you'll be wasted at this company. Why don't you start your own business?' I said: 'But I don't know anything about starting a business!' He said: 'I do!' And that was how it all began …

2.25

A Good morning. And thanks for taking the time to talk to us. We want to talk to you about cookery. That's right, cookery. ... Did you know that cookery books are the second best-selling type of book, outselling romance novels, biographies, self-help, science-fiction ...? In fact, apart from murder mysteries, you name it, they outsell it ... Frankly, the figures are staggering! Roughly 60 million cookery books are bought a year! ... Switch on daytime TV and chances are there'll be cookery programmes on every single channel. In Britain alone, there are around 50 scheduled cookery series! ... Why is cookery such a giant industry? ... Well, we all eat. And a lot of us, it seems, would like to be able to cook. But, sadly, many of us still can't boil an egg.

B That's where we come in. TastePal is a mobile phone app that caters for the 28% of us who, according to a recent survey in the States, just can't cook. Now, TastePal doesn't try to teach you how to cook, because we know you probably don't even have the ingredients in your kitchen to make a decent meal! ... No, the idea is this ... You tell us what you do have in your kitchen cupboards and TastePal comes up with a selection of simple recipes using just those ingredients. We can't guarantee it'll be a culinary masterpiece, but it will be tasty, nutritious and easy to prepare. Plus, if you're going to the supermarket, TastePal will suggest a couple of things you could buy to make it even better!

A Here's a screenshot of the app. As you can see, the user interface couldn't be simpler – with drag-and-drop touchscreen icons for food categories and animated cartoons for how to prepare the meals. Who's our market? Students, young professionals, single people mostly – frequently male. Exactly the right market for a mobile app.

B Now, I guess you're thinking: 'But aren't there apps for this already?' And, indeed, there are – a few. But most of them are little more than digital checklists and recipe instructions – tiny text, difficult to follow. None of them uses animation. And none of them has the extra functions of TastePal. TastePal keeps a log of the meals you like and alerts you when you're running low on what you need to make them. TastePal also alerts you when you're not getting a balanced diet. And it will tell you how to estimate measures if you don't have the right equipment – which we're pretty sure you won't.

A My business partner Jim's a trained chef. And I have six years' experience in designing mobile apps, including two award-winning apps for the iPhone. We're looking for 50,000 euros to cover further development and marketing costs in return for 20% of the business. Thanks a lot.

13 BEING HEARD

2.26

Extract 1
It's a joke, really, this idea that everyone's opinion is valued. I mean, how much can you disagree with the boss? After all, she's the boss!

Extract 2
You often leave a meeting not really knowing what you're supposed to do next, what the action plan is. I usually end up phoning people afterwards to find out what we actually agreed.

Extract 3
Nobody seems to come to the meeting properly prepared. If you want a copy of the report, they don't have it with them. Need to see the figures? They'll get back to you. It's hopeless!

Extract 4
You often get several people all talking at the same time. So no one's really listening to anyone else. They're just planning what they're going to say next. It's survival of the loudest!

Extract 5
They're usually badly organized. Nobody sticks to the point. People get sidetracked all the time. It takes ages to get down to business. As they say: 'If you fail to plan, you plan to fail.'

Extract 6
You know even before you begin who's going to argue with who. The facts don't seem to matter. It's all about scoring points, looking better than your colleagues and impressing the boss.

Extract 7
I try to stop them over-running. We sometimes hold meetings without chairs. That speeds things up a lot! I've even tried showing the red card to people who won't shut up, like in football. Not popular.

Extract 8
Well, to be honest, everybody knows we don't actually decide anything in meetings. The boss already knows what he wants to do anyway!

2.27

Extract 1
A Okay. You've all had a chance to look at the quarterly sales figures.
B Yes. They're terrible.
A Agreed, but if I could just finish. We're 30% down on projections. The question is why?
C Can I just come in here? It seems to me that our marketing strategy is all wrong.
B Now, just a minute. Are you trying to say this is our fault?
C Well, what else can it be? I mean, we're offering generous discounts ...
B Look, sorry to interrupt again, but ...
C No, hear me out. We're offering very generous discounts to our biggest customers as part of our introductory offer. And sales are still slow. Something's going wrong, and I say it's the marketing.

B Well, if you ask me, the problem is the product itself.
C And what is wrong with the product? BabySlim is an innovative addition to our product line.
B Innovative, yes. But there is no market for diet baby food. I said so at the very beginning. Who's going to admit they've got a fat baby?
A You know, maybe she has a point ...

 2.28
Extract 2
A So, that's the position. The company has been officially declared bankrupt.
B Yes.
A And our chief executive officer has been arrested on charges of corruption.
B Yes.
A Of course, our company president has been on television to make a public apology.
B Of course.
A But there was nothing he could do.
B Of course not. Gentlemen, it is a black day in our company's proud history.
A Yes. A very black day. Very, very black.
C Can I just come in here?
B Please, do.
C Well, it's just a suggestion, but shouldn't we all be looking for new jobs?

2.29
Extract 3
A Now, just a minute, just a minute!
B There's no way we're going to accept this!
A Could I just ...?
B They can't make English the official company language!
A Could I just ...?
B If head office thinks we're all going to speak English from now on ...
A Could I just finish what I was saying?
B Frankly, it's bad enough that we have to speak English in these meetings.
A Please! Let me finish. No one is suggesting we can't speak our own language.
B But that is exactly what they are suggesting!
C Can I just say something?
B Go ahead.
C Well, as I understand it, this is only a proposal at this stage.
A That's precisely what I was trying to say – before I was interrupted.
B Now, hang on a second ...
C If I could just finish ... The idea is to introduce English gradually over the next two years ...
B Oh, no! Not while I'm in charge of Human Resources.
A Yes, well, that brings us on to item two on the agenda: restructuring the Human Resources department.

14 SNAIL MAIL

 2.30

1

Erm, well, where's the address? You've completely missed the address out. And what's the 'twenty-twost' of February, Rudi? You mean twenty-second. That should be 'nd', right?

2

'My dear Ms Ramalho' is a bit old-fashioned, don't you think? Sounds like a 19th-century love letter, eh? I don't think you need the 'my'. 'Dear Ms Ramalho' will do. And it's a capital 'T' for 'Thank you'. I know it's after a comma, but it's a capital.

3

So that should be: 'Thank you for your letter of ninth February.' Oh, and 'communication' has got a double 'm', Rudi! Try using the spell check.

4

What's this? 'I am such sorry'? That's 'so sorry', isn't it? Actually, I don't think you need the 'so'. Just 'I'm sorry' sounds better … Okay … 'I'm sorry you were disabled to attend our presentation'? I don't think that's right! 'Unable', I think you mean.

5

'In the mean time …' Oh, I think 'meantime' is one word, not two. Yeah, one word. Oh, what's gone wrong here? 'I enclose a copy of our last catalogue'? That should be 'latest'. The last one's the old one, not the new one.

6

Erm, 'current' is with an 'e', not an 'a' – c-u-double r-e-n-t. And it's a price list, Rudi, not a prize list. With a 'c' not a 'z'. We're not running a lottery!

7

'Information' is singular. You don't need the 's'. So, 'If you would like further information … uh huh … please don't hesitate but contact me again.' That should be 'don't hesitate to contact me again'.

8

Right, nearly finished. 'I look forwards to hearing from you.' That doesn't sound right to me. Wait a minute, it's 'I look forward' not 'forwards'. Yeah. And, er, 'Yours fatefully'. That's 'faithfully' not 'fatefully' – f-a-i-t-h, faithfully … Actually, it isn't, is it? It's 'Yours sincerely' because you've written the woman's name. I'd just put 'Best wishes' if I were you. It's simpler. Er, Rudi, maybe you'd better leave the letter writing to me in future.

15 SOLVING PROBLEMS

 2.31

The first suggestion the company got was a joke really, but it won the $100 bonus. The suggestion was that the bonus should be reduced to $50.

 2.32

Problem 1

After many expensive and unsuccessful attempts to promote the restaurant with posters and T-shirts, the owner, Martha Sanchez, finally came up with a winner. She offered free lunches for life to anyone who agreed to have the name and logo of the restaurant tattooed on a visible part of their body. To date, 50 people have become walking advertisements.

 2.33

Problem 2

A lot of time was wasted on electronic devices that could authenticate signatures and on educating customers of the bank to look after their cheque books. Someone suggested using passwords, but people always forgot them. Finally, the bank manager had a different idea – why not simply put a photograph of the account holder on each cheque?

 2.34

Problem 3

The company quickly realized that there is no way of making industrial cleaners exciting. Special offers and competitions had limited success. So they tried something silly instead. The company's name was changed to the New Cow Corporation. All products were labelled with the New Cow logo, the hotline was changed to 800-BURGERS and its company address to 1 Beef Avenue. Did it work? Well, growing at a rate of 10% a year, New Cow currently employs more than 300 people and enjoys sales of over $80 million.

 2.35

Extract 1

A Okay, we both know the problem. Basically, we can't get retail stores to stock our new product. They say it's too expensive. So the question is: how do we get access to the customer?

B What if we offered it on a sale or return basis?

A No, I don't think so. If we did that, we'd just create cash flow problems for ourselves.

B Hmm. Well, another option would be to sell it direct online.

A It's a possibility, but I really don't think we know enough about e-commerce to take the chance. And if we start bringing in Internet specialists, we could end up spending a fortune.

B Of course, we wouldn't have this problem if we'd priced the product more sensibly in the first place.

 2.36

Extract 2

A Right, our objective for this meeting is to think of ways we can get the supplies we need. As I'm sure you've all heard, our sole supplier is about to go bankrupt!

B Hopefully, it won't come to that, but if it does, we'll certainly have to act fast. Suppose we bought the company out?

A What, and took on all their debts? I don't think so!

C Alternatively, we could just manufacture our own components. I've spoken to our technical department. They say they can do it.

A Yes, but do you have any idea how long it would take to get an in-house production facility operational?

C Well, what choice do we have? Unless we do something, we'll be out of business within six months!

B What I want to know is why our suppliers didn't tell us they were in trouble. If we'd known this was going to happen, we could have had our own production plant up and running by now.

 2.37

Extract 3

A What I want to know is: how do we maintain our profit margins with labour costs rising the way they are?

B Well, it seems obvious, but how about raising prices? I mean, even with a 2% price rise, we'd still be very competitive.

C No, I'm afraid that's not an option. This is an extremely price-sensitive market.

B I know that, but what else do you suggest? If we don't cover our costs, we'll soon be running at a loss.

A Now, let's not panic. The answer could be to shift production to somewhere like South-East Asia. We've talked about it before.

C And close down our plants here? Wouldn't it be easier if we just tried to renegotiate with the unions – get them to accept a lower pay offer?

A If we'd been able to get the unions to accept a lower pay offer, John, we wouldn't be considering outsourcing to Asia.

 2.38

Extract 4

A Now, what on earth are we going to do about all this unsold stock piling up in the warehouses? If we don't move it pretty soon, there'll be no space for new product. And we'll be left with a lot of old product nobody wants! So, ideas? Anybody?

B Well, in my opinion, our product development cycle is way too short. Why don't we delay the new product launch to give us time to sell existing stock?

A This is a technology-driven business, Robert. If we don't continually upgrade our product, the competition will.

B And if we didn't all keep upgrading every three months, we wouldn't have this problem!

C Wait a minute, wait a minute! This old stock, couldn't we just sell it off at a discount to create space for the new stuff? Say, 15%?

A I'd rather not start talking about a 15% discount at this stage, if you don't mind.

C Well, if we'd discounted it sooner, we wouldn't have had to be so generous now.

2.39
Extract 5

A Now, I've brought you all here to discuss a very serious matter. Someone in the company – we don't know who – is passing on information to the competition. I'm sure I don't need to tell you that in a business like ours it is essential we protect our competitive advantage. So, … what do we do?

B Are you telling us we have a spy amongst us?

A If I wasn't, Simon, we wouldn't be here now.

C Well, let's think. We already restrict access to important files, but what about encrypting our most confidential information as well? It's common practice in most companies these days. I'm surprised we don't do it already.

A I'm afraid it's more serious than just downloading data off the company server. This person seems to be recording meetings and private conversations as well.

B You're joking!

A (coughs)

B Erm, sorry, it's just that I can hardly believe this.

C Well, maybe it's time we involved the police. Clearly a crime is being committed here.

A It most certainly is. And I would have called the police in already if I'd thought it would do any good. But, I don't want our spy, whoever it is, to know we know. So, unless we have to, I'd rather see if we can deal with this ourselves first. And who knows? Perhaps we can even turn the situation to our advantage …

2.40
Sony® Ericsson

Whilst on a business trip to New York back in 2001 you find yourself walking down the famous Fifth Avenue when you are approached by an attractive young woman. 'Excuse me,' she says. 'Would you mind taking a picture of me and my boyfriend?' 'Sure,' you reply. 'Thanks a lot!' she smiles and hands you what looks like an ordinary mobile phone, although you notice the screen is full colour. 'But this is a phone, isn't it?' you ask. 'Yeah,' she laughs, 'and a camera! You just press this key here. See? Simple.' You take a couple of shots and remark that it's the first camera-phone you've ever seen. 'Cool, isn't it?' says the boyfriend. 'Latest Sony Ericsson.' You're impressed and decide to check it out next time you're passing a mobile phone store. The rest, of course, is history and today cameras come as standard on every single smartphone.

But what you didn't know at the time is that those two young tourists were actually actors and were being paid to approach passers-by like yourself. They were part of a special campaign by Sony Ericsson. Called 'buzz marketing', the idea was to create publicity for the phone by introducing people to the product and, basically, getting them to want it! In fact, for this particular campaign Sony Ericsson hired 60 actors to do this every day in ten different cities all over the United States.

Buzz, or word of mouth, has now been proven to be the most effective form of marketing in an age when there's so much conventional advertising we've largely learned to ignore it. And, while some say buzz marketing raises ethical questions, the companies who use it stress that the strategy is not to sell but simply to inform. Ethical or not, it's a technique now employed by many of the world's most famous brands. Where product placement places products in movies, buzz marketing places products in your life! And if you think you yourself have never met a buzz marketer – in the street, on the train, at the coffee bar – well, that's the whole point!

2.41
Tata Steel

Tata Steel's managing director, Dr Irani, quickly realized that, whereas in the West there is more provision for those who are made redundant in the form of social security, he had a special responsibility to his own employees. So, he first spent almost a year convincing his people of the need for rightsizing the company.

Then, working in partnership with the workers' union, he developed what he called 'the early separation scheme' or ESS. Within the terms of the ESS, those under 40 years of age who took voluntary early retirement would get their full salary for the rest of their working lives. And older workers would get 20–50% more than their full salary! Furthermore, if they died before reaching retirement age, their families would be paid their salaries for the remaining years. Irani's generosity to his employees looked like madness. And when an Indian industrialist heard about the scheme, he sent him a note saying: 'You either have too much money or not enough brains!'

But Irani knew exactly what he was doing. For the amount the workers who voluntarily left the company got paid remained constant. Had they stayed, it would have gone up annually. And by saving on the extra payroll tax and pension plan contributions, Tata Steel's labour costs declined immediately. Tata ran 40 ESS schemes over the next decade. As a result, by 2004 the workforce had been reduced by 30,000.

But Irani went even further. Instead of offering guaranteed jobs to the children of loyal employees, he began to offer them training at the newly set-up RD Tata Technical Institution. If he could not offer the next generation employment, he could at least increase their employability. And for those who left the company, there was free financial advice and career counselling. Tata is now a textbook case of humane human resource management and a model corporate culture. And this, together with a one billion dollar investment, has made Tata Steel the highly efficient, globally competitive firm it is today.

16 COLLABORATION

2.42

A Okay, look, the problem is this: we simply can't move forward on this project because we never get any answers from the client! I mean, whenever we ask KNP for their input on anything, they just sit on it for weeks without getting back to us. So we fall further and further behind schedule. Frankly, Rolf, it's driving me mad!

B Hmm. Okay, well, thanks, Richard. It sounds like we a have pretty serious communication problem here. Does anyone have any suggestions? Yes, Elaine?

C Erm, it's just a thought, Richard, but maybe you're trying to involve KNP too much.

A How do you mean?

C Well, I mean, you're agreeing objectives with them at the planning meetings, right?

A Yes, of course.

C And then you're asking them for further input between meetings as well?

A Erm, well, it's a complicated project, Elaine. And new issues keep coming up.

C I understand that. But here's an idea. Instead of waiting for them to get back to you on every issue, why not simply go ahead with what you think is best based on what you agreed with them at the meeting and then just ask them to confirm that decision?

A Well, it's an idea. But I still think we need to keep them closely involved in the decision-making process at every stage.

B Richard, I think we've already established that trying to keep the client involved is not working too well. Elaine, I really like your idea of just asking for the final go-ahead on each decision. What I especially like about it is that instead of having to come up with fresh ideas of their own, KNP just has to say yes or no. That's going to make things a whole lot easier! And it would certainly solve the problem of getting them to respond more quickly too.

A What makes you think that?

B Well, they'll know that there's a time constraint on their reply because we're already going ahead with whatever it is. If they still like what we're doing, no problem. But if they don't, well, they'd better get back to us right away or we'll be heading in the wrong direction.

A Hmm, I'm not so sure.

B Well, I like this idea of just asking for the green light at each stage. And if we did that, we could also give them more progress reports: as agreed at our last meeting, we've done this and this; and now we're going to do this – is that still okay with you? From what you say, Richard, it sounds like KNP are not as engaged in this project as we are. Maybe we need to keep them in the picture more. Perhaps another thing we could do is give the decisions we want them to approve a priority rating, so they pay attention to the really important ones. And, Elaine, if we combined your idea with Kevin's idea of setting up a client extranet, there'd be a single website they could always go to to find out what's been done, what's next and what they need to okay. And they could do that with the click of a button.

C Good idea.

B Now, the only thing is: I'm not sure if we could ask for approval on every decision we take. As Richard says, some of these decisions do require client involvement before we take action. If we go ahead and they're not happy, it could waste a lot of time ... and resources. And I'm also a bit worried about KNP feeling we're taking control away from them. Elaine, how do you think we could manage that?

17 EATING OUT

2.43

A So, here we are. Hmm, it's a bit more crowded than usual.

B Nice place. Do you come here often?

A Mm, yes. It's very convenient and the food is excellent, but it looks like we may have to wait for a table today. This place is getting more and more popular ...

A Our table's going to be a couple of minutes, I'm afraid, but we can sit at the bar if you like.

B Oh, okay. I see what you mean about this place being popular.

A Well, we shouldn't have to wait too long. Now, what would you like to drink?

B Oh, just a fruit juice or something for me.

A Okay ... er, excuse me.

B ... So, I'm not really sure how I ended up in financial services.

A Me neither. I studied law at university, but I never wanted to work for a bank. Right. I'll just see if our table's ready.

A Okay, this is their standard menu ...

B Mm. It all looks very good.

A ... and those are the specials. Let me know if you want me to explain anything.

B Thanks. I may need some help. So, what do you recommend?

A Well, they do a great lasagne. But perhaps you'd like something more typically English.

B Mm, yes. And perhaps something a bit lighter.

A Is there anything you don't eat?

B No, not really. I'm allergic to mussels, that's all.

A Oh, that's a pity. The mussels are a speciality. But, erm, you could try the lamb. That's very good here. It comes with potatoes and a salad.

B Mm. That sounds nice. But isn't it a little too heavy?

A Well, you could have it without the potatoes. Or perhaps you'd prefer the cod ...

A Shall we order a bottle of the house red?

B Well, maybe just a glass for me. Could we order some mineral water, too?

A Sure. Sparkling or still?

B This is absolutely delicious. How's yours?

A Not bad at all. More to drink?

B Not for me, thanks. So, how do you think the meeting went this morning?

A Quite well, I think. Of course, we still have a lot of things to discuss ...

A Now, how about a dessert?

B Oh, better not. I'm on a diet.

A Me too. But it doesn't stop me. How about poached peaches? That's not too fattening.

B Right. I'll get this.

A Oh, no, you don't. I'm paying.

B But you paid yesterday, James. It's my turn.

A No, no, I insist. You're my guest.

2.44

Conversation 1

A ... So, Hiro. What's this fugu? It's a kind of fish, isn't it?

B Ah, yes. Er, it's rather unusual, er ...

A Traditional Japanese dish, eh?

B Yes, but, er, it's a little exotic. You may not like it.

A No, no, I like trying new things. Fugu sounds good to me.

B I think you'd prefer something else. Fugu can be ... a little dangerous.

A A bit spicy, you mean? Don't worry about that. I love spicy food.

B No, not spicy. It's, er ... It's poisonous.

A It's what?

B Poisonous.

A Poisonous?

B If it isn't cooked the right way, yes.

A Well, I ...

B Some people love it. And this is a very good restaurant, but 30 people die every year from bad fugu. Really, I think you should try something else.

A Yeah, well, sure. I think you're probably right. Maybe I'll have the tempura instead.

B Yes, tempura. Much better idea, David.

2.45

Conversation 2

A Now, Hans, we thought you might like to try the local speciality.

B Ah, yes?

C Yes, it looks a little strange at first. But you'll love it. You like shellfish, don't you?

B Well, I like prawns. And the mussels we had the other day were excellent.

C Then you'll really enjoy this. It's squid.

B Squid?

C Yes, like octopus, you know?

B Yes, I know what squid is.

C Ah, but this is not just squid.

B No?

A No, this is something really special. It's served in its own ink – as a sauce.

B It's served in ink?

A Yes, you know, the black liquid that squid make.

B Erm, yes. It sounds a bit ... Actually, I hope you don't mind, but could I just have something a bit simpler?

C Well, if you're sure you don't want to try it. It's really very good.

B Yes, I'm sure it is, but, erm ...

2.46

Conversation 3

A Now, is there anything you don't eat, Louise?

B Well, I am on a special diet at the moment, Jean-Claude. I hope that's not a problem.

A No, of course not. This is a very good menu. I am sure we can find something you'll like. What can't you eat?

B Well, I can't eat anything fried. In fact, no fat at all. Nothing made of pastry or cooked in oil. No red meat, of course. Not too much sugar. I can eat white fish but only boiled.

A What about the chicken here? That's very plain and simple.

B Is there a sauce on it?

A Yes, it's a delicious cream and wine sauce.

B No cream, I'm afraid.

A No cream?

B Or wine. I'm not allowed any alcohol at all. Not that I drink much anyway.

A I see. Well, I'm sure they'll serve it without the sauce.

B Hmm. How's the chicken cooked?

A Er, it's roast chicken, I imagine.

B I can only have grilled.

A I'll ask them to grill it.

B Hmm. I'd prefer fish really.

A Well, how about the trout?

B Is it boiled?

A No, baked in the oven.

B Hmm. I may not like it. What does it come with?

A It comes with potatoes and fresh vegetables.

B Oh, I can't eat potatoes. All that carbohydrate! Vegetables are okay. But no beans and ...

18 TELECOMMUNICATIONS

2.47

Extract 1

A Excuse me, Mr Kessler. Mr Gorsky has joined you.

B Ah, thank you. Hello, Jarek.

C Hello, Peter. Sorry, I had a bit of a problem getting through.

B That's okay. We're just waiting for Sulaiman. He's emailed to say he's gone down to Port Rashid to see what's happening with our deliveries and he'll phone in on his mobile from there. So, let's go ahead and start. Welcome to the meeting, everyone. Did you all get a copy of the agenda?

Good ... Okay, before we start, let me introduce Jarek Gorsky. Jarek is the new chief engineer at our sister company in Warsaw. I've asked him to join us today because I'd like his input on how we handle some of these changes to specifications the client is asking for.

C Hello, gentlemen.

B All right, then, let's get started. As you can see, we have several objectives today. The main one, of course, is to agree an action plan that will get us back on schedule within the next three months. I spoke to Mr Al-Fulani yesterday and explained the situation. He's prepared to give us another few weeks to sort out our present difficulties and I have assured him that that is what we will do. I'm sure I don't need to remind you what's at stake here. Now, I'd like to be finished by 10.30, if that's okay, so can we keep our inputs quite short? And let's also try to keep interruptions to a minimum ...

D Er, Peter. Sorry to interrupt, but I suggest we skip item one on our agenda until we hear from Sulaiman.

B Yes, I think that would be best. Let's move straight on to item two ...

2.48

Extract 2

D So just to recap on what we've said. There are some problems we did not foresee between our two main work teams. There's been a language barrier. Our German engineers and Polish workers are speaking mostly German. The Pakistanis are more comfortable in English and are also having some difficulty with our work patterns, which are different from what they are used to in Dubai.

B Thanks, Ernst ... Okay, so, are we all agreed that we need some onsite training to resolve this problem? Can I hear your views, please?

D I agree.

E Agreed.

F Yes, I agree.

C Yeah, I think so.

B Fine.

A Excuse me, Mr Al-Fahim has joined you.

B Ah, thank you. Hello, Sulaiman. How are things at the port?

G Hello, Peter. Not good, I'm afraid. The bad weather here has completely closed the seaports at Jebel Ali and Port Rashid. Nothing is either going in or coming out at the moment. I have my Pakistani team standing doing nothing while we wait for 800 window units and until those are fitted, we can't complete the wiring and plumbing in the hotel complexes.

B Don't we have backup supplies in place for a situation like this, Sulaiman?

G I'm sorry, Peter. This weather is really most unseasonal and we simply could not be fully prepared for it.

B Sorry, Sulaiman, I can't hear you very well.

G Oh, ... Is that better?

B Much better, thanks.

E Er, could I just come in here?

B Karim?

E Yes, it's just that I want to say this is not only a cultural and supply problem. We have had so many changes to specifications – changes almost every week now. The client just keeps changing his mind. And this is making life very difficult for us all.

F Karim's right. We've had to keep revising our work schemes to cope with all the changes.

B Yes, it's a good point. I'll certainly bring all these changes to the attention of Mr Al-Fulani when I next speak to him. They're not in our original contract ... Right, we're running short of time. I think what's needed here with all these delays and changes of plan is a fresh look at this entire project on a logistical level. Ernst, Jarek, can I leave that with you?

C Okay, Peter.

D Yes, sure.

B And keep me posted. I'm beginning to think we may even need to renegotiate our contract with Mr Al-Fulani. Okay, I think we've covered everything for now. Let's schedule another meeting for next week. I'll email you the details. We'll have to finish there. Thanks everybody.

19 NEGOTIATING

2.49

Speaker 1

Spend as much time as possible at the outset getting to know exactly who you're dealing with. Inexperienced negotiators tend to go straight in there and start bargaining. That may be okay for a small, one-off deal, but it's no way to build a long-term business relationship. So create rapport first. This could take several hours or several months! When you're ready to start negotiations, make sure you agree on a procedure before you begin. And while they're setting out their proposals, don't interrupt. Listen. And take notes. Then have lunch! Don't be tempted to make your counter-proposals and enter the bargaining phase until after a good, long break. You'd be surprised how much you can find out over a decent meal. Bargaining, of course, is the critical phase, but it can be surprisingly quick. If it isn't, break off and fix another meeting. Don't try to run marathons. When you do finally get to the agreement stage, agree the general terms, but leave the details to the lawyers – that's what they're there for. Close on a high note and remember to celebrate!

2.50

Speaker 2

Prepare thoroughly. If you don't, you won't know whether to accept an offer and may end up actually arguing with your own side, which is suicide in a negotiation. So, make sure you establish all the points you're going to negotiate and have a clear idea of your opening, target and walk-away position on each. Your opening position, or OP, is your initial offer – on price or whatever. Your TP, your target position, is what you're realistically aiming for. And your WAP, or walk-away position, is the point at which you walk away from the negotiating table. Always be prepared to do that. Know what your fallback position, or FBP, is – what you'll do if you don't reach an agreement. Some people call this your BATNA, your best alternative to a negotiated agreement. You nearly always have a BATNA, however undesirable. But if you really haven't got one, you'd better be good at bluffing or you're going to lose big time!

2.51

Speaker 3

Ideally, a successful negotiation is a kind of joint problem-solving meeting, where we identify each other's interests, wants and needs, and then explore the different ways we could satisfy those. I say 'ideally', because it hardly ever is like that. Win–win negotiation is a great idea, but most people have a simple 'I win – you lose' mentality. So what do you do with the person who simply won't listen, who keeps interrupting, who becomes aggressive, who makes last-minute demands, who won't make a decision? I must have read dozens of books on negotiation tactics. The problem is, so has everybody else. So they don't really work. My only advice is: don't get personal – ever; don't agree to anything until you've discussed everything; don't make any concessions without asking for something in return; ask lots and lots of questions; and don't give in to pressure. Remember, if the answer must be now, the answer must be 'No'.

2.52

Extract 1

A Now, the next thing is: we'd like to see some movement on price. We had a rather lower figure in mind than the one you've quoted us.

B Okay. What sort of figure are we talking about?

A Well, something nearer to seven million euros.

B Now, let me just check I understand you correctly. You're offering us seven million for the whole construction contract?

A That's right.

B And what sort of timescale are we looking at?

A We would expect you to complete the project within 18 months.

B How flexible can you be on that?

A Not very. We were hoping to have the plant fully operational by next September.

B I see ... Can I make a suggestion?

A Go ahead.

B Well, would you be willing to accept a compromise?

A That depends on what kind of compromise you had in mind.

B Well, what if we offered you an alternative? What if you paid us two million in advance, two million mid-contract and another 3.2 million on completion?

A On schedule?

B On schedule. Eighteen months ... Or thereabouts.

A Hmm. So that's 7.2 million euros in all.

B Correct.

A And what if you run over schedule?

B Then there would be a penalty. Let's say 25 thousand euros for each week we ran over schedule.

A Hmm. I'm afraid this doesn't really solve our problem. What we need from you is a guarantee that the project will be finished on time.

B And, as you know, I can only give you that guarantee by bringing in more outside contractors.

A Which ups the price to your original bid of 7.8 million euros?

B Yes.

A At the moment, we do not see this as a viable option.

B Seven point eight million really is my best price on that.

A Well, in that case, I think that's about as far as we can go at this stage.

B Now, wait a minute. We're not going to lose this deal for 600,000 euros, surely ... How about this ...?

 2.53

Extract 2

A Right. We seem to be nearing agreement. But, erm, before we finalize things, can we just run through the main points once more?

B Sure.

A Now, you'll provide a series of eight two-day in-company seminars for our telesales team over the next six months. You yourself will be conducting most of the sessions with two other trainers, using materials especially designed to meet our specific needs and approved by us four weeks prior to the first seminar?

B That's correct.

A And, er, let me get this quite clear, each seminar is to have no more than 16 participants, is that right?

B Yes. We find the seminars are much more effective with smaller groups.

A Hmm, I suppose you're right. It does also mean running more courses, but okay. Now, since we are booking eight seminars, we'll obviously expect a reasonable discount on your usual fee.

B Erm, yes. Could you give us an idea of what you're looking for? Because with this particular course ...

A I would have thought a 15% discount was fair. So that's eight times £3,000 is £24,000 minus 15%, which is, erm, £3,600. And that would come to a total fee of £20,400. And you'd invoice us on completion of the whole series of seminars. Are these terms broadly acceptable?

B Er, well, just a moment. We haven't actually agreed on the discount yet. As I was about to say, with this particular course there wouldn't normally be such a large discount. We offer 10% on five or more of our standard seminars, but this is a specially designed course for your personnel only. Obviously, we have to cover our development costs.

A I should think you could cover them quite easily on just over £20,000, Mr Smart. No, my mind's made up. Fifteen per cent – take it or leave it.

B Well, now, I'm afraid we could only accept this on one condition.

A Which is?

B Erm, we'd want a 25% non-refundable deposit in advance ...

A Done.

B You see, ... erm, sorry?

A Twenty-five per cent deposit – no problem. I'll get accounts to make you out a cheque for, let me see, £5,100 ... Well, that's it. I think we've earned ourselves a drink!

B Erm, well, yes. Nice doing business with you.

 2.54

Right, well, when a team wants to sell a player, they agree a transfer fee. That's the price other clubs have to pay them if they want to buy that player. These vary a lot. For a young, talented player with lots of potential, the transfer fee could be around five to ten million pounds. Obviously, for a real international star, it could be, say, 20 or 30 million. Real Madrid paid Manchester United 80 million for Cristiano Ronaldo, but he's an exception! Now, for a team like Manchester United, that 20 million equals a fifth of the club's annual profit. So buying a player is a big decision.

Okay, so, that's what the player's club gets, but what about the player? Well, every professional player has a FIFA™ agent. FIFA's the governing body for world football. And the agent's job is to negotiate terms with clubs who want to buy the player. The average weekly wage at Manchester United is about £50,000, or two and a half million a year. Wayne Rooney gets £250,000 a week, but, again, he's an exception!

Okay, contracts. Players' contracts can be for two, three or five years, and if a player wants to leave before his contract expires, he has to pay a penalty. But they usually work something out. There's no point having players who don't want to play for you anymore.

So, those are the main points to negotiate in a transfer. Other things might include a percentage of merchandising profits – from sales of shirts, caps, boots with the player's name on them. And foreign players will often want a house and car provided as well, since they may only stay a few years. Some ask for free flights home to visit family. Oh, by the way, all those figures I've mentioned are net, not gross. Footballers don't like to worry about how much tax they're going to have to pay!

20 ASSERTIVENESS

 2.55

Version 1

A Oh, Lars, there you are! Do you have a minute?

B Er, sure.

A Only, I need you to work a little late tonight. I have to get this presentation finished and I need you to help me with some of the slides. Shouldn't take more than a couple of hours. Three at the most.

B Oh, I, er ...

A Problem?

B Er, no. It's just that I was planning ...

A Great. Well, I'll show you what I've done so far. I've indicated where I need you to drop in some graphics ...

B Actually, Carmen, sorry, but would it be okay if we did this tomorrow instead?

A What? But I need it for tomorrow afternoon! I don't want to leave everything till the last minute!

B It's kind of 'last minute' already!

A What's that?

B Oh, nothing. But, erm, the thing is, I'd invited a few friends over this evening – sort of a house-warming party for my new flat, you know. They're coming at seven, and I have to prepare the food and everything.

A At seven! You eat so early in this country! Well, look, Lars, don't you think you should put your job before partying with your friends? You know how it is here. We work to a tight schedule. And it's not like you aren't getting paid overtime for this. Call your friends and tell them to come later. Right now, you have to help me with this presentation! Okay?

B Erm, yes, I know, but, look, sorry, but some of my friends have kids. And it's a workday tomorrow. They can't really stay that late ...

A Lars, hold it right there! Look, I told you when you took this job there'd be a lot of extra work. You said you could handle that. So handle it! Now, come on! I have to get this done by eight. I've got plans myself.

B But ...

A No buts, Lars. Now, call your friends and let's get on.

B Okay, Carmen. Anything you say.

2.56

Version 2

A Oh, hi Lars. Listen, could I ask you a favour?

B Uh-oh, I don't like the sound of this! Let me guess. You want me to work late again?

A Would you? The thing is, I have this presentation to finish for tomorrow and I need someone who's good at producing graphics to help me out with some of the slides. Frankly, you're so much better at this than anyone else in the office, I'd really like it to be you. It shouldn't take more than two or three hours. What do you say? Will you do it?

B Look, Carmen, you're always doing this to me!

A Always doing what?

B Dumping extra work on me at the last minute! Why don't you ever give me any notice when you want me to do overtime?

A Lars, I do usually give you notice. But this presentation just came up. I'm covering for someone who's away on sick leave. And I really need your help.

B Oh, well, that's different then! No problem!

A So you'll do it?

B No, Carmen, I can't. I've got some people coming round this evening. It's my house-warming party, as a matter of fact.

A Oh, really? And you didn't invite me?

B You mean you would have come?

A Of course not. I'm far too busy, Lars – battling on here on my own! It would have been nice to be invited, though.

B Okay, you're invited!

A Sorry, I can't come. I've got this presentation to get ready. And now my top team member's decided to put his social life first, it's going to take all night!

B Look …

A Oh, don't worry about it, Lars. I'll ask Joanna instead.

B The new kid?

A The new kid, yes. She's very competent, actually. And very keen to help out. The way you used to be, Lars! In fact, I'm thinking of sending her to the Rio conference with Angelique.

B Hey, I thought I was supposed to be going to Rio with Angelique!

A Well, that was before you lost your can-do attitude, Lars. I need someone in Rio who'll be an asset not a liability!

B Okay, okay. I'll give you an hour, all right? Let's see how much of your presentation we can get done by seven. Then I have to go!

A Thanks a million, Lars! I owe you one!

 2.57

Version 3

A Ah, Lars. Can you spare me a moment? I've got a favour to ask you.

B Sure.

A It's about this presentation I have to get ready for tomorrow's meeting.

B Oh, yes?

A Yes, I realize it's rather short notice, but could you possibly stay on for a couple of hours to help me out with some of the slides? I'd really appreciate it. It's just the graphics I need help with, actually, I've got the rest of it pretty much covered.

B Ah, now that could be a bit difficult, Carmen. You see I have some friends coming round this evening.

A Oh, really?

B Yes, it's my house-warming party, actually. Got a few friends coming over to celebrate, you know. Normally, I'd be happy to help out, but tonight I can't.

A Of course, your new flat! I forgot. Congratulations!

B Thanks. It's nice to have my own place at last!

A Of course. Well, now, I appreciate that you've got plans. And I didn't know until today I was even doing this presentation. But there we are. So Lars, I'd really like you to help me out – even if it's just for an hour. You know how important this presentation is.

B I understand that, yes. But I have these guests coming at seven. Before that I have to cook and get things ready. So you see I just can't help you this evening.

A It sounds like you have a busy evening ahead! Okay, I understand this is very inconvenient for you. I'm not happy about it myself, to be honest. It's my evening gone too. And I would prefer it if you were able to help me out. You're a lot better at designing graphics than I am, so that would save a lot of time.

B I really can't help you this evening, Carmen. It would be unfair to cancel my party now at the last minute with some of my guests probably already on their way over.

A This is a problem, isn't it? Naturally, I'm disappointed that you can't at least postpone your party for an hour or two. I don't often ask you to do overtime. And I'd really like your input on this slideshow.

B I could look at it first thing in the morning if that's any help. But tonight I can't.

A Okay, Lars, well, I'd better find someone else to give me a hand this time, then. Maybe Joanna can spare me some time.

B Yes, Joanna's really good with graphics. I'll ask her if you like. And, look, my party shouldn't go on too late. A lot of my guests have kids and it's a workday tomorrow. If you email some of the data over to me, I'll take a look at it

before I go to bed. Then we should be able to finish it off really quickly in the morning. How about that?

A Yes, that would certainly be some help. I'll do that.

B And I guess we could both come in half an hour early in the morning to give ourselves a bit more time.

A Good idea. Thanks, Lars. I'm glad we managed to sort this out. Enjoy your party! See you in the morning.

Macmillan Education
4 Crinan Street
London N1 9XW
A division of Macmillan Publishers Limited
Companies and representatives throughout the world

ISBN 978-0-230-45520-7

Designed by emc design limited
Cover design by emc design limited
Cover illustration/photograph by Getty Images/E+
Picture research by Sally Cole

The publishers would like to thank the following people, schools and institutions for their help in developing this third edition: Pat Pledger, Pledger Business English Training, Hamburg; Louise Bulloch, Intercom Language Services, Hamburg; Elbie Picker and David Virta, Hamburg; William Fern, KERN AG IKL Business Language Training & Co. KG, Frankfurt; Belén del Valle, ELOQUIA, Frankfurt; Katrin Wolf, Carl Duisberg Centren, Cologne; Andrina Rout, Fokus Sprachen und Seminare, Stuttgart; Gerdi Serrer, ILIC, Paris; Sylvia Renaudon, Transfer, Paris; John Fayssoux; Kathryn Booth-Aïdah, Araxi Formations Langues, Paris; Fiona Delaney and Allison Dupuis, Formalangues, Paris; Francesca Pallot and Susan Stevenson, Anglesey Language Services, Chatou, France; Paul Bellchambers, Business and Technical Languages (BTL), Paris; Louise Raven, marcus evans Linguarama, Stratford-upon-Avon.

Many thanks also to all the teachers around the world who took the time to complete our *In Company* online questionnaire and who have contributed to the development of the *In Company* series.

The authors and publishers would like to thank the following for permission to reproduce their photographs:

Photo acknowledgements
Adidas.com p21(tl); **Alamy**/Ace Stock Ltd p8, Alamy/Amana Images inc p47(br), Alamy/J.Belanger p123(2), Alamy/Colinspics p33(tl), Alamy/T. Gartside London p31, Alamy/JL Images p32(t), Alamy/C.Pondy p87, Alamy/Radius Images p37, Alamy/E.Rooney p33(tr), Alamy/tetra images p133(ml), Alamy/P.Titmuss p33(bl), Alamy/Trekand shoot p33(bm), Alamy/Zoo Imaging Photography p33(cl); **Andertoons**/M.Anderson p74(t); **Brand X Pictures** p16(tl); **Cartoonstock**/J. di Chiarro p98(tr), Cartoonstock/M.Shapiro p50(tr), Cartoonstock/J.Hawkins p26(tr), Cartoonstock/V.Shirvanian p122(tr); **Corbis**/Blend Images pp17(t), 47(bl), 74(b), Corbis/M.Barbour/Demotix p23, Corbis/J.Doberman p123(l), Corbis/F.Frei pp2, 6, Corbis/R.Gomez p47(tl), Corbis/T.Graham p102, Corbis/T.Grill p30(cr), Corbis/Hero Images p44, Corbis/Hiya Images p99,

Corbis/R.Kaufman p85, Corbis/S.Marcus p78, Corbis/M.Mawson p32(b), Corbis/Ocean pp9(bl), 91, Corbis/Sullivan p47(tr), Corbis/Sygma p46, Corbis/M.Taner p33(c), Corbis/C.Liewig/Tempsport p119(c), Corbis/K. Tiedge p60, Corbis/B.Vogel p57, Corbis/Wavebreak Media Ltd p17(c); **FLPA**/K. Knipser/Imagebroker p133(bl); **Getty Images**/AFP p67, Getty/ All Canada Photos p123(4), Getty/Blend Images p26(bl), Getty/F1online p119(l), Getty/Flickr p22, Getty/Gallo Images p34, Getty/Hemis.fr p105, Getty/Iconica p27, Getty/Image Bank p139, Getty/Johner Images p51, Getty/Lonely Planet pp2, 6, 7, 115, Getty/Look p30(bc), Getty/Manchester United p119(r), Getty/Photoalto p122(bl), Getty/Photodisc p117, Getty/ Riser pp17(b), 75, 92, Getty/Stockbyte p56(tcl), Getty/Stockfood Creative p103, Getty/Stone pp54, 94, 108(l), 108(r), Getty Tao Images p133(tl), Getty/Taxi p39, Getty/UpperCut Images p56(bcl); **Guy Kawasaki/ Alltop.com** p68; **Photodisc**/Getty p56(bcr); **Plainpicture**/Cultura p116, Plainpicture/Erickson pp13, 16(br), 80, Plainpicture/H.Hoogte/I.Loonen p98(bl), Plainpicture/K.Synnatzschke pp14, 38; **Puma.com** p21(cl); **Sony Mobile Communications** p95; **Superstock**/Blend Images pp9(tr), 112, Superstock/L.Le Bon p123(3), Superstock/Corbis p40. Superstock/Cultura Ltd p129, Superstock/Eyecandy Images p30(br), Superstock/Fotosearch p50(bl), Superstock/Glow Images p30(bl), Superstock/Hemis.fr pp62, 63, Superstock/Image Source pp33(br), 81, 109, Superstock/A.Hare/Loop Images p33(tm), Superstock/Minden Pictures p56(tcr).

Commissioned photographs by Paul Bricknell p28; Nick Miners pp52, 53, 76, 77, 100, 101, 124, 125.

The author and publishers are grateful for permission to reprint the following copyright material:

Bruce Tulgan has given approval for Macmillan Education to use material from 'Financial Times Guide to Business Travel; Material from 'E-writing' by Dianna Booher, copyright © Dianna Booher 2001, used with permission, reprinted courtesy of Booher consultants, www.booher. com; Material used from www.ecogeek.com; Material from website www. firstdirect.com, reprinted by permission of First Direct; Geert Hofstede, Gert Jan Hofstede, Michael Minkov, 'Cultures and Organizations, Software of the Mind', Third Revised Edition, McGraw Hill 2010, ISBN: 0-07-166418-1. © Geert Hofstede B.V. quoted with permission; Material from 'Make Meaning in Your Company' by Guy Kawasaki, dated 20.10.04, copyright © Guy Kawasaki 2004, reprinted with approval; Material from 'The NY-LON Life' by Michelle Jana Chan, dated 13.11.00, copyright © Michelle Jana Chan 2000, reprinted with approval; Material from 'Riding the Waves of Culture' by Fons Trompenaars and Charles Hampden-Turner, copyright © Nicholas Brealey Publishing 1993 and The McGraw-Hill Companies Inc., reprinted with approval; Material from 'The Complete Idiot's Guide to Winning Through Negotiation' by John Ilich, copyright © John Ilich 1999, published by Alpha Books, reprinted by permission of the publisher; Extract from 'Getting Past No: Negotiating with Difficult People' by William Ury, published by Random House Business Books, 1991, reprinted by permission of The Random House Group Limited & The Sagalyn Literary Agency.

Printed and bound in Thailand

2018 2017 2016 2015 2014
10 9 8 7 6 5 4 3 2